Gumtau/Kurschatke
Firnkes/Kammerer

Englisch Übungsbuch

7. / 8. Klasse

Englisch Übungsbuch
7./8. Klasse

Autoren:
Hannes Gumtau, Wolfgang Kurschatke,
Friedrich Firnkes, Hilmar Kammerer

1. Auflage 2007 (1,01)

Einbandgestaltung: Petra Wöhner, Stuttgart
Illustrationen: Hans Limo Lechner, Pastetten
Layout: Hans Limo Lechner, Pastetten
Satz: PC-Print, München; L&N Litho, Waiblingen
Druck: Mediengruppe UNIVERSAL
Grafische Betriebe Manz und
Mühlthaler GmbH, München
Printed in Germany
ISBN 978-3-12-828305-0

Inhalt

Vorwort

Liebe Schülerin, lieber Schüler,

diejenigen von euch, die bereits mit *Englisch Übungsbuch 5./6. Klasse* gearbeitet haben, können diese Seite getrost überlesen. Denn wir haben diesen zweiten Band genauso wie den Band davor aufgebaut, so werdet ihr euch ohne Mühe zurechtfinden können. Für alle, die das erste Mal mit „Englisch Übungsbuch" üben, hier einige Hinweise zur Arbeit mit dem Buch.

Zunächst einmal die gute Nachricht: Ihr müsst das Buch keineswegs von vorn bis hinten durcharbeiten. Jedes Kapitel und auch jedes Unterkapitel können für sich bearbeitet werden. Die genauen Themen findet ihr in den Inhaltsverzeichnissen zu den einzelnen Lernbereichen aufgeführt. Schaut also in eure Hefte oder fragt eure Lehrerin oder euren Lehrer, wo ihr die meisten Fehler macht, und wählt dann die entsprechenden Kapitel aus. Zu vier Lernbereichen bieten wir euch wieder „Futter" an:

Grammatik
Rechtschreibung
Wortschatz
Prüfungstraining

Den Übungen gehen immer Beispiele voran, die euch zeigen, wie bestimmte Formen im Englischen gebraucht werden. In dem farbig unterlegten Kasten bekommt ihr Hinweise dazu, was ihr beachten müsst, wenn ihr die Übung bearbeitet. Diesen Teil solltet ihr aufmerksam durchlesen, denn er hilft euch, die Übung besser zu verstehen und damit auch leichter zu bearbeiten.

Mithilfe des Lösungsteils könnt ihr eure Ergebnisse überprüfen.

Wir haben nicht alles, was in einem Schuljahr behandelt wird, aufgegriffen, sondern nur die Themen, die häufig zu Fehlern führen. Je nach Schulart und Bundesland kann ein Thema vorkommen, das erst in der nächsten Klasse behandelt wird. Dann könnt ihr diese Seiten problemlos überspringen.

Viele Wiederholungsübungen (Revision) zu Themen der 6. Klasse helfen euch, den neuen Stoff besser zu verstehen. Außerdem habt ihr vielleicht das eine oder andere aus dem letzten Schuljahr auch schon wieder vergessen.

Die Autoren und der Verlag wünschen euch viel Spaß mit dem Buch und in Zukunft eine bessere Englischnote.

Lernbereich GRAMMATIK

Zeichenerklärungen

Achtung

Vorsicht Falle!

Korrigiere die Fehler!

Übung im Heft

Fachausdrücke

Englisch:	Deutsch:	Beispiel:
adjective	Adjektiv, Eigenschaftswort	tall, beautiful
comparative	Komparativ	taller, more beautiful
superlative	Superlativ	tallest, most beautiful
adverb	Adverb	quickly, fast
emphasizing pronoun	verstärkendes Pronomen	myself, themselves
gerund	Gerund	flying
modal verb	modales Hilfsverb	can, could
noun	Substantiv, Hauptwort	friend
singular	Singular, Einzahl	a friend
plural	Plural, Mehrzahl	two friends
possessive adjective	Possessivpronomen (adjektivisch gebraucht)	my, our
possessive pronoun	Possessivpronomen (substantivisch gebraucht)	mine, ours
prop word	Stützwort	one, ones
reciprocal pronoun	reziprokes Pronomen	each other
reflexive pronoun	Reflexivpronomen	myself, ourselves
verb	Verb, Zeitwort	go, talk
past perfect	Plusquamperfekt	he had written
past progressive	Verlaufsform im Imperfekt	we were waiting
present progessive future	Verlaufsform im Präsens mit futurischer Bedeutung	they are flying

1 Artikel – Substantiv

1 **Write the plural form of the words.**

-s		-es		unregelmäßig	
girl →	girl **s**	box →	box **es**	man →	**men**
house →	house **s**	lady →	ladi **es**	woman →	**women**
ball →	ball **s**	potato →	potato **es**	child →	**children**
		leaf →	leav **es**	tooth →	**teeth**
				foot →	**feet**

Revision

Den **Plural** der Substantive bildest du, indem du **-s** anhängst. Nach **Zischlauten** (s, sh, ch, x) und einigen Substantiven auf **-o** hängst du **-es** an. Bei einem **Konsonanten + -y** schreibst du **-ies.** Bei einigen Substantiven mit der Endung **-f** oder **-fe** bildest du den Plural mit **-ves.** Unregelmäßige Formen musst du auswendig lernen.

a) In London .... (taxi) are black and .... (bus) are red. A lot of .... (man) and .... (woman) are on their way to their .... (office). The .... (lorry) make a lot of noise.

b) All the .... (child) go to school. Some of them ride their .... (bike). Most of the .... (teacher) come by car.

c) In Anne's school there are eighteen .... (class). In each class there are about thirty .... (pupil). The .... (boy) and .... (girl) like to go to .... (party) at .... (weekend).

Schreibregeln siehe Rechtschreibung Seite 66 – 68

Fill in *one* or *ones*. 2

Which **ball** do you like? — *Welchen Ball möchtest du?*
The red **one.** — *Den roten.*
Are those your **friends?** — *Sind das deine Freunde?*
Yes, the tall **ones** over there. — *Ja, die Großen dort.*

Revision

Das Stützwort (= prop word) **one** für Singular oder **ones** für Plural verwendest du, wenn du ein schon genanntes Substantiv (z. B. ball, friends) nicht wiederholen willst.

a) Which bike is yours? – The black . . . .

But there are four black . . . . – The . . . . with the white stripes.

b) I'd like to have three balls. – Red . . . . or yellow . . . . ? –

Two red . . . . and a yellow . . . . , please.

c) Look at the girls over there. The . . . . on the bike is my friend Jenny and the

. . . . who are walking are Clare and Betty.

Say it in English. 3

a) Sage, dass du neue Sportschuhe brauchst. Deine alten sind hässlich.

b) Sage, dass Clare fünf Kleider probierte und dass sie ein blaues und zwei grüne kaufte.

c) Sage, dass diese Orangen teuer sind und dass du die billigen haben möchtest.

4 Use the s-genitive.

New York **'s** underground
at the butcher **'s**
a two hours **'** rest

America **'s** history
at my uncle **'s**
this week **'s** magazine

Den **s-Genitiv** verwendest du auch bei Orts- und Zeitangaben. Bei bestimmten Wendungen bleibt der Ort ungenannt, z. B. at the butcher's (shop), at my uncle's (house). Beachte den Unterschied bei Zeitangaben, z. B. this week's magazine (Singular) und a two hours' rest (Plural).

The Potters

a) Yesterday Mr Potter worked hard and he then had ....
(a two hours, rest)

b) He went to .... (the newsagent) first and bought
.... (magazine, this month).

c) His wife asked him to bring .... (today, paper) as well.

d) After that he went to .... (the baker) to buy some bread and
then he got some medicine at .... (the chemist).

e) In the evening, Mr Potter watched TV and he saw ....
(weather forecast, today).

f) Mrs Potter told her husband that she was going to spend a weekend at her ....
(aunt) in London.

g) There she'd very much like to use .... (underground, London).

h) She's going to visit a museum about .... (history, Britain).

Complete the sentences. (Nouns in the singular) 5

Andy's **hair** **is** too long.	*Andys* ***Haar(e)*** ***ist (sind)*** *zu lang.*
His **knowledge** of English **is** good.	*Seine* ***Englischkenntnisse*** ***sind*** *gut.*
This **is** good **news.**	*Das* ***sind*** *gute* ***Nachrichten.***

Einige **Substantive** haben im Englischen nur die Singularform:

damage – Schaden, furniture – Möbel, information – Information(en)
progress – Fortschritt(e), homework – Hausaufgabe(n)

Folgende **Substantive** werden trotz der Pluralform als **Singulare** verwendet:

news – Nachricht(en), maths – Mathematik, physics – Physik, politics – Politik

Dies bedeutet: Die dazugehörenden Bestimmungswörter (this), Verben (is) und Pronomen (his) stehen im Singular.

a) The Wards are getting new .... (Möbel). They bought .... (them / it) at a big store.

b) Mr Ward's .... (Kenntnisse) of English .... (are / is) not very good.

c) He isn't making good .... (Fortschritte) at night school.

d) He hasn't much time to do his .... (Hausaufgaben). He only did .... (them / it) yesterday because he had a day off. So it wasn't .... (much / many) .... (Hausaufgaben).

e) The .... (Informationen) in the English lessons .... (are / is) very important. Mr Ward shouldn't miss .... (them / it).

f) Mr Ward thinks the .... (Nachrichten) .... (are / is) awful.

g) However, he is very interested in .... (Politik).

6 **Translate.** (Nouns in the plural)

These **trousers are** dirty. Andy needs **a** new **pair of** trousers and **two pairs of** shorts.	*Diese **Hose ist** schmutzig.* *Andy braucht **eine** neue **Hose*** *und **zwei** kurze Hosen.*

Einige **Substantive** haben im Englischen nur die **Pluralform.** Wenn du die genaue Anzahl nennen willst, stellst du **a pair of/pairs of** voran. Die dazugehörenden Bestimmungswörter (these) und Verben (are) stehen im Plural.

glasses	– *Brille(n)*	**scissors**	– *Schere(n)*
jeans	– *Jeans*	**shorts**	– *kurze Hose(n)*
outskirts	– *Außenbezirk(e)*	**stairs**	– *Treppe(n)*
pyjamas	– *Schlafanzug(züge)*	**tights**	– *Strumpfhose(n)*
		trousers	– *lange Hose(n)*

a) Schau, meine Schwester trägt eine neue Brille.

b) Sie benutzt die Schere, um das Papier zu schneiden.

c) Ist das Andys Schlafanzug?

d) Andy trägt im Sommer keine langen Hosen, sondern nur kurze.

e) Er braucht eine neue Jeans.

f) Sein Vater kauft eine lange Hose und zwei Jeans.

g) Andys Freund wohnt in einem Außenbezirk von Manchester.

h) Die Jungen machten großen Lärm. Sie rannten die Treppe auf und ab.

2 Pronomen – Mengenbezeichnungen

Fill in the missing pronouns. 7

Revision

This isn't **my** bike *Das ist nicht mein Fahrrad.*	**Mine** is white. *Meins ist weiß.*
Is this **our** car? *Ist das unser Auto?*	Yes, it's **ours.** *Ja, es ist unseres.*

Die **substantivisch** gebrauchten **Possessivpronomen** (possessive pronouns) **mine, yours, his, hers, its, ours, yours, theirs** beziehen sich auf ein vorangehendes Substantiv, das du nicht wiederholst. Sie stehen **allein.**
Die **adjektivisch** gebrauchten **Possessivpronomen** (possessive adjectives) **my, your, his, her, its, our, your, their** stehen **vor** einem Substantiv.

a) This isn't the Potters' car. .... is much older.

b) Whose idea was it? – I told you, it was ....

c) Whose bike is it? – It's Bob's. It's ....

d) I can't find my dictionary. Can I have ...., Simon?

e) We have had our lunch. Have you had .... ?

f) I've written to .... penfriend. Has Claire already written to .... ?

g) Can we use your car? .... has broken down.

h) Peter isn't only a friend of .... brother, he is also a friend of ....

i) It was not only my fault. It was .... (Daniel and Tina), too.

j) Whose footballs are those in the net? Are they .... (Darren and Jenny)? –

No, ... are at home.

8 Fill in the correct form of *oneself.*

I can see **myself** in the mirror. *Ich kann **mich** im Spiegel sehen.*
Susan taught **herself** to play the guitar. *Susan brachte **sich** Gitarrespielen bei.*

Reflexivpronomen:

Singular		Plural	
(I)	myself	(we)	ourselves
(you)	yourself	(you)	yourselves
(he)	himself	(they)	themselves
(she)	herself		
(it)	itself		

Die **Reflexivpronomen** (reflexive pronouns) verwendest du, wenn das **Subjekt** (z. B. Susan) und das **Objekt** (z. B. herself) dieselbe Person (oder Sache) bezeichnen.

a) Mary hurt .... when she fell off her bike.

b) The cat was scratching .... behind the ear.

c) The children enjoyed .... at the party yesterday.

d) Tony introduced .... to the girls he didn't know.

e) Ian and Jean taught .... to play the piano.

f) You can see .... in the clear water, children.

g) Simon dressed .... very carefully before he went out.

h) Can we make .... useful in the garden?

i) After you have helped your mother, you can make .... comfortable, boys.

Fill in the correct form of *oneself.* 9

I know New York well because I have been there **myself.**
The **boys** made the model plane **themselves.**

*Ich kenne New York gut, weil ich **selbst** dort gewesen bin.*
*Die Jungen haben das Modellflugzeug **selbst** gebaut.*

Hier verwendest du das Reflexivpronomen, um ein Substantiv (z. B. the boys) hervorzuheben. Man nennt es **verstärkendes Pronomen** (emphasizing pronoun).

a) I think you can do all the exercises . . . . , Bob.

b) Did Tony speak to the headmaster . . . . (selbst)?

c) I asked . . . . why I could't understand what he said.

d) Geoff . . . . saw the Queen when he was in London.

e) His wife didn't believe that he had seen the Queen . . . .

f) Joan did all the preparations . . . . (selbst).

g) The children did all the housework . . . .

h) We like the house . . . . but it's not very convenient (geeignet).

i) When we moved there we decorated all the rooms . . . .

10 Translate. Fill in the correct form of *oneself,* if necessary.

Do you **remember** your last holidays?
Erinnerst *du* ***dich*** *an die letzten Ferien?*

We **met** in London.
Wir ***trafen uns*** *in London.*

Viele Verben sind im Deutschen **reflexiv**, im Englischen aber **nicht reflexiv**, z. B.:

to join	– *sich anschließen*	**to wonder**	– *sich fragen*
to happen	– *sich ereignen*	**to complain**	– *sich beschweren*
to meet	– *sich treffen*	**to imagine**	– *sich vorstellen*
to remember	– *sich erinnern*	**to refuse**	– *sich weigern*
to feel	– *sich fühlen*	**to sit down**	– *sich setzen*

The youth club

a) Katie schloss sich vor zwei Wochen einem Jugendklub an.

b) Beim ersten Treffen stellte sie sich allen Jungen und Mädchen vor.

c) Die Gruppe trifft sich jeden Freitagabend.

d) Sie amüsieren sich beim Tanzen und Spielen.

e) Katie kann sich nicht erinnern, solch nette Leute vorher getroffen zu haben.

f) Sie fühlt sich in dem Klub sehr wohl.

g) Letztes Wochenende trafen sich die jungen Leute im Klub.

h) Katie fragte sich, wie viele Leute kommen würden.

i) Katie und ihre Freundin machten alle Arbeit für die Party selbst.

j) Die Gäste amüsierten sich und bedienten sich beim Essen selbst.

k) Die Nachbarn beschwerten sich nicht, weil sie selbst gerne laute Rockmusik hören.

l) Katie stellt sich vor, nächste Woche wieder eine Party zu organisieren.

m) Ihre Freundin wird sich nicht weigern, ihr zu helfen.

Fill in the correct reflexive or reciprocal pronoun. 11

Katie and Lucy are good friends.
Katie und Lucy sind gute Freundinnen.

They always help **each other.**
Sie helfen ***sich*** *immer (gegenseitig).*

Wenn du eine **wechselseitige Beziehung** ausdrückst (sich gegenseitig, einander), verwendest du im Englischen das **reziproke Pronomen** (reciprocal pronoun) **each other.**

Katie and Lucy see **themselves** in the mirror. (... sehen **sich** ...)

They can't see **each other** when it's dark. (… können **einander** ...)

Good friends

a) Katie und Lucy are good friends. They have known . . . . for many years.

b) They always do their homework together. They help . . . .

c) Yesterday Katie had to do her homework . . . . because Lucy was ill.

d) Next Sunday they are going to go to a party. They are sure they'll enjoy . . . .

e) When the two girls are on holiday, they write letters and postcards to . . . .

f) When Lucy is in Germany she teaches . . . . German.

g) Katie and Lucy go to the same school. They see . . . . every day.

12 Fill in *some* or *any* and their compounds.

Revision

There is **someone** at the door.	*Da ist **jemand** an der Tür.*
Have you seen **anyone**?	*Hast du **jemand** gesehen?*
I don't want **anything** to drink.	*Ich möchte **nichts** zu trinken.*
Can I have **some** more cake, please?	*Kann ich bitte noch **etwas** Kuchen haben?*
Yes, of course.	***Ja**, natürlich.*

Du verwendest **some** und die Zusammensetzungen (compounds) in **bejahenden Sätzen**, **any** und die Zusammensetzungen bei **Frage** und **Verneinung**. **Some** und die Zusammensetzungen verwendest du auch in **Fragen**, wenn du die Antwort **Ja** erwartest.

Alone in the house

Last night Peter's parents went out.

a) Peter's mother said: "There's .... to eat in the fridge (Kühlschrank). Would you like .... biscuits?"

b) Peter answered: "Yes, please. I'd like .... biscuits, but I don't want .... to drink."

c) When his parents had gone, Peter heard a noise .... in the house and said to himself: "There must be .... in the house."

d) When he went upstairs, he couldn't see ...., because there was no light.

e) "Where are the matches", he thought, "they must be ...."

f) He thought: "I wish .... was with me."

g) "Perhaps I could phone ...., but I can't find my friend's number ....".

h) "So it'll be better if I watch .... on TV."

i) "I'll have a look if there is .... interesting on tonight."

3 Adjektive – Adverbien

Revision

Fill in the correct forms of the adjectives. 13

Grundstufe:	tall	clever	beautiful	good
Komparativ:	tall **er**	clever **er**	**more** beautiful	**better**
Superlativ:	the tall **est**	the clever **est**	**the most** beautiful	**the best**

Beim **Adjektiv** gibt es **drei Arten der Steigerung:**

1. mit **-er/-est** bei kurzen einsilbigen und vielen zweisilbigen, die auf **-y, -er, -le, -ow** enden (z. B. happy, clever, simple, narrow).
2. mit **more/most** bei anderen zweisilbigen und allen mit mehr als zwei Silben (z. B. careful, wonderful).
3. **unregelmäßige,** z. B. good – better – best; bad – worse – worst; much / many – more – most; little – less – least; far – farther – farthest.

Bob's class

a) Bob is . . . . than Tom, but Tony is the . . . . in class. (clever)

b) Paul says Maths lessons are . . . . Today's lesson was the . . . . one of the week. (boring)

c) Mr Lloyd is a . . . . teacher. He is . . . . many other teachers. The pupils say he is the . . . . teacher in the school. (good)

d) The headmaster is . . . . , although he isn't the . . . . person of the teaching staff. Two teachers are . . . . he is. (old)

e) Some pupils are . . . . at English, but Martha is the . . . . of all. (bad)

f) Martha is a . . . . girl. She is one of the . . . . girls in our class. (beautiful)

14 Say it in English. (Make comparisons.)

Geoff is **as** tall **as** Paul.	*Geoff is so groß wie Paul.*
Paul is **not as** tall **as** Ian.	*Paul ist nicht so groß wie Ian.*
Ian is **taller than** Geoff.	*Ian ist größer als Geoff.*
He is **the tallest** in class.	*Er ist der Größte in der Klasse.*

Du hast verschiedene Möglichkeiten, einen Vergleich auszudrücken.

The more your learn, **the** better you'll be at school.
Je mehr du lernst, desto besser wirst du in der Schule sein.

Du erzählst einem Freund, dass

a) euer Haus nicht so groß ist wie seins.
b) dein Vater älter ist als seiner.
c) ein Opel nicht so schnell ist wie ein Jaguar.
d) ein Porsche der Schnellste von allen ist.
e) ein Porsche weniger kostet als ein Jaguar, aber mehr als ein Opel.
f) dein Fahrrad so gut ist wie seins.
g) du schneller fahren kannst als er.
h) du, je mehr du trainierst, desto weiter springen kannst.
i) dein Bruder am weitesten von allen Schülern springt.

15 Correct the mistakes.

a) John is older as his cousin. ....

b) Martha is intelligenter than her sister. ....

c) Keith is bader in English than Bob. ....

d) But he is not as bad than John. ....

Choose the correct form of the adverb. 16

Mrs Grant is a **wonderful** singer.
*Frau Grant ist eine **wunderbare** Sängerin.*
She is also a **good** actress.
*Sie ist auch eine **gute** Schauspielerin.*

She sings **wonderfully.**
*Sie singt **wunderbar**.*
She acts very **well.**
*Sie spielt sehr **gut.***

Du bildest das **Adverb** in der Regel mit dem **Adjektiv** (z. B. wonderful) + ly. **Besondere Formen** sind z. B.: good – well (gut); fast – fast (schnell); hard – hard (schwer); fantastic – fantastically (phantastisch); friendly – in a friendly way (freundlich).

On a train

a) An old lady was sitting .... (quiet) on her seat, when suddenly a group of young people entered the carriage and shouted .... (loud).

b) The young men didn't get on .... (good) with each other.

c) The laughed .... (wild) and jumped around .... (mad).

d) At first the old lady spoke to the boys .... (friendly), but when they didn't answer .... (polite), she asked them .... (angry) to leave the carriage .... (quick).

e) In the end the group left the train .... (noisy).

Beachte die Schreibung der Adjektive auf -y, z. B. angry → angrily.

17 Adjective or adverb?

Revision

John is a **quick** worker.
A Porsche is a **fast** car.

He always works **quickly**.
It goes very **fast**.

Mit dem **Adjektiv** beschreibst du, wie jemand oder etwas **ist**.

Mit dem **Adverb der Art und Weise** (adverb of manner) beschreibst du, wie etwas **geschieht**.

On the bus

a) At the railway station the old lady left the train . . . . (quick) and walked . . . . (slow) to the bus station.

b) The . . . . (impolite) group of young boys took the bus, too.

c) One of them was a . . . . (rude) boy. He spoke to the old lady . . . . (rude).

d) At first the old lady answered . . . . (friendly), but after a while she spoke to the boys very . . . . (angry).

e) Most of the other passengers were . . . . (quiet). They read their papers . . . . (quiet).

f) The old lady knew that she was in a . . . . (terrible) situation, because the group was shouting at her . . . . (terrible, loud). She was . . . . (horrible) afraid.

Write the comparative and superlative forms of the adverbs. 18

Grundstufe:	fast	easily	well
Komparativ:	fast **er**	**more** easily	**better**
Superlativ:	fast **est**	**most** easily	**best**

Einsilbige Adverbien und **early** steigerst du mit **-er/-est**, andere auf **-ly** mit **more/most**. Die **unregelmäßigen Steigerungsformen,** z. B. badly – worse – worst, much/a lot – more – most, (a) little – less – least, musst du auswendig lernen.

a) hard

. . . .

. . . .

b) happily

. . . .

. . . .

c) badly

. . . .

. . . .

d) early

. . . .

. . . .

e) wonderfully

. . . .

. . . .

f) strongly

. . . .

. . . .

Correct the mistakes. 19

a) Susan sang beautifully than Martha. . . . .

b) Roger drives as badlier as John. . . . .

c) Bob drives badliest of all. . . . .

d) Mrs Ward drives more careful than her husband. . . . .

e) Peter reads littler than his brother. . . . .

20 Fill in the correct forms (adjective or adverb).

Katie **seemed** **tired** after the party,
but she **looked** very **happy.**

Katie schien nach der Party müde zu sein,
aber sie schaute sehr glücklich aus.

Nach **einigen Verben**, die einen Zustand oder eine Eigenschaft ausdrücken, steht ein Adjektiv und kein Adverb:

be	– *sein*	**become / get**	– *werden*
feel	– *sich fühlen*	**look**	– *aussehen*
seem	– *scheinen*	**smell**	– *riechen*
sound	– *klingen*	**stay**	– *bleiben*
taste	– *schmecken*		

Football

a) Geoff: You know football is an . . . . (easy) game. You can join our team . . . . (easy).

b) Ian: Yes, it seems to be . . . . (easy), but for me it's quite . . . . (difficult).

c) Geoff: Our forwards are very . . . . (quick). They can kick the ball . . . . (quick) into the opponent's half.

d) Ian: I sometimes wait . . . . (nervous) for the beginning of a match, but when we're playing I never feel . . . . (nervous).

e) Geoff: I must say you don't look . . . . (nervous) even before the match. I think you'll play . . . . (perfect).

f) Ian: Do some of your players get . . . . (tired) after sixty minutes?

g) Geoff: No, they don't. It sounds . . . . (strange), but they take their sport very . . . . (serious) and they train very . . . . (hard).

4 Verben

Use the simple past and its negation. 21

The girls **were** in the room, but the boys **weren't** there.
All the pupils **talked,** but Tom **didn't talk.**
All the cars **stopped,** but the bus **didn't stop.**
All the boys **wrote,** but the girls **didn't write.**

Revision

Du bildest das **simple past** wie folgt: Bei **regelmäßigen Verben** hängst du **-ed** an, bei **unregelmäßigen Verben** musst du die Formen **auswendig** lernen.
Die **Verneinung** bildest du, wenn kein Hilfsverb (z. B. be, can) vorhanden ist, mit **did + not + Infinitiv** des Verbs.

a) All the children laughed, but Betty didn't laugh. *laugh*

b) Alex . . . . by bike, but John . . . . by bike. *come*

c) Mr Brown . . . . the film, but his wife . . . . the film. *see*

d) Simon . . . . the bus, but Lucy . . . . the bus. *catch*

e) David . . . . a recorder, but John . . . . one. *buy*

f) Charles . . . . a picture, but Clare . . . . one. *draw*

g) Mr Ward . . . . the question, but Mrs White . . . . it. *repeat*

h) Mr Dent . . . . a car, but Mr Clark . . . . a car.
He . . . . a bus. *drive*

i) Mrs Thomson . . . . , but Mrs Parker . . . . *relax*
She worked.

j) Mr Green . . . . his house, but Mr Grey . . . . his. *sell*

k) Tom . . . . the answer, but Bob . . . . it. *know*

l) Mary . . . . the film, but Martha . . . . it. *like*

22 Ask questions and give answers in the simple past.

Ian **worked** last night	When **did** he **work**?
His wife **was** at home.	**Was** she at home?
She **wrote** letters.	What **did** she **write**?

Revision

> Du bildest die Frage im **simple past** ebenfalls mit **did**, wenn kein Hilfsverb (z. B. was) da ist.

a) When .... you .... the letter? I .... it last week. ***write***

b) When .... Nelly .... home? She .... home at ten. ***come***

c) Where .... you .... Tom? I .... him in town. ***see***

d) When .... Geoff ...... to the pub? He .... there last night. ***go***

e) When .... the telephone ....? It .... at six. ***ring***

f) When .... you at home? I .... at home all day. ***be***

g) What .... you ....? I .... a salad. ***choose***

h) What .... you ....? I .... a sandwich. ***eat***

i) What .... he ....? He .... a letter. ***post***

j) What .... she ....? She .... her key. ***lose***

k) Who .... you ....? I .... my mother. ***call***

l) How much .... you ....? I .... two pounds. ***pay***

m) Where .... they ....? They .... at the opera. ***meet***

n) What .... she ....? She .... good-bye. ***say***

o) What .... he ....? He .... a car. ***steal***

p) Where .... they ....? They .... in the lake. ***swim***

q) Who .... he ....? He .... his teacher. ***ask***

It happened yesterday. (Use simple past.) 23

Du übst das **simple past** mit regelmäßigen und unregelmäßigen Verben.

A visit

Revision

a) Yesterday Mrs Wood .... (come) to see the Stones.

b) Mr Stone .... (ask): "When .... you .... (leave) home?"

c) Mrs Wood .... (answer): "I .... (leave) at 6 and I .... (go) by bus."

d) They .... (have) tea together and then they .... (talk) about the children.

e) Billy .... (watch) TV and Susy .... (read) a book.

f) They .... (not, sit) in the kitchen, they .... (sit) in the living room, where there .... (be) a nice fire in the open fireplace.

g) In the evening they .... (drink) a glass of wine and .... (eat) some biscuits, but they .... (not, have) any sandwiches.

h) At ten o'clock Mrs Wood .... (say) that she .... (want) to go home, but she .... (leave) at eleven o'clock.

i) Mr Stone .... (give) her a lift in his car.

j) When Mr Stone .... (drive) home again, he .... (lose) his way, but finally he .... (can) recognise where he .... (be).

24 Use the present perfect.

Revision

The blackboard is clean.	I **have** **cleaned** it.
The dog is wet.	It **has** **been** out in the rain.
We are happy.	We **have** **won** the match.

Du bildest das **present perfect** mit **have/has** + **past participle** (Partizip Perfekt).
Das Ergebnis ist **sichtbar.**

Give the result.

a) The boys' room is in a mess. They .... it. *not clean*

b) Helen's dress is new. She .... it. *just, buy*

c) John wants to post a letter. He .... it. *finish*

d) The windows are open. The pupils .... them. *open*

e) Bob's homework is done. He .... it. *copy*

f) Clare takes the book back to the library. She .... it. *read*

g) Peter knows all the words. He .... them. *learn*

h) Mary is tired. She .... all night. *not, sleep*

i) The train isn't there. It .... the station. *leave*

j) Tom is in hospital. He .... his leg. *break*

Teacher: *"Simon, your work has certainly improved. There are only ten mistakes here."*
Simon: *"Oh, good, Miss."*
Teacher: *"Now, let's have a look at the second line, shall we?"*

Translate. Use present perfect and *already* – *not ... yet* – *ever* – *never* – *often*.

25

Have you **already** **seen** the new film?	No, I **have** **n't** **seen** it **yet.**
Have you **ever** **been** to England?	No, I' **ve** **never** **been** there, but I' **ve** **often** **been** to Ireland.

Du bildest Sätze mit **present perfect** in Verbindung mit **already** (schon), **not ... yet** (noch nicht), **ever** (schon einmal), **never** (noch nicht), **often** (schon oft).
Der **genaue** Zeitpunkt ist hier nicht wichtig, aber es liegt immer ein **Bezug zur Gegenwart** vor.

Friends

a) Tom fragt seinen Freund Simon, ob er das Buch schon gelesen hat.

Tom: ...

b) Simon antwortet, dass er noch keine Zeit hatte.

Simon: ...

c) Tom fragt ihn, ob er schon oft Kriminalgeschichten im Fernsehen gesehen hat.

Tom: ...

d) Simon antwortet, dass er noch nicht oft Fernsehen geschaut hat.

Simon: ...

e) Simon fragt Tom, ob er schon einmal ein Buch von Agatha Christie gelesen hat.

Simon: ...

f) Tom antwortet, dass er den Namen noch nie gehört hat.

Tom: ...

g) Tom fragt Simon, ob er schon einmal bei Madame Tussaud's gewesen sei.

Tom: ...

h) Simon sagt, dass er schon zweimal dort war, aber dass er das Chamber of Horrors noch nicht besucht hat.

Simon: ...

26 Complete the sentences. (Use present perfect and *since* or *for*.)

How long **has** Tony **been** ill?

– He **has been** ill **for** a month.
– He **has been** ill **since** February.

Revision

Du übst das **present perfect** in Verbindung mit **since** (seit) und **for** (seit). **Since** bezieht sich auf den **Zeitpunkt**, zu dem eine Handlung begonnen hat, **for** auf den **Zeitraum**, den sie schon andauert.

a) Ian .... (be) busy .... two months.
He .... (not, write) to Paul .... Easter.

b) His wife .... (be) ill .... July. She ....
(be) in bed .... a month.

c) Mrs Potter .... (know) Ian .... almost three
years. They .... (be) friends .... Christmas.

d) Mrs Potter's shop .... (be) open now .... two
hours. It .... (be) open .... 9 o'clock.

e) Jack .... (not, do) any homework .... March.
He .... (not, be) to school .... over two weeks.

f) Jack .... (not, see) Mary .... ages.
Mary has got a new bike. She .... (have) it ....
her birthday.

Present perfect or simple past? 27

Look, the Wards **have bought** a new car.

Have you **ever** **seen** a cricket match?
No, I **have** **n't** **seen** a match **yet.**

How long **have** you **been** friends?
We'**ve been** friends **since** we were boys.
We'**ve been** friends **for** many years.

Bob **bought** a car in **1995.**

When **were** you in Edinburgh?
I **was** there **last year.**

When **did** Mr Brown **come**?
He **came** an hour **ago.**

Revision

Mit dem **present perfect** berichtest du über etwas, das gerade geschehen ist und sich auf die Gegenwart auswirkt, bzw. über etwas, das noch nicht abgeschlossen ist.
Signalwörter: since, for (schon seit), ever (schon einmal), yet, up to now, so far, always (schon immer), how long ...?

Du berichtest mit dem **simple past** über Vorgänge, die in der Vergangenheit zu einem bestimmten Zeitpunkt geschehen sind.
Signalwörter: in 1995, last ..., ago, when ...?

Judy (= J) and Martha (= M)

a) J: . . . . you . . . . (enjoy) the party yesterday?

M: Yes, I . . . . Tim . . . . (not, dance) at all.

J: There . . . . (be) a wonderful band and they . . . . (play) great music.

M: That's true. I . . . . (never, hear) such good music before.

b) J: . . . . ever . . . . (you, be) to Scotland?

M: No, I . . . . (not, be) there yet, but I . . . . (be) in Ireland last August.

c) J: When . . . . (you, see) Mr Traynor?

M: I . . . . (not, see) him for a long time, but I . . . . (see) his wife a week ago.

28 Use present perfect progressive and *since* or *for.*

Lisa: How long **have** you **been living** in Reading?
George: I **have been living** here for three years now.

Lisa: How long **has** Alice **been working** in that shop?
George: She **has been working** there since last summer.

Du bildest das **present perfect progressive** (Verlaufsform im present perfect) mit **have/has been + -ing-Form** des Verbs.
Du verwendest diese Zeit, wenn du sagen willst, dass der **Verlauf** einer Handlung bis in die Gegenwart reicht.

a) How long .... (Bob, wait)?
– He .... three hours.

b) How long .... (your friends, stay) with you?
– They .... with us .... May.

c) How long .... (you, go) to this school?
– I .... here .... three years now.

d) How long .... (you and Alan, play) tennis?
– We .... two and a half hours.

e) How long .... (Geoff, study) German?
– He .... it .... many years.

f) How long .... (it, rain) today?
– It .... 11 o'clock.

g) How long .... (this girl, cry)?
– She .... half an hour now.

Complete the dialogue. (Use present perfect or present perfect progressive and since or for.) 29

We **have been** here all day.
Wir sind schon den ganzen Tag hier.

How long **have** you **had** this bike?
Wie lange hast du dieses Fahrrad schon?

We **have been learning** all the time.
Wir lernen schon die ganze Zeit.

How long **have** you **been cycling** today?
Wie lange radelst du heute schon?

Du verwendest das **present perfect** bei Verben, die einen **Zustand** beschreiben, z. B. be (sein), have (haben), know (kennen), want (wollen), like (mögen), believe (glauben), see (sehen).
Das **present perfect progressive** verwendest du, wenn du das **Andauern** oder den **Verlauf** einer Tätigkeit oder Handlung betonen willst.

At the disco

a) Patrick: How long . . . . (you, have) this job, Simon?

b) Simon: I . . . . (have) it . . . . 3 years now.

c) Patrick: . . . . (you, ever, think) about doing anything else?

d) Simon: No, I . . . . (always, want) to become a disc jockey and I . . . . (like) this job . . . . I started.

e) Patrick: How many VIPs . . . . (you, see) here?

f) Simon: Well, there . . . . (be) quite a lot of them. Some of them . . . . (come) here . . . . a long time.

g) Patrick: And would you say they . . . . (enjoy themselves) with the music you play?

h) Simon: I think so. I . . . . (always, choose) the latest hits.

30 Translate. (Mixed tenses: Simple past, present perfect, present perfect progressive.)

Du musst nun zwischen verschiedenen Zeitformen wählen. Achte auf **Signalwörter** und darauf, ob eine Handlung **abgeschlossen** ist, noch **andauert** oder das **Resultat vorliegt**. Denke daran, dass es im Deutschen egal ist, ob du ich **ging** oder ich **bin gegangen** sagst.

Mr Ward

a) Herr Ward lebt schon sei vielen Jahren in Macclesfield.

b) Sein Freund, Herr Müller, hat ihn im letzten Sommer besucht und sie hatten eine schöne Zeit in England.

c) Herr Müller lernt schon seit drei Jahren Englisch.

d) Herr Ward und seine Familie haben viele Sehenswürdigkeiten (sights) in Nordengland gesehen, aber sie waren noch nicht in York. Letztes Wochenende haben sie Durham besucht.

e) Wie lange spielt Herrn Wards Sohn Jerry schon in der Fußballmannschaft? – Er spielt dort seit einem Jahr.

f) Herr Ward versucht seit Tagen seinen Freund anzurufen, aber er hat ihn nie erreicht. Er machte Urlaub in Italien.

g) Herr Ward hat vor zwei Jahren Urlaub in Österreich gemacht, und danach hat er seinen Freund in Bayern besucht.

h) Herr Ward arbeitet seit zwei Jahren in einer Autofabrik (car factory). Davor hat er in einer Autoreparaturwerkstatt (garage) gearbeitet.

i) Wie lange ist er schon Mechaniker? – Er ist seit zehn Jahren Mechaniker.

Mother: *"Alan! You have been fighting in the playground again, haven't you? You have lost your front teeth?"*
Alan: *"I haven't lost them, Mother. They are in my back pocket."*

Complete the sentences. 31

Use **simple past** or	**past progressive**
It **was** cold last night.	It **was getting** warmer by the next morning.
	What **were** you **doing** at nine o'clock?
	– I **was sleeping.**
The telephone **rang** when	Mr Ward **was watching** TV.

Du bildest das **past progressive** mit **was/were** + **-ing-Form** des Verbs. Mit dem **past progressive** beschreibst du einen Vorgang in der Vergangenheit, der über einen bestimmten Zeitraum (z. B. was becoming warmer) verlief, oder eine gerade **laufende Handlung** (z. B. was watching), die durch eine andere (z. B. rang) **unterbrochen** wurde.

a) Mrs Ward . . . . (cook) dinner when her husband . . . . (come) home. Mr Ward asked: "What . . . . (you, do) at 9 o'clock this morning?" – "I . . . . (shop) at the supermarket."

b) While Joanne . . . . (wait) at the bus stop, her friend Martha . . . . (arrive). Joanne . . . . (wait) for her friend because she . . . . (want) to go to the cinema with her. When the bus . . . . (come), they . . . . (still, talk) together.

c) When the girls . . . . (leave) the bus, the sun . . . . (shine). They . . . . (hurry) because it . . . . (get) late.

d) In the evening while the girls . . . . (walk) to the bus stop, it . . . . (rain).

32 Form sentences.

Use	**simple past**	and	**past perfect**	
Jenny	**watched**	the film after she	**had done**	her homework.
Jason	**was**	late for School because	**he had missed**	the train.

Du bildest das **past perfect** (Plusquamperfekt) mit **had + past participle** (z. B. done, missed). Du verwendest das **past perfect** zusammen mit dem simple past, wenn du über Handlungen oder Vorgänge berichtest, die noch vor einem Zeitpunkt in der Vergangenheit stattgefunden hatten.
Frage und **Verneinung** sind einfach: She had not done.
Had he missed?

A week in Manchester

Mr Garner went to see his friend Mr Potter last autumn.

a) **Sunday morning:** arrive at the airport / take a bus to town

After he had arrived at the airport he took a bus to town.

b) **Sunday afternoon:** arrive at the house / Mr and Mrs Potter welcome him

. . . .

c) **Monday:** visit a gallery in the afternoon / have a long and good breakfast

. . . .

d) **Tuesday:** go on a boat trip / have a drink at a pub in the evening

. . . .

e) **Wednesday:** go to a concert in the evening / take a walk along the river

. . . .

f) **Thursday:** The Potters give a party / buy a lot to drink and eat

. . . .

g) **Friday:** Mr Garner pack his suitcase / say good-bye to the Potters

. . . .

h) **Saturday:** spend a day in Frankfurt / go home

. . . .

Use past perfect and simple past. 33

Beachte, dass das **past perfect** weiter zurückreicht als das **past**.

a) After John . . . . (leave) the underground he . . . . (not, know) where he . . . . (be).

b) When John . . . . (lose) his way, he . . . . (ask) a policeman.

c) After the policeman . . . . (tell) him where to go, he . . . . (find) the next bus stop.

d) Before the bus . . . . (arrive), John . . . . (have) a look at the timetable.

e) As soon as the bus . . . . (stop), he . . . . (jump) onto the platform.

f) Although he . . . . (take) some extra money with him, he . . . . (not, have) enough.

g) After he . . . . (get) the ticket, he . . . . (see) that he . . . . (cannot) pay the fare.

h) Luckily John . . . . (meet) a friend he . . . . (not, see) for many years.

i) After John . . . . (ask) his friend for some money, he . . . . (give) him a pound.

34 Complete the sentences.

Revision

Use **going to-future**	or	**will-future**
Take an umbrella It **is going to rain.**		I think it **will** also **rain** tomorrow.
Tim **is going to give** a birthday party.		He **will be** fourteen next Saturday.

Du verwendest das **going to-future**, wenn du einen **Plan** oder eine **Absicht** hast.
Mit dem **will-future** drückst du aus, dass du **Vorhersagen** und **Vermutungen** für die Zukunft hast. Häufige Wörter hierfür sind: hope (hoffen), to be sure (sicher sein), think (denken), suppose (vermuten), perhaps (vielleicht), probably (wahrscheinlich).

a) Where are you going? – I . . . . (buy) tickets for the theatre.

b) What did the weather forecast say? – The report said: "It . . . . (be) a warm and sunny day, but in the evening there . . . . (be) some showers."

c) What . . . . (you, do) next weekend? – I phoned my friend. We . . . . (spend) a day in London. Perhaps we . . . . (visit) the zoo. We . . . . (return) late at night.

d) Why is Robert learning Russian? He . . . . (study) in Moscow next term.

e) Has your uncle already arrived? – No he hasn't. The train . . . . (probably, not come) on time. I . . . . (meet) him at the station.

f) Wait a moment. I . . . . (help) you.

Make sentences. Use the present progressive future. 35

Tom **is playing** squash tonight.
His friend **is coming** to see him tomorrow.

Du verwendest das **present progressive** auch, wenn du ausdrückst, dass du in der **Zukunft** etwas **fest geplant** hast. Meist steht eine Zeitbestimmung (z. B. tonight, tomorrow) dabei, die die Zukunft angibt.

a) Peter / come / see / his friend / tomorrow.

....

b) Mrs Ward / take / her children / to the zoo / on Sunday.

....

c) They / have breakfast / at 9 o'clock.

....

d) Mr Ward / is / stay / at home / tonight?

....

e) He / travel / to London / on Sunday.

....

f) Mr Ward / go / to a concert / in the evening.

....

g) They / play / Mozart.

....

h) Mr Ward / take / a train / to get to London.

....

i) He / come back / on Monday morning.

....

j) He / stay / at a hotel / on Sunday night.

....

36 Fill in the gaps using a gerund.

Travelling by plane is exciting.	*Reisen mit dem Flugzeug ist aufregend.*
Mr Potter enjoys **flying.**	*Herr Potter fliegt sehr gern.*
He likes to look around airports.	*Er schaut gerne auf Flughäfen herum.*

Diese **-ing-Form** (Gerund) kann als **Subjekt** eines Satzes (z. B. travelling) oder als **Objekt** (z. B. flying) stehen.
Das Gerund steht nach **bestimmten Verben**:

avoid	– *vermeiden*
enjoy	– *genießen, sehr gern tun*
finish	– *aufhören*
mind	– *etwas dagegen haben*
keep	– *weitermachen*
stop	– *aufhören*

Nach folgenden Verben kann entweder die **-ing-Form** oder der **to-Infinitiv** stehen:

begin	– *anfangen*
hate	– *hassen*
like	– *gern tun*
prefer	– *lieber tun*

Flying as a hobby.

a) Mr Clifford likes . . . . (travel) by plane.

b) He always says that . . . . (fly) is great fun.

c) He enjoys . . . . (walk) round the airport, but his wife avoids

. . . . (go) on holiday this way.

d) She doesn't mind . . . . (stay) at home while her husband enjoys

. . . . (look) at all the planes.

e) . . . . (go) by train is Mrs Clifford's hobby.

f) She never stops . . . . (look) at timetables.

g) She prefers . . . . (travel) in fast trains.

h) Finally Mr Potter has finished . . . . (talk) about his favourite hobby.

Write one sentence by using a gerund and the correct preposition if necessary.

37

Mr Potter is **fond of** travelling to foreign countries.
He **thought of** visiting Australia next summer.
The best **chance of** going on holiday is flying by plane.

Du verwendest die **-ing-Form** (Gerund) nach **Präpositionen** (z. B. of). Diese können verbunden sein mit einem **Adjektiv**:	**afraid of** – *Angst haben* **fond of** – *gern tun* **good at** – *gut sein in* **interested in** – *interessiert an* **tired of** – *genug haben von*
mit einem **Verb**:	**think of** – *daran denken* **succeed in** – *Erfolg haben* **look forward to** – *sich freuen auf*
mit einem **Substantiv**:	**chance of** – *Gelegenheit zu* **difficulty (in)** – *Schwierigkeiten zu* **way of** – *Art und Weise (zu)*

A flight to Australia

a) Mr Clifford wanted to travel to Australia. He was fond of it.
Mr Clifford was fond of travelling to Australia.

b) Mr Clifford could not find out the cheapest flight. He had difficulty.

c) At last he got a flight in September. He succeeded.

d) He didn't fly with a small airline. He was not interested.

e) Mr Clifford didn't want to miss his plane. He was afraid.

f) He waited at the airport for a very long time. He was tired.

g) He wanted to stay in Australia for two months. He thought of it.

h) He came back in October. He had a chance.

i) He hoped to see his wife soon. He was looking forward to it.

38 Use the passive.

Mr Potter's car **is checked** regularly.	*Herrn Potters Auto wird regelmäßig untersucht.*
It **must be repaired** by a mechanic.	*Es muss von einem Mechaniker repariert werden.*
It **can be used** soon.	*Es kann bald benutzt werden.*

Du bildest das **Passiv** (passive) mit einer Form von **to be** (im present: am, is, are) und dem **past participle** (Partizip Perfekt).
Wenn du sagen willst, wer eine Handlung ausführt, verwendest du **by** (z. B. by a mechanic). Du kannst das Passiv auch mit **modalen Hilfsverben** (z. B. can, must) **+ be + past participle** bilden.

At a garage

a) Mr Green owns a garage.

A garage . . . .

b) He must repair a lot of cars.

. . . .

c) He should check the engines.

. . . .

d) Mr Green does all the work by himself.

. . . .

e) Mr Green can't repair all types of cars.

. . . .

f) He mustn't drive buses.

. . . .

g) Mr Green writes the bills.

. . . .

h) The customers seldom pay the bills on time.

. . . .

Complete the sentences. Use the passive (past). 39

A man **was run over** last night. *Gestern Abend wurde ein Mann überfahren.*
Two people **were taken** to hospital. *Zwei Leute wurden ins Krankenhaus gebracht.*

Im **simple past** bildest du das **Passiv** mit **was/were + past participle.**

An accident

a) An old woman .... (knock down) by a taxi last weekend.

b) The main road .... (block) for an hour.

c) The woman and the taxi driver .... (take) to hospital.

d) A doctor .... (call) when they arrived there.

e) The woman's leg .... (operate on) immediately.

f) The driver .... (send) home after two hours.

g) The next day the woman .... (visit) by her husband.

h) The following day the driver .... (question) by the police.

i) The taxi .... (repair) in a garage.

j) The bill for the repairs .... (send) to the driver.

k) The cost of the hospital .... (not pay) by him.

Correct the mistakes. 40

a) The taxi was drove by Mr Garner. ....

b) The accident were not seen from the police. ....

c) Mr Garner was send to hospital. ....

d) The doctor was operated on by the woman. ....

41 Make sentences in the passive. (Present perfect)

The boys **have been called** all morning. — *Die Jungen sind schon den ganzen Morgen gerufen worden.*

The letter **hasn't been written** yet. — *Der Brief ist noch nicht geschrieben worden.*

Im **present perfect** bildest du das **Passiv** mit **has/have been** + **past participle**.

A mess in the classroom. (Say what has happened.)

a) pupils / make / a mess / in the classroom.

A mess has been made in the classroom by the pupils.

b) throw around / paper / all over the floor.

. . . .

c) boys / break / some chairs.

. . . .

d) one of the boys / catch / form teacher.

. . . .

e) off the wall / knock / a picture.

. . . .

f) two girls / injure / piece of chalk.

. . . .

g) a book / hit / a boy.

. . . .

h) bad things / write / on blackboard.

. . . .

i) Mike's book / tear / to pieces.

. . . .

j) the form teacher / call / the headmaster.

. . . .

Form sentences. Use the passive. (Future) 42

Mr Garner's car **will be repaired.** *Herrn Garners Auto wird repariert werden.*
Mr Garner **will be asked** some questions. *Man wird Herrn G. einige Fragen stellen.*

Das **will-future** bildest du im **Passiv** mit **will be** + **past participle**.

A new house. (Say what will be done.)

a) the walls / paint ....

b) the rooms / decorate ....

c) a new garage / build ....

d) the roof / repair ....

e) the floor / clean ....

f) a new kitchen / buy ....

g) friends / invite ....

Say it in English. 43

Du **musst nun** verschiedene Zeiten im Passiv bilden.

Du berichtest über einige Ereignisse. Du sagst, dass ...

a) dein Fahrrad gestohlen worden ist.
b) deine Uhr gestern repariert wurde.
c) das neue Kino in einer Woche eröffnet werden wird.
d) das Spiel von deiner Mannschaft verloren wurde.
e) das nächste Spiel gewonnen werden muss.
f) der neue Spieler nicht bezahlt werden kann.

5 Modalverben

44 Fill in must – mustn't – needn't.

Revision

Must heißt müssen. **Mustn't** heißt nicht dürfen.
Needn't heißt nicht müssen/nicht brauchen.

a) We .... hurry. It's late. You .... buy a ticket because I've got one. Passengers .... smoke in the underground.

b) At the zoo you .... keep to the rules. You .... feed the animals.

c) Peter .... practise the guitar tonight, but he .... do any maths homework. They did it at school.

d) Mr Grey .... forget to pay back the money he borrowed from his bank. He .... pay it at the end of this month, but he .... pay it this week.

e) Clare is ill. She .... go to school. She .... stay at home, but she .... stay in bed.

45 Say it in English.

Sage, dass,

a) Herr Grey hier nicht parken darf, weil der Platz frei bleiben muss.
b) Herr Weiß sich nicht beeilen muss, weil er nicht um 8 Uhr im Büro sein muss.
c) Herr Potter um 6 Uhr zu Hause sein muss und nicht zu spät kommen darf.

Use other tenses of the modal verbs. 46

John **must** help his father.
muss
He **needn't** clean the kitchen.
muss nicht
He **mustn't** go out tonight.
darf nicht
He **can** go out in the afternoon.
darf
He **can** walk to his friend's.
kann

He **had to** help him yesterday.
musste
He **didn't have to** clean the hall.
musste nicht
He **was not allowed to** go out last night.
durfte nicht
He **will be allowed to** go out at the weekend.
wird dürfen
He **will be able to** see his friend soon.
wird können

Von den **Modalverben** (modale Hilfsverben) **must, needn't, mustn't, can** kannst du nicht alle Zeiten bilden. Die **„Ersatzformen" have to** (für must), **not have to** (für needn't), **not be allowed to** (für mustn't) und **be able to/be allowed to** (für can) kannst du für alle Zeitformen verwenden.

a) John **must** get up at seven. Yesterday he . . . . at six. Tomorrow he . . . . at nine.

b) Clare **needn't** help with the housework from Monday to Friday. She . . . . last weekend because her mother did all the work. She . . . . next Sunday because it's her birthday.

c) John **mustn't** watch TV tonight. He . . . . see a film yesterday. He . . . . watch TV when he has school next morning.

d) John **can** use his father's bike. He . . . . it during his next holidays. He . . . . take his father's rucksack last weekend.

e) Clare **can** play the guitar. She . . . . in a band next summer. She . . . . a little tune two years ago.

6 Satzarten

47 Form questions. Ask for the underlined parts.

	Does	Peter read books?
	Has	he finished this book?
	Did	Robin live in Sherwood Forest?
Where	**were**	his men at first?
Who	**did**	Robin ask to live with him in the forest?
		Who wanted to catch them?
		What happened in Nottingham?

Revision

Yes-/No-Fragen beginnen mit einem **Hilfsverb** (z. B. has). Ist kein Hilfsverb da, nimmst du **do/does** im **simple present**, **did** im **simple past**. Vor dem Hilfsverb kann bei anderen Fragen ein Fragewort stehen (z. B. where). Wenn du nach dem **Subjekt** eines Satzes fragst (z. B. who), umschreibst du nicht mit **do/does** oder **did**.

Robin Hood

a) Peter is reading a book about Robin Hood.

. . . .

b) He has never read such a book before.

. . . .

c) The book is very interesting.

. . . .

d) Robin Hood lived in Sherwood Forest.

. . . .

e) Robin and his men fought against the Sheriff of Nottingham.

. . . .

f) The Sheriff couldn't catch them because they hid in the forest.

. . . .

g) Robin and his men went to Nottingham on a Sunday morning.

. . . .

Ask for the underlined parts. 48

Mr Grant **dreamt about** a terrible monster.
What did Mr Grant **dream about** ?

His familiy was **laughing at** him.
Who was his family **laughing at** ?

Revision

Im Fragesatz stellst du die **Präposition** (z. B. about), genau wie im Aussagesatz, hinter das **Verb.**

Loch Ness Monster

a) Mr Grant is interested in strange stories.

b) One day he heard about the monster in Loch Ness.

c) He read all books he could find about it.

d) Mr Grant was looking forward to his holiday in Scotland.

e) Last summer he made a journey to Loch Ness.

f) There he was waiting for the monster.

g) Dark clouds came from the west.

h) Suddenly an enormous creature came out of the water.

i) Mr Grant was very much afraid of what he saw.

j) In the end he woke up in his tent.

49 Fill in *who, which / that* or *whose.*

The boy who is standing over there is my friend.
The boat which / that has sunk is ours.
The boy whose brother is in the team is Tom Brown.

Who bezieht sich auf **Personen**, **which** auf **Sachen**. **That** kann auch für Sachen stehen, manchmal für Personen. **Whose** verwendest du, um die Zugehörigkeit, den Besitz auszudrücken. Es steht für Personen und Sachen.

The boat race

a) Jim Brown is one of the sportsmen . . . . study at Oxford.

b) His friend John studies also in a town . . . . has a famous university.

c) They take part in the boat race . . . . takes place on the Thames.

d) They are among the best sportsmen . . . . are chosen by the coach.

e) They use boats . . . . are very light.

f) The race . . . . takes place in March is a great attraction.

g) The Oxford team . . . . colour is dark blue is strong this year.

h) John . . . . the Cambridge team didn't know before is the best man.

50 Correct the mistakes.

a) Jim whose is John's friend studies at Oxford. . . . .

b) The boat who is standing over there belongs to Jim's team. . . . .

c) John which trains very hard is also a good student. . . . .

d) This is Sally who sister is my friend. . . . .

Fill in *who, which* or *that* and leave out the pronoun if possible. 51

The boy	**who**	you see over there is my friend.
The girl		you see over there is my sister.
The boat	**which / that**	they use today is not theirs.
The boat		they use today is old.

Hier sind **who** und **which/that Objekt** des Relativsatzes. Du kannst sie weglassen. Man nennt diese Relativsätze **contact clauses.**
Denke daran, dass du **who** und **which/that** nicht weglassen darfst, wenn sie **Subjekt** des Relativsatzes sind.

a) Oxford and Cambridge are old towns . . . . are famous for their universities.

b) The Oxford-Cambridge boat race is an event . . . . a lot of people like to see.

c) It's always an exciting race . . . . the spectators (Zuschauer) come to watch.

d) The Oxford team is the team . . . . won last year.

e) These are the new boats . . . . were especially designed for the race.

f) John Brown is one of the students . . . . the coach chose for the team.

g) John has a brother . . . . is twenty years old.

h) The team . . . . had the best start was that of Cambridge.

52 Join the two sentences. Use a relative clause and leave out the pronoun.

We were talking **about** a boy.
This is the boy who we were talking **about.**
This is the boy we were talking **about.**

I have been looking **for** a bike.
The bike which I have been looking **for** is Peter's.
The bike I have been looking **for** is Peter's.

Du kannst auch hier das Relativpronomen **weglassen**, wenn es als Objekt einer Präposition steht. Die Präposition steht, wie im englischen Hauptsatz, **hinter** dem Verb.

a) Do you like the boats? The spectators are looking at them.

Do you like the boats the spectators are looking at?

b) The boats are expensive. The teams are sitting in them.

....

c) The "dark blue" team is sitting in the boat. We were talking about it.

....

d) Is that the Oxford team? The reporter is speaking to them.

....

e) The teams are at the start. The crowd is cheering at them.

....

f) The coach is very good. The Cambridge team is listening to him.

....

g) The result was the same last year. I told you about.

....

53 Translate into English.

a) Die Mannschaft, deren Coach Amerikaner ist, trainiert sehr oft.
b) Das ist das Boot, das Oxford gehört.
c) Das Boot, das die Universität bezahlt, ist teuer.
d) Jim hat einen Freund, der in Cambridge studiert.

Form sentences. Use if-clauses. (Typ 1) 54

– If there **is** enough snow, we **will go** skiing tomorrow.
– If you **come** with us, I **can show** you my new skis.
– If the sun **shines**, **come** with us.

Revision

Im **if-Satz Typ 1** (if-clause) drückst du aus, dass in **Zukunft** etwas geschehen wird, wenn (if) eine bestimmte Bedingung erfüllt wird.
Im Hauptsatz kannst du statt **will** ein anderes **modales Hilfsverb** (z. B. must, can) oder einen **Imperativ** (z. B. **come** with us) verwenden.

a) the children hurry / catch the train

b) it rain / they not stay / outside

c) the boys and girls / go by train / they / can / travel / together

d) the train be / not crowded / everyone / have a seat

e) the children be / hungry / eat / sandwiches

f) they be / fit / can / climb / mountains

g) the boys / not get wet / they / take / waterproofs

h) they / go on / a tour / must / start / early in the morning

55 Complete the conversation. Use if-clauses. (Typ 2)

- If I **had** time, I **would walk** to town.
- If Tony **was** at home, he **could watch** the film.
- If we **went** to London, we **might see** the Queen.

Im **if-Satz Typ 2** drückst du aus, dass etwas geschehen oder sein könnte, wenn eine Bedingung (If I had ...) erfüllt werden würde. Im Hauptsatz kann statt **would** auch ein anderes **modales Hilfsverb** (z. B. could, might) stehen.

Money

a) Jack: What would you do if you . . . . (have) no money?

Alan: If I . . . . no money, I . . . . (gamble) in Las Vegas.

b) Jack: Where . . . . (you, go) if you . . . . (win) a lot of money?

Alan: If I . . . . a lot of money, I . . . . (travel) around the USA.

c) Jack: What . . . . (you, like) to see?

Alan: If I . . . . (have) the chance, I . . . . (cross) Death Valley.

d) Jack: Where . . . . (you, can) book your holiday?

Alan: If I . . . . (find) a good travel agent's, I . . . . (book) it there.

e) Jack: I . . . . (come) with you if I . . . . (have) enough money.

Alan: It . . . . (be) very nice if we . . . . (can) travel together.

Finish the sentences. Use if-clauses. (Typ 1 u. 2) 56

Du musst nun überlegen, welchen Typ von **if-Satz** du verwendest.

A journey to Scotland

a) You should take your car with you if you . . . . (want) to visit Scotland.

b) The weather . . . . (be) fine if you come in August.

c) You . . . . (must, go) to a travel agent's if you are planning a journey.

d) If you came this year, you . . . . (can, see) the Edinburgh Festival.

e) If you . . . . (cannot, come) . . . . (tell) us in time.

f) You could travel by plane if flights . . . . (be) cheaper.

g) If I am in Scotland in August, I . . . . (meet) you in Edinburgh.

Say it in English. Use direct speech. 57

Bob fragt seinen Freund, ob ...

a) er ihn am Flugplatz abholen kann, wenn er mit dem Flugzeug käme.

Ian antwortet, dass ...
b) er mit dem Auto kommt, wenn seine Ferien lang genug sind.
c) er die Highlands besuchen würde, wenn er die schönste Route finden würde.

Bob sagt ihm, dass ...
d) Ian in ein Hotel gehen solle, wenn er Camping nicht mag.
e) er zur Insel Skye fahren könnte, wenn er genug Zeit hätte.

7 Wortstellung im Satz

58 Make sentences with the correct word order.

S	AdH	V	AdO	AdZ
Geoff	usually	sings	at the pub	on Friday evenings.

AdZ	S	AdH	V	AdO
On Sunday	they	never	go	to the pub.

Revision

Im **Aussagesatz** lautet die **Wortstellung**: Adverb der Zeit (AdZ) – Subjekt (S) – Adverb der Häufigkeit (AdH) – Verb (V) – Adverb des Ortes (AdO) – Adverb der Zeit (AdZ).
Das **Adverb der Zeit** kann am Beginn oder Ende des Satzes stehen.
Das **Adverb der Häufigkeit** steht zwischen Subjekt und Verb oder nach dem 1. Hilfsverb (z. B. can) und hinter einer Form von to be (z. B. is): *He **is sometimes** tired on Monday morning.*

a) Geoff / holidays / in summer / take / often / in Wales

b) to pubs / he / usually / in the evening / go

c) Geoff / the National Gallery / sometimes / like to visit / in Aberystwyth

d) usually / the Welsh / English / speak / but / they / never / forget / their Welsh language

e) always / try / Geoff / Welsh / to understand

Answer the questions. (Sentences with two objects.) 59

	indirektes Objekt	direktes Objekt	
The postman brought	Mr Potter	a letter	(not a parcel).

	direktes Objekt	indirektes Objekt	
The postman brought	a letter	to Mr Potter	(not to Peter).

Im Englischen gibt es Verben (z. B. bring), nach denen **zwei Objekte** stehen können. Normalerweise steht das indirekte Objekt (z. B. Mr Potter) **vor** dem direkten (z. B. a letter). Wenn du das indirekte Objekt **betonen** willst, steht es am **Ende**.
Wörter mit **zwei** Objekten:

bring	– *bringen*	**give**	– *geben*
offer	– *anbieten*	**pass**	– *reichen*
sell	– *verkaufen*	**send**	– *schicken*
show	– *zeigen*	**tell**	– *erzählen*
write	– *schreiben*		

a) What did Janet send Mr Bates? (a letter)

....

b) Who did the postman give the letter? (Peter, not Mr Bates)

....

c) What did Janet tell her friend? (an adventure)

....

d) Who did Mrs Bates offer a cigarette to? (the postman, not his wife)

....

e) What did Robert show his sisters? (the pictures)

....

f) What did Mr Cooper pass his wife? (her glasses)

....

g) What does Monica teach her? (German)

....

60 Form sentences. (Two objects)

Mr Potter said hello **to his friend.** (indirektes Objekt)

Geoff explained the problem **to Mr Potter.** (indirektes Objekt)

Bei **einigen Verben** stellst du das **indirekte Objekt** immer mit **to** an das **Satzende**:

add	– *hinzufügen*	**deliver**	– *liefern*
describe	– *beschreiben*	**explain**	– *erklären*
introduce	– *sich vorstellen*	**prefer**	– *vorziehen*
say	– *sagen*		

a) The painter added .... (a tree, picture).

b) The postman delivers .... (Mr Bates, a letter).

c) Sheila described .... (the accident, girl-friend)

d) Can you explain .... (me, that problem)?

e) Tom introduced .... (Mrs White, himself).

f) The girls like tea. They prefer .... (coffee, tea).

g) We said .... (her, nothing).

61 Correct the mistakes.

a) Geoff explained Mr Potter the problem. ....

b) Sarah added the list to the words. ....

c) Mr Potter showed his wife it. ....

d) Mr Evans introduced himself the class. ....

e) John described me the way. ....

Wörterliste der Übersetzungen Deutsch – Englisch

abholen	fetch	Mannschaft	team
Amerikaner	American		
amüsieren	amuse	Nachbar	neighbour
anprobieren	try on	nett	nice
Autofabrik	car factory	organisieren	organize
Autowerkstatt	garage		
		parken	park
beeilen	hurry	Platz	place
benützen	use		
bezahlen	pay	reparieren	repair
billig	cheap		
brauchen	need	schneiden	cut
Büro	office	schnell	fast
		solch	such
eröffnen	open	sondern	but
		spät	late
fahren	drive, go	Spiel	match
Fahrrad	bicycle, bike	Spieler	player
Ferien	holiday	springen	jump
Flughafen	airport	stehlen	steal
Flugzeug	plane		
Freundin	girl-friend	Tanzen	dancing
		teuer	expensive
Gast	guest	tragen	wear
gehören	belong to	trainieren	train
genug	enough	Treffen	meeting
gewinnen	win		
Gruppe	group	Uhr	watch
Jugendklub	youth club	verlieren	lose
Kino	cinema	wie viele	how many
Kosten	cost	Woche	week
		Wochenende	weekend
Lärm	noise	wohnen	live
laut	loud		
Leute	people		

Lernbereich RECHTSCHREIBUNG

1 Großschreibung – Bindestrich – Apostroph

2 Schreibregeln

3 Schwierige Wörter

4 Unterschiede zur deutschen Schreibweise

Diese Übungen solltest du gründlich durcharbeiten, wenn du schlechte Diktate geschrieben oder bei anderen Aufgaben Punkte verloren hast, weil du Wörter falsch geschrieben oder verwechselt hast. Die Regeln der Rechtschreibung werden mit schon bekannten Wörtern wiederholt und mit neuen Vokabeln weitergeführt.

1 Großschreibung – Bindestrich – Apostroph

Do you know London? Say where it is. 1

The **T**ower of **L**ondon
the **H**ouses of **P**arliament
Hyde **P**ark
Victoria **S**tation

Queen **E**lizabeth II
the **Q**ueen

BBC
ITN

Große Anfangsbuchstaben: Offizielle Bezeichnungen (Gebäude, Plätze, Staßen), politische Begriffe und Titel, Abkürzungen.

a)	The Prime Minister lives	1	in Trafalgar Square
b)	There are lots of offices and banks	2	on the river Thames.
c)	There is a famous street market	3	in Portobello Road.
d)	The Rock Circus is	4	in Downing Street.
e)	The Houses of Parliament are	5	in Piccadilly Circus.
f)	Nelson's Column is	6	in Baker Street.
g)	The Crown Jewels are	7	in Buckingham Palace.
h)	The Queen lives in	8	in the Tower of London.
i)	Big Ben is	9	in the City of London.
j)	Madame Tussaud's is	10	next to the Houses of Parliament.

!!!

Vielleicht brauchst du einen Stadtplan von London (in deinem Schulbuch oder im Atlas), um die Aufgaben zu lösen. Präge dir die richtige Schreibweise aller Personen, Orte und Sehenswürdigkeiten ein.

2 Put capital letters in the correct places.

Große Anfangsbuchstaben: Ländernamen und ihre Ableitungen, offizielle Bezeichnungen, Monate, Wochentage, Feste.

a) Buckingham palace is the official London residence of her majesty the queen.

Palace ....

Revision

b) The city of London is the financial centre of great britain.

....

c) Downing street is the official residence of the british prime minister.

....

d) The Guiness World of Records exhibition is situated in the fantastic Trocadero centre in piccadilly circus.

....

e) The Houses of Parliament consist of the house of commons and the house of lords.

....

f) Notting Hill Gate in the west of London is famous for its carnival in august.

....

g) The thames barrier protects London against the rising water level.

....

h) The White Tower was built as a royal palace for william the conqueror about 1078. Tourists can visit it nearly every day of the year; it is closed only on christmas eve, christmas day and new year's day.

....

....

Make one word out of two. 3

swimming-pool
Schwimmbecken

Einige zweiteilige Wörter werden mit **Bindestrich** geschrieben.

basin • clock • known • pan • skate • skating

a) ice –
b) to roller –
c) wash –
d) well –
e) alarm –
f) frying –

playground
Spielplatz

Andere zweiteilige Wörter werden **zusammen**geschrieben.

bed • bike • board • class • earth • key
mate • motor • name • quake • room • room • sur

g)
h)
i)
j)
k)
l)

physical education
Sportunterricht

Die meisten zweiteiligen Wörter werden im Englischen **getrennt** geschrieben.

assistant • club • name • recorder • room • year

m) family
n) cassette
o) leap
p) shop
q) dining
r) drama

Achte auf Unterschiede zum Deutschen:
Es besteht kein Zusammenhang zwischen deutscher und englischer Schreibweise!

4 Put two or three words together.

Bilde Wörter, die aus zwei oder drei Teilen bestehen. Überlege dir die richtige Schreibweise: **mit Bindestrich – zusammen – auseinander?**

a) A .... is a place where young people can meet.

b) You can buy newspapers at a ....

c) You sleep in a .... when you are camping.

d) For an English pupil German is a ....

e) Two roads meet at a ....

f) The postman puts the letters into the ....

g) A son's wife is called ....

h) Jane paid for the book with a .... note.

bag
box
centre
cross
daughter
five
foreign
in
language
law
letter
news
pound
roads
sleeping
stand
youth

5 Write the full words.

125	a hundred and twenty-five
2,763	two thousand, seven hundred and sixty-three
35th	thirty-fifth

Beachte den **Bindestrich** zwischen Zehnern und Einerzahlen. – Bei 100 oder 1000 kannst du a hundred/a thousand oder one hundred/one thousand sagen. – Die Tausender werden mit einem Leerraum oder einem Komma abgetrennt, z. B. 2 763 oder 2,763.

a) 21
b) 94
c) 101
d) 228
e) 1,111
f) 30th
g) 31st
h) 99th
i) 101st
j) 234th

Mind the apostrophe 6

What ' s that over there?
It ' s a black bike.
He ' s got a green one.
I don ' t know.
And the girls ' bikes are yellow.

Let ' s have a look.
It can ' t be Peter's bike
Who ' s got a black bike?
The boys haven ' t got black bikes.

Der Apostroph steht im **s-Genitiv** ('s bei einem Besitzer; -s' bei mehreren Besitzern und einem Wort, das den Plural auf -s bildet*) **und in Kurzformen**.
* 's schreibst du, wenn der Plural nicht auf -s endet, z. B. **men's** bikes.

a) Do you know the ...boys'... (boy) names? – Yes. ...They're... (They are) Paul and Simon. .... (Paul) sister plays tennis in my club.

b) Do you know the .... (girl) name? – Yes. .... (She is) called Lisa. .... (She has) worked for our school magazine since May.

c) .... (who has) got a moped? – That boy in front of the café. .... (He is) called Jason. .... (He is not) from here, he comes from Blenville.

d) Jason often plays the guitar at .... (children) parties. He also likes reading. .... (He has) just finished a book about .... (London, history).

Two fleas were walking out of a cinema when they discovered it was raining hard. "Shall we walk?" said one flea. "No", said the other, "let's take a dog."
(flea) (Floh)

* Übungen zum s-Genitiv findest du auch auf der Seite 10.

2 Schreibregeln

7 Add -s or -es.

-s?	book	disco	roof		put	
	book **s**	disco **s**	roof **s**		put **s**	
oder						
-es?	speech	potato	half	wife	fetch	go
	speech **es**	potato **es**	halv **es**	wiv **es**	fetch **es**	go **es**

-s enden der regelmäßige **Plural** von Substantiven (z. B. books) bzw. die 3. Person Singular von Verben im **simple present** (z. B. he/she/it puts).

-es schreibst du nach **Zischlauten** (z. B. speeches, boxes, buses, quizzes, bushes), bei einigen Substantiven auf **-o** (z. B. potatoes, tomatoes – aber: discos, pianos, studios, photos) und den Verben go und do. Einige Substantive auf **-f** und **-fe** haben den Plural auf **-ves** (z. B. halves, calves, shelves, wives, lives, knives) – andere bilden eine normale Pluralform auf **-s** (z. B. roofs, cliffs).

!!! life [ai] → lives [ai] (das Leben)
to live [i] → he lives [i] (er lebt)

Fill in the plural.

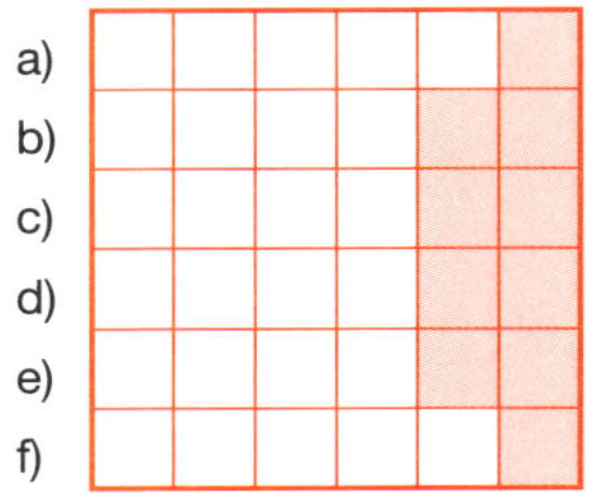

a) radio
b) leaf
c) bush
d) knife
e) calf
f) cliff

He/she/it does it.

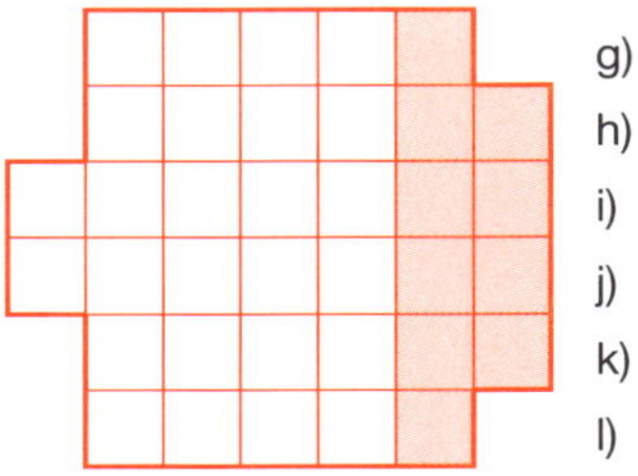

g) beat
h) push
i) teach
j) watch
k) miss
l) talk

-ys or -ies? 8

journe **y**	enjo **y**	**y** oder **i** ?	dictionar **y**	marr **y**
journe **ys**	enjo **ys**		dictionar **ies**	marr **ies**

-ys enden der **Plural** von **Substantiven** (journeys) bzw. die **3. Person Singular** von Verben im **simple present** (he/she enjoys).

-ies schreibst du, wenn **vor dem -y** am Wortende ein Konsonant steht (z. B. dictionaries, he/she marries).

Fill in the plural.

a)
b)
c)
d)
e)
f)
g)
h)
i)

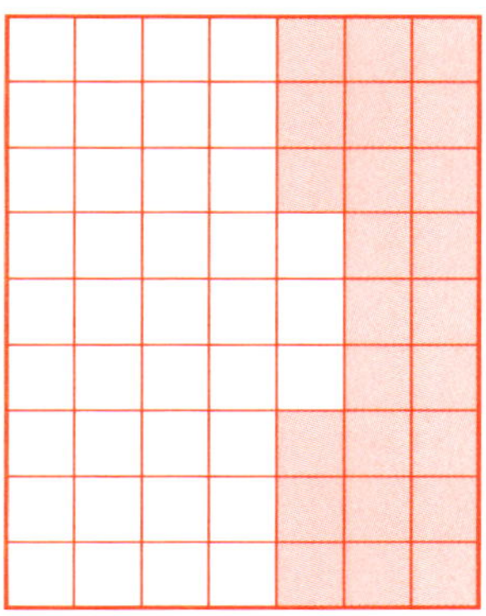

He/she/it does it.

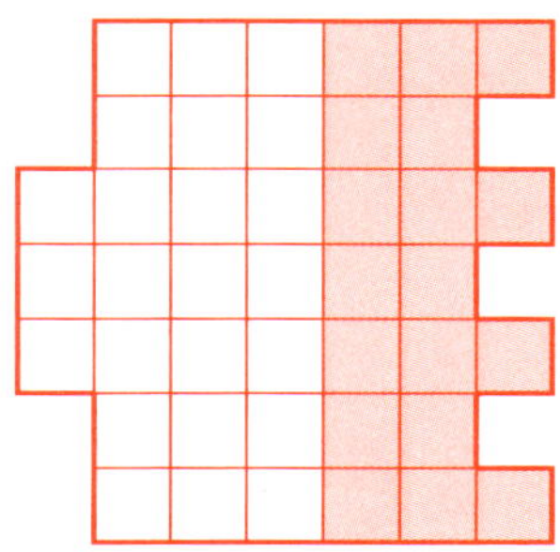

j)
k)
l)
m)
n)
o)
p)

a) a ferry
b) a party
c) a diary
d) a jersey
e) a monkey
f) a valley
g) a story
h) a hobby
i) a reply

j) I tidy
k) I stay
l) I study
m) I enjoy
n) I hurry
o) I play
p) I copy

9 y or i?

enjo **y**
enjo **yed**
enjo **ying**

happ **y**

y oder **i** ?

marr **y**
marr **ied**
marr **ying**

happ **ier**
happ **iest**
happ **ily**

-yed	enden das simple past und past participle bei den regelmäßigen Verben, wenn vor dem **-y** ein Vokal ist (enjoy).
-ied	schreibst du, wenn vor dem **-y** ein Konsonant steht (z. B. married).
-y	bleibt immer vor der Endung -ing, also enjoying und marrying.
y	wird zu **-ier** bzw. **-iest**, wenn du zweisilbige Adjektive auf -y steigerst (aber: grey, greyer, greyest – vor dem -y ist ein Vokal!).
y	wird zu **-ily**, wenn du vom Adjektiv das Adverb ableitest.

Überlege dir die richtige Form der Wörter, z. B. a) – d) die Fragen sind im **simple past**: Antworte in dieser Zeit, e) die Frage ist im **past progressive**, f) nach dem 'fond of' folgt die **-ing-Form**, g) die **Steigerungsform** von 'busy' ist gefragt, h) bilde das **adverb of manner** von 'happy'.

a) What did you **study**, Jane? – I . . . . the map.

b) Where did you **stay** last weekend? – We . . . . at a youth hostel.

c) What did you **carry** in this box, Tom? – I . . . . an old TV.

d) Why did you **hurry** last night? – We . . . . because we wanted to get the bus.

e) What **were you doing** yesterday in the afternoon? – I was . . . . (try) to write an essay but my friend Sheila came.

f) What is your hobby, Peter? – I'm **fond of** . . . . (play) rugby.

g) Manchester and Liverpool are busy towns in England. – But London is **the** . . . . (busy) **of all**.

h) Susan **is smiling** . . . . (happy). – She has passed her test.

Two consonants? 10

Konsonant verdoppeln?	sto **p**	prefe **r** *	trave **l**	swi **m**	ho **t**
	sto **pp** ed	prefe **rr** ed	trave **ll** ed	swi **mm** er	ho **tt** er
	sto **pp** ing	prefe **rr** ing	trave **ll** ing	swi **mm** ing	ho **tt** est
tal **k**	shou **t**	conque **r** *	kee **p**	chea **p**	
tal **k** ed	shou **t** ed	conque **r** ed	kee **p** er	chea **p** er	
tal **k** ing	shou **t** ing	conque **r** ing		chea **p** est	

Nach einem einzelnen, betonten Vokal wird ein einzelner Endkonsonant vor den Endungen **-ed, -ing** bei Verben bzw. **-er, -est** bei Adjektiven verdoppelt. Dies gilt auch für abgeleitete Wörter auf **-er, -ing**, z. B. swim → swimmer, swimming. Bei prefer ist die Endsilbe betont – deshalb wird das -r verdoppelt; bei conquer ist die Endsilbe nicht betont – also keine Verdoppelung des -r. Ein -l wird im britischen Englisch immer verdoppelt (im AE: traveled, traveler). Beachte die normale Schreibung auch bei **shout**, **keep** und **cheap** (2 Vokale!), **talk** (2 Endkonsonanten!).

Fill in the right words.

a) Tom is … (sit) under a tree.
b) Jane likes … (swim).
c) Let's go … (shop).

d) Bill is … (cut) onions.
e) Peter has … (drop) a vase.
f) What are you … (plan)?
g) The car … (skid); it was icy.
h) The … (rob) escaped.
i) Susan is … (thin) than Helen.
j) The … (travel) got on his train.
k) Who's the best … (run)?
l) Jack is the … (fit) in our club.
m) Tom … (answer) yesterday.

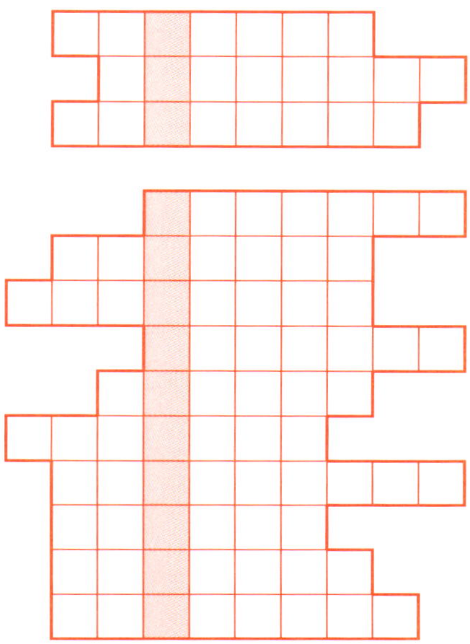

11 Fill in ll or l in the gaps.

ll oder l ?			
	fu ll	a ll	ti ll
	wonderfu l	a l most	unti l

Beachte die besondere Schreibweise von **full, all und till** – im Gegensatz zu den Zusammensetzungen. Denke auch an die Verdoppelung von „l“ vor Endungen, z. B. control – controlled/controlling/controller im britischen Englisch.

a) What a beautifu . . . . day. I'm glad school is a . . ready over.

b) It was a sucessfu . . . . day for Peter. He a . . most won the race.

c) We must stay at school ti . . . . six o'clock. We must a . . so come tomorrow morning.

d) Your paper is fu . . . . of mistakes, Tom. You must repeat the exercise unti . . . . you understand it.

e) Susan can't go out today a . . though the sun is shining. She broke her leg and must stay in bed ti . . . . next week.

f) This is a very usefu . . book. It's fu . . . . of interesting texts.

g) The trave . . . ers bought their tickets at a trave . . . . agency.

h) Put your books a . . . . together on the desk, girls.

i) Jack doesn't like school, he has stopped working a . . together.

Teacher: *“Jeff, your writing is dreadful. Why do you write so badly?”*

Jeff: *“So you won't notice the spelling mistakes, Miss.”*

-e or not? 12

-e	practis **e**	practis **e**	danc **e**	larg **e**	larg **e**
fällt weg!	practised	practising	dancer	larger	largest

Ein stummes -e am Wortende fällt vor den Endungen **-ed** bzw. **-ing** bei Verben sowie **-er** bzw. **-est** bei Adjektiven weg. Dies gilt auch für abgeleitete Wörter auf **-er**, z. B. to dance (tanzen), dancer (Tänzer/in).

-e	complet **e**	advertis **e**	chang **e**
bleibt!	complet **e** ly	advertis **e** ment	chang **e** able

Das -e bleibt aber vor der Endung **-ly**, wenn du aus dem Adjektiv das Adverb bildest, z. B. complete → complet**e**ly*, und bei abgeleiteten Wörtern auf **-ment** oder **-able**.

cano **e** → canoeing
queu **e** → queueing
hous **e** → housework

Bei diesen Übungen musst du auch deine Kenntnisse in der Grammatik anwenden und die Wörter in Klammern in die richtige Form bringen, z. B. a) nach fond + of folgt die **-ing-Form**, b) Look… verlangt **present progressive**; nach look forward + to folgt wieder die **-ing-Form**.

a) Sheila was .... (surprise) when she met her old friend Barbara.

Barbara isn't fond of .... (write), so they had no contact.

b) Look. Tom is .... (leave). He wants to be home early.

He is looking forward to .... (practise) the guitar this afternoon.

c) Susan enjoys .... (be) with her friends.

They often go .... (dance) or .... (swim).

* Übungen zum **Adverb** findest du auf den Seiten 21 – 24, zur **-ing-Form** auf den Seiten 32 – 41.

3 Schwierige Wörter

13 Choose the right word.

write		right
	[rait]	
schreiben		*richtig*

Du übst **Homophone:** Wörter, die gleich ausgesprochen, aber verschieden geschrieben werden und eine andere Bedeutung haben.

buy	by
father	farther
hole	whole
lain	lane
sail	sale
throne	thrown
threw	through
weak	week
wear	where
whose	who's

a) We travelled ~ car.

.... by ....

b) The boys were too tired to go ~

....

c) Father made a ~ in the wall.

....

d) lie, lay, ~

....

e) This old car is not for ~

....

f) throw, threw, ~

....

g) The river Avon runs ~ Stratford.

....

h) Our team is too ~ to win.

....

i) They ~ school uniforms in England.

....

j) That's a nice hat. – I wonder ~ it is.

....

Fill in the right words. 14

right + write [rait]	ride [raid]

Schwierigkeiten bereiten nicht nur **echte Homophone** (wie z. B. right + write), sondern auch **Wörter mit ähnlicher Aussprache**, aber verschiedener Schreibung und Bedeutung (wie z. B. ride).

a) right / write / ride

Susan is going to . . . . a letter to her cousin.

Tom wants to . . . . to school on his bike.

Has Jason found the . . . . telephone number?

b) their / there / they're

Who are the girls over . . . . ?

. . . . Jane and Jill.

. . . . waiting for . . . . bus.

c) also / although

The boys went out . . . . it was very cold.

The girls . . . . played in the garden.

d) want / won't

The Millers . . . . to buy a new car.

But they . . . . buy it if it is too expensive.

!!! won't = will not

e) rarely / really

I . . . . don't know what this means.

Tom . . . . gets up before ten in the morning.

f) know / no / now

Do you . . . . the answer?

I'm sorry, ...

I don't think I can solve the problem . . . .

"Why were you speeding, madam?"
asked the traffic cop.
"Well, officer", came the reply,
"my brakes are bad and I wanted
to get home before I had an accident."

brake – Bremse
break – Pause

15 Find the missing words.

hour
knife
wrong

bus**i**ness
Chris**t**mas
ev**e**ry

throu**gh**
thum**b**
autum**n**

Wir üben **Wörter mit stummen Lauten** am Wortanfang, mitten im Wort und am Wortende. Du sprichst sie nicht – darfst sie aber beim Schreiben nicht weglassen.

a) Sicily is an …
b) Put the plates in the …
c) We go to bed in the …
d) A young cow is a …
e) You write with … on the board.
f) The Houses of … are a famous building in London.
g) The Nelson … stands in Trafalgar Square.
h) English is a … language for German pupils.

16 Find twelve words with a silent letter.

answer	biro	climb	dialect	ever
fifteen	ground	hour	interest	jump
knife	listen	mustn't	neighbour	often
perhaps	quick	racket	sandwich	talk
umbrella	valley	whose	youth	zoo

Difficult words with [e]. 17

Fred head said friend any

Du übst verschiedene Schreibweisen für den Laut [e].

a) r . . . . . d	b) pl . . . . . sure	c) s . . . . . d
d) m . . . . . ny	[e]	e) l . . . . . mon
f) w . . . . . pon	g) l . . . . . sure	h) s . . . . . s

a) a colour
b) Thank you. – It's a ~
c) He … (say) yesterday.
d) a lot of
e) a yellow sour fruit
f) A gun is a ~
g) spare time
h) she … (say)

Difficult words with [i:]. 18

Steve sleeve believe please ceiling

Du übst verschiedene Schreibweisen für den Laut [i:].

a) make fun of
b) Do you … in Father Christmas?
c) Food made from milk
d) this (plural)
e) a high temperature of the body
f) to get (a present)
g) the inside of the roof of a room
h) The … keep order in town.

a) t . . . . . se	b) bel . . . . . ve	c) ch . . . . . se
d) th . . . . . se	[i:]	e) f . . . . . ver
f) rec . . . . . ve	g) c . . . . . ling	h) pol . . . . . ce

19 Difficult words with [u:].

who	shoe	too	two
June	blue	fruit	group

Du übst verschiedene Schreibweisen für den Laut [u:].

a) right, correct
b) anything that can be eaten
c) not to win
d) to pick out from a number of persons or things
e) a small boat
f) you can draw straight lines with it
g) to go from one place to another
h) you can drink apple ~

a) tr	b) f . . . . . d	c) l . . . . . se
d) ch . . . . . se	[u:]	e) can . . . . .
f) r . . . . . ler	g) m . . . . . ve	h) j . . . . . ce

20 Difficult words with [ei].

take raise day eight

Du übst verschiedene Schreibweisen für den Laut [ei].

a) a birthday ~
b) you can go by ~
c) not yesterday and not tomorrow
d) a list of facts and figures
e) to find out how heavy a thing is
f) someone who sells paper, pens, ink
g) a country in Southern Europe
h) to stop sleeping

a) c . . . . . ke	b) tr . . . . . n	c) tod . . . . .
d) t . . . . . ble	[ei]	e) w . . . . . gh
f) st . . . . . tioner	g) Sp . . . . . n	h) w . . . . . ke

4 Unterschiede zur deutschen Schreibweise

Translate. 21

camera *__K__amera*	archite**c**t *Archite**k**t*	cir**c**us *Zir**k**us*	De**c**ember *De**z**ember*	
	passiv**e** *Passiv*	list *List**e***		
comfortab**le** *komfortab**el***	theat**re** * *Theat**er***	Iri**sh** *iri**sch***	astronom**y** *Astronom**ie***	**y**oung *__j__ung*

* Im amerikanischen Englisch: theater.

> Gewisse Unterschiede zur deutschen Schreibweise treten häufig auf und du findest zahlreiche weitere Beispiele zu jedem Muster. Beachte auch die Regeln für große Anfangsbuchstaben (im Englischen wird nicht jedes Substantiv großgeschrieben!).

a) We know a lot about … *(Grammatik):*
… *(Aktiv)* and … *(Passiv).*
… *(Perfekt)* and … *(Futur),*
… *(Infinitiv)* and … *(Partizip),*
… *(Subjekt)* and … *(Objekt).*

b) Here are some jobs:
… *(Doktor)* and … *(Detektiv),*
… *(Architekt)* and … *(Kapitän),*
… *(Sekretärin)* and … *(Mechaniker).*

c) Here are some drinks:
… *(Kaffee)* and … *(Kakao),*
… *(Limonade)* and … *(Tee).*

d) These are subjects at school:
… *(Physik)* and … *(Chemie),*
… *(Biologie)* and … *(Mathematik),*
… *(Geografie)* and … *(Musik).*

e) In … *(Geografie)* we learn a lot about:
… *(Afrika)* and … *(Amerika),*
… *(Asien)* and … *(Australien).*
… *(Irland)* and … *(Schottland),*
… *(Temperatur)* and … *(Klima).*

f) Peter goes shopping in the … *(Supermarkt):*
… *(Orangenmarmelade)* and … *(Zucker),*
… *(englische Schokolade),*
… *(Zigaretten)* and … *(Tabak).*

false *(falsch)*

Tückische Vokale:

marm**a**lade	l**e**monade	Parl**i**ament	t**o**bacco	s**u**n
calend**a**r	hous**e**wife	Fr**i**day	c**o**ffee	S**u**nday
thous**a**nd	Ir**e**land		seld**o**m	s**u**mmer
assist**a**nt			c**o**coa	

22 Translate.

a) Maschine
b) Oktober
c) Toilette
d) Parlament
e) Adresse
f) Marmelade
g) Kopie
h) tausend

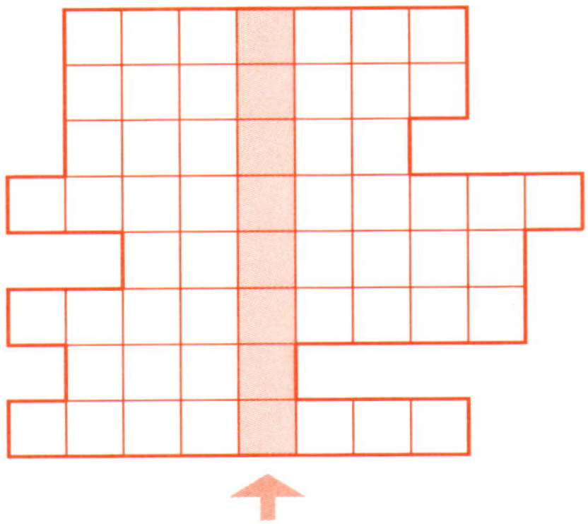

All children like . . . .

i) Joghurt
j) Mikrofon
k) Trompete
l) Detektiv
m) Hausfrau
n) Schokolade
o) Karotte
p) Rakete

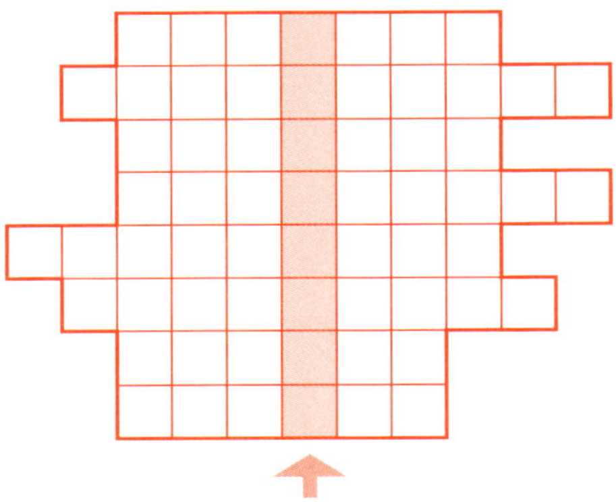

Most children hate . . . .

"Jeff won't be at school today,"
said a voice on the telephone.
"He's not very well."
"Who's that calling?" asked the school secretary.
"My dad."

Find twelve mistakes and correct them. 23

Saturday is Stuart's favourite day because he cleans windows and earns some pocket money. Last weak he wanted to clean Mrs Clays windows. He left his home on his bike at half past eight and carryed with him a small ladder and a bucket.

In Station Street he didn't notice some oil on the road. He skided[1] and fell of his bike. The bucket fell off two and made a loud noise. Some people stopped and looked at him, and some began to laugh. Stuart wasn't injured, but his face was red. He got up and checked his bike. Their were some scratches[2] on it and there was a nail in the back tyre[3]. It had a puncture[4]. Stuart pushed his bike to the bike shop next to the supermarket. The assistent managed[5] to repair it immediatly, but Stuart was late now.

At eleven o'clock he nocked at Mrs Clay's door. "Hello, Stuart. Your late. But never mind. Did you walk here?" "No, I didn't", Stuart replied. "I came by bike. But sometimes walking is faster then going by bike."

1 skid – *ausrutschen*
2 scratch – *Kratzer*
3 tyre – *Reifen*
4 puncture – *Reifenpanne, Loch im Reifen*
5 managed – *hier: schaffte es*

Lernbereich WORTSCHATZ

* Tipps

1 Wörter sammeln und ordnen

2 Wörter einsprachig erklären

3 Wörter richtig anwenden – Communication

TIPPSTIPPSTIPPS

Die Übungen auf den folgenden Seiten helfen dir, englische Wörter besser zu behalten und auch selbst anzuwenden.
Wir möchten dir noch einmal vorschlagen, eine **Lernkartei mit Vokabelkärtchen** anzulegen.*
Die Kärtchen hierfür könnten so aussehen:

Vorderseite des Kärtchens	*Rückseite des Kärtchens*
letter I write a ~ to my penfriend	Brief def.
to write writer writing	schreiben noun
early late	früh opp.
to start to begin	anfangen syn.

Du sammelst nicht nur neue Vokabeln und ihre deutsche Bedeutung, wie wir dies im **1. Lernjahr*** gezeigt haben, sondern erweiterst deine Angaben um **synonyms** (z. B. to *start – to begin*), **opposites** (z. B. *early* – früh; *late* – spät), **definitions** *(I ~ a letter to my pen-friend)* oder Wörter aus derselben **Wortfamilie** (z. B. *to write* – schreiben; *writer* – Schriftsteller/in; *writing* – Schreiben, Schrift). Die nötigen Informationen und Beispiele entnimmst du den Wörterlisten deines Schulbuches und den folgenden Übungen.

1 Wörter sammeln und ordnen

1 Fill in the right words: clothes – computer – school.

Ordne die Substantive den drei Oberbegriffen **Kleidung – Computer – Schule** zu.

biro • book • boots • copy • coat • costume
glove • joystick • lead • order • pencil • pens
plug • printer • ruler • satchel • screen
shirt • sweater • symbol • trousers

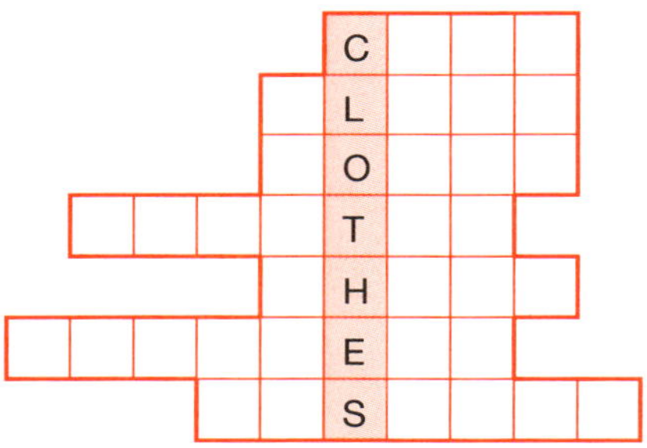

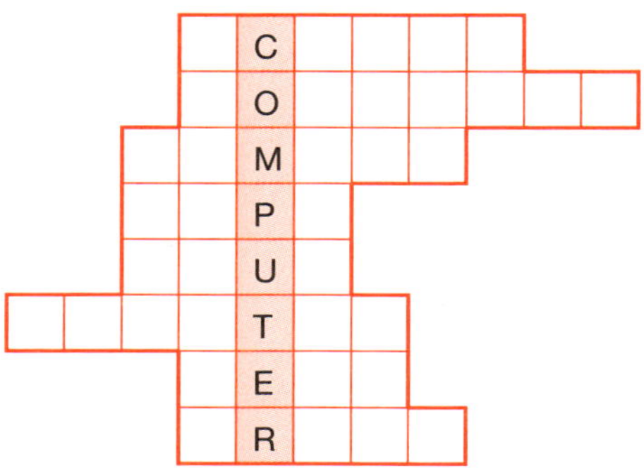

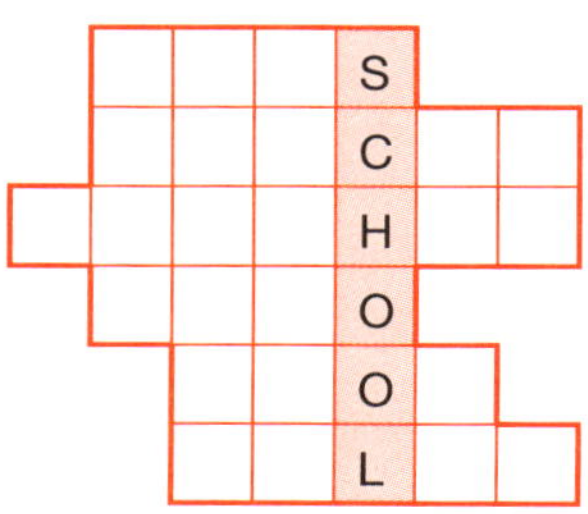

Clothes and computer. Make two groups of twelve words each. 2

Du kannst schwierige Wörter leichter behalten, wenn du sie **nach Sachfeldern ordnest.** Du erweiterst deshalb zwei Gruppen – Kleidung und Computer –, indem du auch Verben und Adjektive zuordnest.

breakdown • central unit • to change • to click on • to connect to copy • denim • disk • fashion • fashionable • to fit • jumper keyboard • mouse • order • to press • to print • to put on • to save scarf • to sew • to take off • to wear • well-dressed

a)

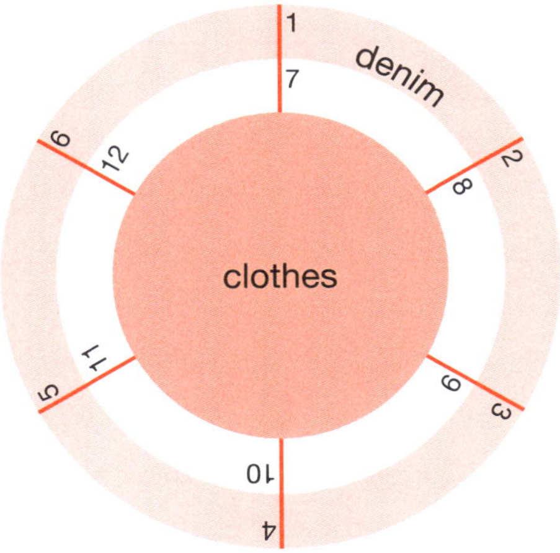

b)

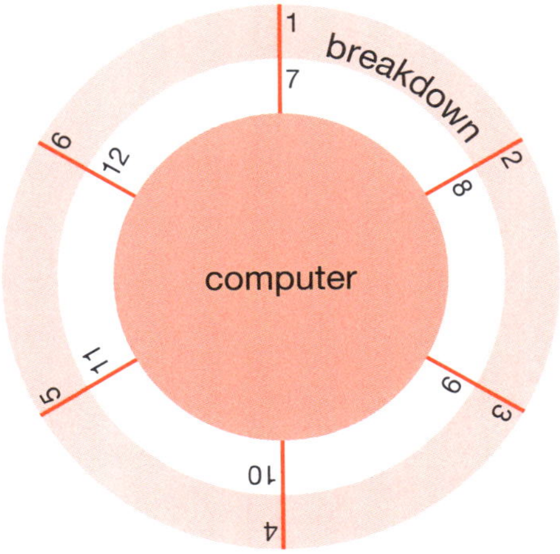

3 Complete the time-table.

Trage in den Stundenplan ein: bestimmte Zeiten und Schulfächer. Da manche Fächer mehrstündig sind, bleiben Lücken im Plan.

	MON	TUES	WEDS	THU
9.00	a)			
9.00 – 10.00	d)	h)	n)	
10.00 – 10.40	e)	k)		
10.40 – 11.00	b)			
11.00 – 11.40	f)	l)	m)	
11.40 – 12.20	g)			
12.20 – 1.40	c)			
1.40 – 2.20	i)	j)	o)	
2.20 – 3.00				
3.00 – 3.40				

a) All the pupils come together for . . . . at 9 o'clock.
b) There is a twenty-minute . . . . from 10.40 to 11.00 o'clock.
c) Pupils can eat their . . . . at school or at home.
d) In . . . . they learn what happened a long time ago.
e) In . . . . they hear about England and other countries.
f) In . . . . the pupils learn about Jesus.
g) They learn about electricity in . . . .
h) In . . . . they study numbers.
i) They sing or play an instrument in . . . .
j) They do . . . . in the gymnasium.
k) In . . . . they study their mother tongue.
l) In . . . . they learn about food.
m) They draw pictures in . . . .
n) They learn a foreign language (It's spoken in France).
o) They play hockey, soccer or tennis in . . . .

History • RE (Religious Education) • French • Music • Geography • lunch • Maths • break • Home Economics • PE (Physical Education) • Science • Assembly • English • Art • Games

Complete the table. 4

Du führst das Wortspiel ‚Stadt – Land – Fluss' mit englischen Vokabeln durch. Du kannst für dich allein (z. B. mit Stoppuhr!) oder mit Freunden/Freundinnen spielen.

	animal	name	job	activity	country	plant
	ant	Andrew	assistant	archery	Austria	apple
	budgie	Brian	baker	badminton	Brasil	banana
	cat	Christopher	chimney-sweep	canoeing	Canada	cherry
d						
e						
f						
g						
h						

Mache in deinem Übungsheft weiter!
Überlege dir auch andere Oberbegriffe (z. B. subjects at school, parts of the body, colours, clothes …)!

Einige Tipps mit Umschreibungen.

d (an animal like a small horse), (you can do it in a swimming pool), (a police officer who finds out how a crime has happened), (a country north of Germany), (a small flower).

e (a strong bird), (someone who does electrical work), (the Irish Republic), …

f (a clever wild animal with red hair and a thick hairy tail), (a member of a fire brigade), (Paris is the capital), (roses and daisies are ~).

g (It is kept for its milk, meat and skin), (He or she shows you the way in another town), (exercises that make the body strong), (a fruit like a large yellow orange).

h (a very large animal that lives in African rivers), (a man or woman at the head of a school), (an evergreen tree with small red berries and prickly leaves – think of Christmas!).

5 Which words fit in?

Wähle die passenden Verben zu den Oberbegriffen aus.

bringen

to bring – *herbringen, mitbringen*
to take – *wegbringen, hinbringen*

a) . . . . these roses away, Bill, they are ugly. . . . . those daffodils here and put them on the table.

b) Mr Davenport . . . . his grandson to the kindergarten, so he is never at home when the postman . . . . him the mail in the morning.

c) Did you . . . . your guitar, Sharon? We could play together. There's plenty of time, and I'll . . . . you to the bus stop in my car.

kochen

to cook food – *Essen zubereiten/kochen*
to make tea – *Tee kochen*
to boil water – *Wasser kochen*
to boil in water – *im Wasser kochen*

d) The water in the kettle is . . . . Sheila, can you . . . . the tea?

e) Who's going to . . . . the meal?

f) Andy will . . . . a lovely breakfast of bacon and eggs.

g) Anne will . . . . some eggs.

Revision

fahren? h) Can you … a bike? i) The buses … every ten minutes. j) Tom always … home by bus. k) Sheila … to work in her new car.

sehen? l) Tom … a great film yesterday. m) … who's coming. n) Can you … the sign over there?

hören? o) I always wake up when I … my alarm clock. p) Do you often … music in the evening?

Find a suitable verb. 6

to ? homework → to **do** homework
to ? a goal → to **score** a goal

Es ist eine große Hilfe, wenn du Vokabeln nicht isoliert lernst, sondern auch überlegst, mit welchen Wörtern sie zu kombinieren sind. Diese **Wortkombinationen** (Kollokationen) entsprechen nicht immer dem Deutschen!

falsch: ~~make~~ your homework – *mache deine Hausaufgabe*
~~shoot~~ a goal – *schieß ein Tor*

catch • give • grow • have • lay • light • make • take

a) .... the table b) .... potatoes

c) .... a cigarette d) .... a bus or train

e) .... a rest f) .... a speech

g) .... a lift h) .... a photo

Which noun belongs to which verb? 7

to attend ? → to attend **school**

Du suchst ein **Substantiv**, das gut zum **Verb** passt, z. B. to attend school *(die Schule besuchen)*.

a) to practise → 4) the flute
b) to miss
c) to iron
d) to fill in
e) to mend
f) to explain
g) to knit
h) to click on

1) the school bus
2) a form
3) a shirt or trousers
4) the flute
5) a broken watch
6) a pullover or socks
7) a difficult problem
8) the symbols

to explain *(etwas erklären)*
to explain sth. **to** sb. *(jdm. etw. erklären)*

8 Find words for people.

to begin	*anfangen*	→	beginn**er**	*Anfänger/in*
to visit	*besuchen*	→	visit**or**	*Besucher/in*
police	*Polizei*	→	police**man**	*Polizist*
		→	police**woman**	*Polizistin*
to cook	*kochen*	→	cook	*Koch, Köchin*

Du sammelst **Berufsbezeichnungen**: männliche und weibliche Formen auf **-er** bzw. **-or**, Männerberufe mit der Endung **-man** und Frauenberufe mit der Endung **-woman**. Manchmal hat das Verb dieselbe Form wie das Substantiv.

a) to conjure
b) to teach
c) to report
d) to deal
e) to drive
f) to paint
g) to invent
h) to bake
i) post
j) business
k) football
l) sing

9 Find the nouns.

to print	*drucken*	→	print**er**	*Drucker (Gerät)*
to build	*bauen*	→	build**ing**	*Gebäude*
to advertise	*werben für*	→	advertise**ment**	*Inserat, Anzeige*
to suggest	*vorschlagen*	→	suggest**ion**	*Vorschlag*
to invite	*einladen*	→	invit**ation**	*Einladung*
to define	*definieren*	→	defin**ition**	*Definition, Erklärung*
to work	*arbeiten*	→	work	*Arbeit*

Du bildest andere **Substantive**, die Sachen oder Begriffe bezeichnen: Endungen **-er, -ing, -ment, -ion, -ation** oder **-ition**. Manchmal hat das **Verb** dieselbe Form wie das **Substantiv**.

a) to state
b) to express
c) to paint
d) to spell
e) to cross
f) to draw
g) to mean
h) to swim
i) to shop
j) to drink
k) to telephone
l) to move
m) to begin
n) to end
o) to visit
p) to inform

meaning – *Bedeutung*
Meinung – opinion

Some difficult nouns. 10

to live [i]	*leben*	→	life [ai]	*Leben*
to choose	*wählen*	→	choice	*Auswahl*

Verb und **Substantiv** einer Wortfamilie unterscheiden sich manchmal stark voneinander.

a) to enter
b) to sell
c) to pronounce
d) to think
e) to advise
f) to describe
g) to fly
h) to please

Find the adjectives. 11

fashion	*Mode*	→	fashion**able**	*modisch*
colour	*Farbe*	→	colour**ed**	*farbig, gefärbt*
wind	*Wind*	→	wind**y**	*windig*
danger	*Gefahr*	→	danger**ous**	*gefährlich*
to use	*benutzen*	→	use**ful**	*nützlich*
		→	use**less**	*nutzlos*
to complete	*fertigstellen*	→	complete	*vollständig*

Du bildest **abgeleitete Adjektive**,
z. B. mit den Endungen **-able, -ed, -y, -ous** oder **-ful/-less.**

a) crowd
b) to tidy
c) friend
d) to correct
e) luck
f) beauty
g) to lock
h) to change
i) cloud
j) power
k) to follow
l) to marry
m) to rain
n) sun
o) success
p) wonder

"What's your father's occupation[1]?" asked the school secretary on the first day of the new term.
"He's a ***conjurer****[2], Miss", said the new boy.*
"How interesting. And what is his favourite trick?"
"He saws people in half."
"Oh, no. And now the next question.
Any brothers and sisters?"
"Not full ones. One half-brother and three half-sisters."

[1] *Beruf,* [2] *Zauberkünstler*

12 Complete the list.

Du sammelst die bekannten Vokabeln einer Wortfamilie in einer Tabelle. Nicht immer findest du zu einem Verb 3 weitere Wörter, wie etwa bei to help *(helfen)* – help *(Hilfe),* helper *(Helfer/in)*, helpful *(hilfreich)*. Du könntest die Sammlung erweitern.

Verben	Substantive		Adjective
	Personen	Sachen/Begriffe	
a) to help	helper	help	helpful
b) to love			
c) to use			
d) to begin			
e) to write			
f) to visit			
g) to rob			
h) to listen			
i) to build			
j) to paint			
k) to live			
l) to succeed			
m)			young
n)			different
o)		fashion	
p)		danger	

2 Wörter einsprachig erklären

People and their jobs. 13

A disc jockey → plays records in a disco or on the radio.
Disc jockeys → play records in a disco or on the radio.

Du führst typische Tätigkeiten an und vermeidest allgemeine Angaben, die auch auf jeden anderen zutreffen, z. B. A disc jockey *likes pop music*. Achte auf die **Pluralendung** und **Verbform** (Disc jockeys play), wenn du von mehreren Personen berichtest.

a) A customer
b) A fireman
c) A doctor
d) Shop assistants
e) A programmer
f) A milkman
g) A postman
h) An instructor
i) An apprentice
j) Reporters

1 comes when you are ill.
2 delivers the milk every morning.
3 shows you how to do a certain sport.
4 goes into a shop to buy something.
5 delivers letters and parcels.
6 puts out fires.
7 is learning to do a job.
8 write for a newspaper or a magazine.
9 help customers and sell things in a shop.
10 works with computer software.

Vehicles. 14

A lorry ... ? → It's a large motor cart for carrying heavy goods.

Du erklärst **Verkehrsmittel**, indem du angibst, **wozu** man sie braucht oder **wie** sie aussehen.

a) A coach — It's a bus …
b) A minibus — It's a …
c) A chairlift — It takes you …
d) A caravan — It's a vehicle with …
e) A van — It's a large motor car …
f) A camping bus — It's a bus …
g) A ferry — It's a boat …

Customer: *"This loaf is lovely and warm."*
Baker: *"So it should be, Madam. The cat's been sitting on it all morning."*

15 Buildings.

A skyscraper … → is a very tall building.

Du erklärst **Gebäude**, indem du typische Eigenschaften (Aussehen, Verwendung) anführst.

- joined at one side to another house
- with no upstairs
- stands alone and has a garden around it.
- a large building with lots of flats and offices
- stands in a row of houses

a) A bungalow is a house with no upstairs ....

b) A detached house ....

c) A semi-detaches house is ....

d) A block of flats is ....

e) A terraced house ....

16 Rooms.

A lounge … → is a room in the house **where** you sit and relax.

Du erklärst **Räume** nach dem Muster: **Angabe der Örtlichkeit + where + Zweck**. Suche aus beiden Kästen je eine Information!

1 a room in the house • a big room in a youth hostel • a large room in a school • a hall • a workshop

2 you and your classmates have your meals • you and your family sleep • a lot of people sleep • you do exercises for the body • cars are repaired

a) A canteen is ....

b) A dormitory is ....

c) A bedroom is ....

d) A gymnasium is ....

e) A garage is ....

Find synonyms. 17

right? *richtig*? correct?

Is this answer **right**?
Well, the first sentence is **correct**, but the second is **wrong**.

Du erklärst die Bedeutung von Vokabeln, indem du Wörter mit (fast) der gleichen Bedeutung findest: **synonyms** (= Synonyme). Eine andere Möglichkeit der einsprachigen Worterklärung wäre es, ein **opposite** anzugeben (z. B. wrong – right): Dies kannst du auf den Seiten 95 – 97 üben.

a) to repair
b) to begin
c) to go away
d) very good, super
e) to ride one's bike
f) pleased
g) correct
h) terrible
i) to go into
j) to destroy

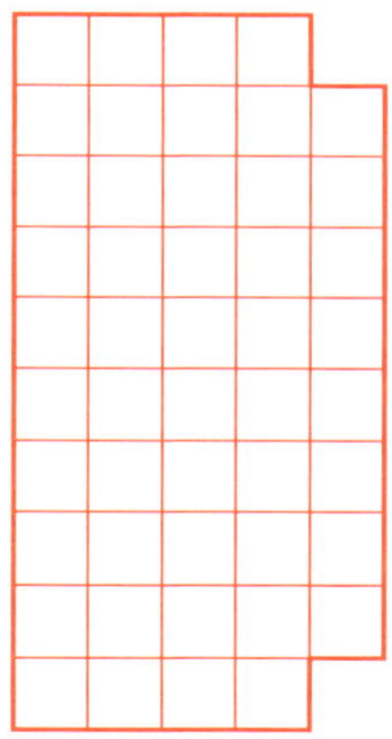

Fill in words that mean the same as each of them. 18

a) Paul **enjoyed** the film. His girl friend . . . . it too.

b) The policeman **noticed** a thief. He . . . . him from his car.

c) What do you do in your **spare** time, Bill? I usually go fishing in my . . . . time.

d) The show on TV was **terrific**. It was really . . . .

e) Who is the **top** player in your soccer team? I think Alan is our . . . . player.

19 Explain the words in bold print.

Can you **repeat** that?
Can you **say** that again?

What did he **answer**?
What did he **reply**?

Du erklärst **Wörter**, indem du die **Bedeutung** umschreibst (to explain – erklären; to paraphrase – umschreiben), wie z. B. *to repeat*, oder du findest ein **synonym**, wie z. B. bei *to answer*.

a) Tom is **exhausted** after the long run.	1 very dirty
b) The Bakers have a **huge** garden.	2 well and strong
c) It was **filthy** in the shed.	3 very tired
d) All the players are **fit**.	4 very big
e) Our teacher was **annoyed**.	5 have a lot to do
f) The police came **at once**.	6 quite angry
g) The children **are busy**.	7 right away
h) The police came **immediately**.	8 famous
i) I met a **well-known** writer.	9 at once

Beim Wiederholen könntest du die rechte Spalte abdecken und die Lösungen ohne Hilfen finden.

20 Match the words and definitions.

Du suchst die entsprechende Erklärung in Liste 2.

List 1: words	**List 2: definitions**
a) to attend	1 not to wake up in time
b) to earn	2 to be fond of
c) to repeat	3 to take things out of a bag
d) to leave	4 to talk about
e) get off a bus	5 speak or write a little about
f) to agree	6 to ask somebody to come
g) to invite	7 to say yes
h) to mention	8 to leave a bus
i) to oversleep	9 to go away
j) to like	10 to get money for work
k) to unpack	11 to go to
l) to discuss	12 to say or do something again

Find the opposites. 21

Jason is quite **short**
but Peter is **tall.**

Oft kannst du ein Wort durch ein **opposite** erklären. Wie du bereits weißt, ist ein opposite ein Wort mit entgegengesetzter Bedeutung (manchmal auch **antonym** genannt).

a) long
b) clever
c) sad
d) rich
e) boring
f) loud
g) never
h) dry

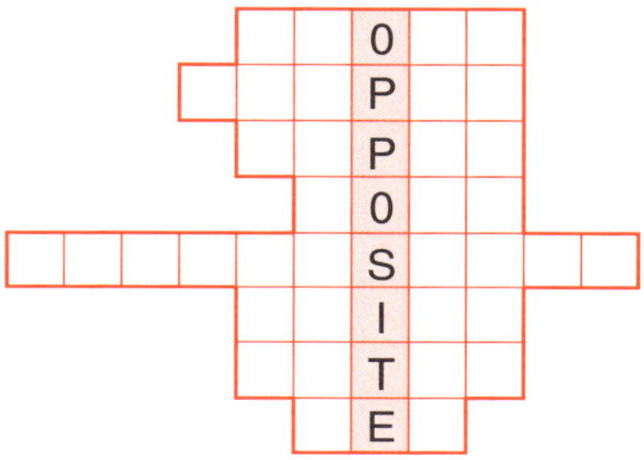

i) to forget
j) expensive
k) light
l) to look for
m) easy
n) beginning
o) friendly

Teacher: *"Do you write with your right hand or your left hand, Billy?"*
Billy: *"Well, I usually write with a pen."*

22 Complete the texts by using opposites.

Achte auf die **Wortart** (z. B. Verb, Substantiv, Adjektiv) und **Form** (z. B. -ing-Form, he/she ...s, simple past) deines **opposites**.

a) Do you **love** classical music, Ken?

I . . . . it.

b) Why are you **shouting**, boys? Mum is sleeping.

Can't you . . . . ?

c) Where do they **sell** these T-shirts?

I'd like to . . . . one.

d) Tell me the **truth**, Barbara.

I can't stand . . . .

e) We **lost** the last soccer match.

I'm sure we'll . . . . next time.

f) Please **leave** the door **open**, Jane.

Don't . . . . it.

g) Why do you **pull** the trolley, Ann?

You must . . . . it.

h) The **entrance** is over there.

But where is the . . . . ?

i) Don't **stop** jogging.

. . . . running.

j) I'd like **something** to eat,

but there's . . . . in the fridge.

k) This is a **serious** story.

I like . . . . stories better.

l) Shall we do the homework **together**?

I think I'll do it . . . .

m) I'm not going to wear **the same** dress at two parties.

Why don't you buy a . . . . one?

Put in the feminine form. 23

Du wiederholst einige bekannte Wörter für Verwandte und Berufe. Achte auf die genaue **Form** der **opposites**, z. B. e) man (Singular), g) men (Plural).

a) son
b) wife
c) uncle
d) husbands
e) man
f) son-in-law
g) men
h) king
i) waiter
j) policeman
k) prince
l) steward

Give the opposites. 24

Revision

a) a **good** plan
b) a **dangerous** road
c) **better** than
d) the **last** day
e) the **best** result
f) **low** temperatures
g) a **positive** answer
h) a **funny** man

i) **inside** the house
j) **after** lunch
k) **against** the plan
l) we are **together**
m) **with** our friends
n) **in front of** the door
o) **up** the hill
p) **under** the table

Use prefixes to find the opposites. 25

happy	*glücklich*		**un happy**	*unglücklich*
correct	*richtig*		**in correct**	*unrichtig, falsch*
possible	*möglich*		**im possible**	*unmöglich*
to load	*aufladen*	**to**	**un load**	*abladen*
advantage	*Vorteil*		**dis advantage**	*Nachteil*

Mit den Vorsilben **un-**, **in-/im-/ir-** bzw. **dis-** kannst du viele **opposites** bilden. Siehe auch die Übungen zur Wortbildung auf Seite 88.

a) friendly
b) usual
c) patient
d) to agree
e) to pack
f) interesting
g) comfortable
h) lucky
i) regular

Leider geht das nicht immer so leicht: **important** (wichtig) ist z. B. kein opposite des nicht existierenden Wortes ~~portant~~.

26 Test: Which words in the text tell you that ...

How to get there The Tower of London is situated on the River Thames next to Tower Bridge.

BY UNDERGROUND: The Circle or District lines to Tower Hill station.

BY BUS: London Transport buses: numbers 15, x15, 25, 42, 78, 100, D1, D9, D11.

Also served by regular sightseeing tours.

"In truth there is no sadder spot on the earth."

THOMAS BABINGTON MACAULAY (19TH CENTURY HISTORIAN)

For more than 900 years, The Tower has stood proud over London. So if you want a taste of history during your visit, come to The Tower. Because The Tower is London.

Opening Hours

1st March 1995 ~ 31st October 1995:

09.00 - 18.00 Monday ~ Saturday
10.00 - 18.00 Sunday

1st November 1995 ~ 29th February 1996:

09.00 - 17.00 Monday ~ Saturday
10.00 - 17.00 Sunday

Last tickets sold one hour before closing.

If you wish to see all The Tower's attractions, you are advised to leave at least two hours for your visit.

Tower closed: 24th-26th December, 1st January.

a) The Tower of London is not far from Tower Bridge.

. . . .

b) The Tower is not open at Christmas.

. . . .

c) You can get there by tube.

. . . .

d) The Tower is a very unhappy place.

. . . .

e) One hour isn't enough time to see all the interesting sights.

. . . .

Du sollst den Text (hier: Prospekt des Tower of London) gründlich durchlesen und dann die Textstellen herausfinden, welche die Angaben bestätigen. Du sollst also versuchen, einen englischen Text einsprachig zu erklären – mit *synonyms* oder *opposites* oder *paraphrases*.

3 Wörter richtig anwenden

False friends. Translate into English and German. 27

Paul stays at the gymnasium.
~~*Paul steht am Gymnasium.*~~
Paul bleibt in der Turnhalle.

Falsche Freunde nennt man Wörter, die so ähnlich wie deutsche Wörter aussehen, aber etwas anderes bedeuten.

Englisch:		Deutsch:
a)	⇦ Flur floor ⇨	....
b)	⇦ Rock rock ⇨	....
c)	⇦ Note note ⇨	....
d)	⇦ Kaffee café ⇨	....
e)	⇦ Art (und Weise) art ⇨	....
f)	⇦ Platz nehmen take place ⇨	....
g)	⇦ City, Stadtzentrum city ⇨	....
h)	⇦ Bank (Sitzbank) bank ⇨	....
i)	⇦ (Kartoffel-)Chips chips ⇨	....
j)	⇦ also also ⇨	....

28 False friends. Translate into German.

who? ✕ *wer?*
where? ✕ *wo?*

why? ✕ *warum?*
because ✕ *weil*

Du wiederholst ‚falsche Freunde'.

a) *Where* is Peter Wright?
b) What do you want to *become*, Jason?
c) Can you hear the *bell*?
d) The *rent* is only 100 £.
e) The *plate* is wonderful.
f) I *wonder* why Jane hasn't come.
g) Our *local* football team is good.
h) I saw a *snake* in the grass.
i) Mother bought a *biscuit*.
j) Susan sat on the *bank* of the river.

Little Angie: *"Mum, does God go to the bathroom?"*
Mum: *"No, dear. Why do you ask?"*
Little Angie: *"Well, this morning I heard Dad knock on the bathroom door and say, "Oh, God, are you still in there?"*

29 Don't mix them up.

although? till? while?

Du übst ‚kleine Wörter'.

although • because • as soon as but • if • so • still • till • while

bis • deshalb • während • aber wenn • weil • sobald als • obwohl • noch

a) Patrick and Jane didn't go for a walk last Sunday . . . . it was raining.

b) Susan watched a thriller last night . . . . she was very tired.

c) George will visit his aunt in Canada . . . . he gets an invitation from her.

d) Andy is away, ... he can't come to my birthday party.

e) Jane has got to work . . . . ten o'clock tomorrow.

f) Jason always listens to records . . . . he is doing his homework.

g) Ann started to read the story a few days ago, ... she hasn't finished it yet.

h) She will return the book . . . . she has read it.

i) Are you . . . . hungry? You've eaten so much.

Write the numbers in words. 30

1 one	1. first	11 eleven	11. eleventh	10 ten	10. tenth
2 two	2. second	12 twelve	12. twelfth	20 twenty	20. twentieth
3 three	3. third	13 thirteen	13. thirteenth	30 thirty	30. thirtieth
4 four	4. fourth	14 fourteen	14. fourteenth	40 forty	40. fortieth
5 five	5. fifth	15 fifteen	15. fifteenth	50 fifty	50. fiftieth
6 six	6. sixth	16 sixteen	16. sixteenth	60 sixty	60. sixtieth
7 seven	7. seventh	17 seventeen	17. seventeenth	70 seventy	70. seventieth
8 eight	8. eighth	18 eighteen	18. eighteenth	80 eighty	80. eightieth
9 nine	9. ninth	19 nineteen	19. nineteenth	90 ninety	90. ninetieth
				100 a hundred	100. a hundredth

Du wiederholst die **Grundzahlen** (z. B. twelve) und die **Ordnungszahlen** (z. B. twelfth) und achtest auf die Tücken der Rechtschreibung!

a) How many days has January got?
b) How many days has February got?
c) How many months has a year got?
d) How many weeks has a year got?
e) How many days has a year got?
f) How many days has a leap-year got?
g) How many pence are there in a pound?
h) How many cents are there in a dollar?
i) How many inches are there in a foot?
j) How many feet are there in a yard?

leap-year – *Schaltjahr*

Write the date. 31

20/6/97 (USA: 6/20/96)
20th June 1997

June 20th, 1997 (v. a. USA)

Schreibe das Datum, wie man es spricht:
June the twentieth, nineteen ninety-seven
oder: the twentieth of June, nineteen ninety-seven
June twentieth, nineteen ninety-seven

a) 14/5/95 …
b) 1/4/97 …
c) 2/12/95 …
d) 3/8/90 …
e) 10/10/96 …

D	1st	= first
	2nd	= second
A	3rd	= third
	4th	= fourth
T	21st	= twenty-first
	22nd	= twenty-second
U	23rd	= twenty-third
M	24th	= twenty-fourth

Policeman: *"I'll have to report you, sir. You were doing at least eighty miles an hour."*
Motorist: *"Nonsense, constable – I've only been driving for ten minutes."*

32 Time expressions: Fill in the correct prepositions, if necessary.

at	eight o'clock	**in**	the morning	**on**	Monday	–	today
	midnight		the afternoon		my birthday		yesterday
	the weekend		the evening		April 1st		tomorrow
	Easter		spring		Easter Sunday		last night
	night		1997		Christmas Eve		next week

Du wiederholst Präpositionen für **Zeitangaben: at** (+ Uhrzeit, Wochenende, Fest); **in** (+ Tageszeit, Jahreszeit, Jahr); **on** (+ Wochentag, Datum, Festtag), ohne **Präposition** (heute, gestern, morgen, letzte ..., nächste ...).

MADAME TUSSAUD'S
THE PROMENADE PIER CAFE

Buses – 2, 13, 18, 27, 30, 74, 82, 113, 159, 176

★ Madame Tussaud's is open from 10 a.m. to 5.30 p.m. every day except Christmas Day.
★ Doors open earlier every weekend, on Bank Holidays and during the Summer Season.
★ Admission prices include VAT.
★ Children 4 years and under admitted free.
★ Souvenir Shop. ★ Combined tickets for Madame Tussaud's and the London Planetarium are available at a reduced rate. ★ Discounts for groups of 10 or more.
Apply to: Group Booking Office, Madame Tussaud's, Marylebone Road, London NW1 5LR.
Telephone: 071-935 6861
★ Promenade Pier Café – tea, coffee, hot and cold buffet.
★ Souvenir Photographs available. ★ Personal photography encouraged.

from ... to – *von ... bis*
about – *ungefähr*

a) Madame Tussaud's opens . . . . 10 a.m. and closes . . . . 5.30 p.m.

b) It is open . . . . 10 a.m. . . . . 5.30 p.m.

c) It is closed . . . . Christmas Day.

d) Doors open earlier . . . . the weekend, ... Bank Holidays and

. . . . summer.

e) There are long queues at the booking office . . . . the morning. You should buy

your ticket . . . . a day before your visit.

Fill in the correct prepositions. 33

to go	**by** bus	to send **by** post	to go **on** foot	to go **for** a walk
to come	**by** ferry		**on** a bike	
	by train		**on** horseback	
	by air			
	by car			

Du übst **Präpositionen**, mit denen du angibst, wie jemand geht/fährt/reist bzw. wie etwas befördert wird. Achte auf das **by** in Passivsätzen!

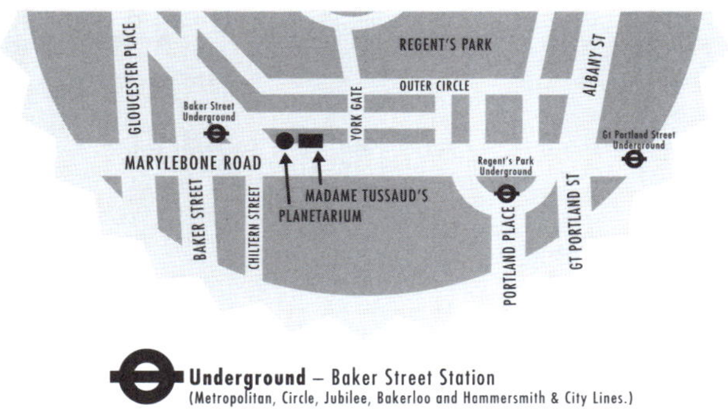

MADAME TUSSAUD'S
BAKER STREET

Sharon Davenport and two friends from abroad want to go to Madame Tussaud's.

a) How can we get . . . . Madame Tussaud's, Sharon?

If you want to go . . . . Underground, you must get off . . . . Baker Street Station. Madame Tussaud's is . . . . the station. Or we can go . . . . bus, there are several buses, 2, 13 or 18. **Buses** – 2, 13, 18, 27, 30, 74, 82, 113, 159, 176

You can go as far as Regent's Park Underground Station and then go . . . . foot, it isn't far.

b) What can we do afterwards?

We can go . . . . Regent's Park to have a little rest. We could go . . . . a walk or even rent a bike and go . . . . bike for an hour or so.

34 You want to say thank you.

Thanks
Thanks very much/ Thanks a lot.

Du bedankst dich bei Freunden.

Thank you.
Thank you very much.

Du bedankst dich bei Bekannten und Fremden.

That's all right.
Not at all.
Don't mention it.
It's a pleasure.
You're welcome.

Du antwortest auf Dank *(Bitte sehr; gern geschehen; nicht der Rede wert).*

!!! Nicht: Please

It's Sharon's 13th birthday.
She got lots of presents from her friends (Patsy, ...) and neighbours (Mr Lewis, ...).

a) Sharon: "Oh, this book is very interesting, Patsy, ..."

Patsy: ". . . . . I'am glad you like it."

b) Sharon: ". . . . . for the present, Mr Lewis. I'll buy a cassette for the money."

Mr Lewis: ". . . . . I hope you'll find a nice one."

35 Say it in English.

a) „Vielen Dank für deine Hilfe, Jason."
„Gern geschehen."

b) „Vielen Dank, Frau Wilson. Das Buch ist wirklich interessant."
„Bitte sehr."

c) „Es war nett, dass Sie mich im Auto mitgenommen haben, Herr Brooks. Vielen herzlichen Dank."
„Aber bitte, nicht der Rede wert."

You need help. 36

Will you help me?
Would you do something for me?
Can you open the door for me?
Can / Could I have something to drink?

Du bittest jemanden um Hilfe.
Could I ...? ist etwas höflicher als *Can I ...?*

Yes, all right.
Yes, OK.
Yes, of course.

Du kommst gerne einer Bitte nach.

I'm sorry, but I can't at the moment.
I'm afraid I haven't got time right now.

Du lehnst eine Bitte höflich ab
und gibst einen Grund dafür an.

You're in London and you need help.
Put the sentences in order.

a) Thank you very much.
b) Yes, of course.
c) Is Rock Circus near here?
d) Excuse me. Can you help me?
e) No. It's only five minutes on foot.
f) Oh yes. Go straight ahead and take the first turning on the right.
g) You're welcome.
h) Is it far?

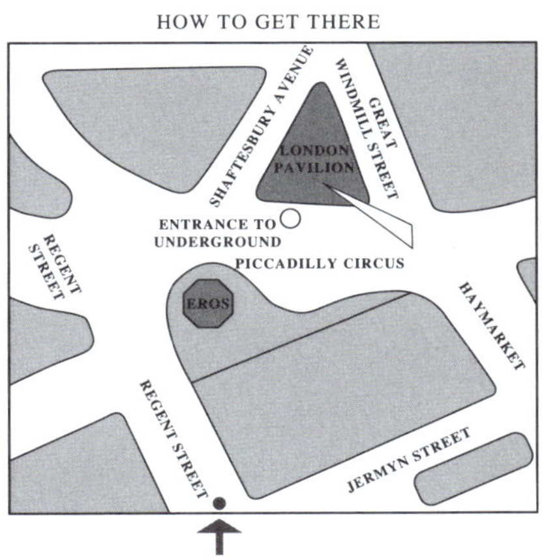

Say it in English. 37

a) „Kann ich noch eine Tasse Tee haben, Jane?"
„Ja, natürlich."
b) „Würden Sie mir die Hausaufgabe noch einmal erklären, Herr Brook?"
„Aber ja. Welche Übung ist es denn?"
c) „Könntest du den Brief für mich in den Briefkasten werfen?"
„Tut mir leid. Ich bin in Eile."
d) „Hilfst du mir bitte, Andy? Die Kiste ist sehr schwer."
„Leider kann ich im Augenblick nicht. Ich warte auf meine Mutter."

38 Say that you are sorry.

I'm sorry, I'm late. I'm so sorry. I'm very sorry. That was my fault.	Du entschuldigst dich.
That's all right. It doesn't matter.	Du zeigst Verständnis.
Excuse me. May I ask you a question? Pardon? Can you repeat that? Sorry? Can you say that again?	Du unterbrichst ein Gespräch und möchtest nicht unhöflich erscheinen. Du hast etwas nicht richtig gehört oder verstanden und fragst nach.

a) *Peter hat seine Hausaufgabe vergessen und entschuldigt sich. Sein Klassenlehrer, Mr Fox, zeigt Verständnis dafür und bittet ihn, die Übung am nächsten Tag zu zeigen.*

Peter: "I've forgotten . . . ."

Mr Fox: "That's . . . ."

b) *Susan kommt zu spät in den Unterricht. Sie berichtet ihrer Englischlehrerin, Miss Potter, dass sie den Bus verpasst hat. Miss Potter meint, dies sei nicht so schlimm.*

Susan: " . . . ."

Miss Potter: " . . . ."

c) *Jane hat ein Wort nicht verstanden und bittet ihren Mathelehrer, Mr Circle, den Satz zu wiederholen.*

Jane: " . . . ."

d) *Miss Potter und Mr Circle unterhalten sich vor einem Klassenzimmer. Alan braucht den Schlüssel für das Klassenzimmer und unterbricht die beiden.*

Alan: " . . . ."

"Alan, where's your homework?"
"What homework, Sir?"
"The essay that was due in today[1]."
"Sorry, Sir, I've lost my memory."
"I'm sorry to hear that. When did it happen?"
"When did what happen, Sir?"

[1] due in today – zu heute auf

Describing people. 39

What does she/he look like? What do they look like? Can you describe her/him/them?	**Du fragst nach dem Aussehen** einer Person und **erhältst eine Beschreibung**, z. B. mit diesen Angaben:
She's quite tall.	*– Körpergröße*
She's got short brown hair.	*– Haare*
She's got blue eyes.	*– Augen*
She was wearing glasses.	*– Brille*
The girl was wearing a red blouse and a black skirt.	*– Kleidung*
How old is she/he?	**Du fragst nach dem Alter** und bekommst **Antwort**:
She's between 15 and 18 years old.	*– zwischen 15 und 18*
He's already 19.	*– schon 19*
She's almost 16.	*– beinahe 16*
He's about 20.	*– ungefähr 20*

Lindsey is describing her friend Donna:

a) Donna's got . . . . hair. Her eyes are . . . . She's quite . . . . and . . . . She usually wears red . . . . and a yellow . . . . Donna is . . . . fourteen years old.

Choose between: almost • blue • fair • jeans • long • sweater • tall • thin

Mike has to give a description of his father:

b) My father is rather . . . . and quite . . . ., because he eats too much. His hair is . . . . and . . . . He's got . . . . eyes. He has a . . . . and he wears . . . . He's . . . . forty years old.

Choose between: about • beard • brown • fair • fat • glasses • long • short

40 Opinions.

What do you think of it? What do you think about the problem? What's your opinion of / about her?	Du willst wissen, was dein Gesprächspartner meint.
I think / I believe / I feel it's ... In my opinion it's ...	Du sagst, was du meinst.
I agree with you I think so, too. Yes, you're right.	Du stimmst einer Aussage zu.
I'm not so sure.	Du weißt nicht so recht.
I'm afraid I can't agree. I'm afraid I disagree.	Du widersprichst höflich.
I don't agree. No, you're wrong.	Du widersprichst ausdrücklich.

Say it in English.

Dein Vater unterhält sich mit einem Gast aus der englischen Partnerstadt. Du bist der Dolmetscher.

a) *Dein Vater will wissen, was Mr Scott vom deutschen Fußball hält.*
My father wants to know …

b) *Er meint, dass Deutschland Favorit bei der Europameisterschaft ist.*
Mr Scott thinks …

c) *Dein Vater widerspricht freundlich und fügt hinzu, dass seiner Meinung nach Holland die bessere Mannschaft habe.*
My father …

d) *Mr Scott will sich nicht so festlegen. Er glaubt, dass Holland nicht mehr so gut ist wie vor zwei Jahren.*
Mr Scott …

What to say in certain situations. 41

a) Du sprichst einen Unbekannten an.	1 Thank you.
b) Du findest etwas interessant.	2 What a pity.
c) Du findest etwas schrecklich.	3 The same to you.
d) Du bedauerst etwas.	4 What a surprise!
e) Du bietest etwas an.	5 That's awful.
f) Du bist sehr erstaunt.	6 Here you are.
g) Du bedankst dich.	7 Not at all.
h) Du antwortest auf ein Dankeschön.	8 How do you do.
i) Du erwiderst gute Wünsche.	9 Excuse me.
j) Du hältst etwas für gut.	10 How interesting.
k) Du willst wissen, wie es jemandem geht.	11 Good idea.
l) Du begrüßt einen Erwachsenen.	12 How are you?

Find the five mistakes and correct them. 42

a) Jason became a camera for his birthday. . . . .

He's made nice photos with it. . . . .

b) Sharon often plays tennis on the afternoon. . . . .

c) *Patrick bedankt sich bei Sheila für das Buch. Sheila meint, das sei schon in Ordnung:*

P: "Thanks a lot for the book."
S: "Please." . . . .

d) What colour has your new car, Mr James?
It's black. . . . .

Lernbereich PRÜFUNGSTRAINING

	Grammatik	Rechtschreibung	Wortschatz	
1. Test				111
	Plural vermischte Zeiten Steigerung Gerund nach Adj. + Präp. Gerund nach Verb + Präp. some/any	-er/-or Pluralendungen	synonyms opposites Definitionen ‚kleine Wörter'	
2. Test				116
	one/ones if-Sätze vermischte Zeiten Gerund als Subjekt Gerund nach Verben	l/ll Konsonanten verdoppeln	opposites Seine Meinung sagen Wörter richtig anwenden	
3. Test				121
	adjective/adverb reflexive pronoun each other	Großschreibung e (advertisement, nicely) -ly (happily, awfully)	opposites definitions Umschreibung	
4. Test				125
	modal verbs passive questions Steigerung	Großschreibung Apostroph homophones (there/their)	opposites synonyms definitions Seine Meinung sagen	

Tipps

* Diese Tests entsprechen in Umfang und Anforderungen etwa deinen schriftlichen Prüfungen (Klassenarbeiten, Schulaufgaben).
* Betrachte sie deshalb als eine Art Prüfungstraining und bearbeite sie in 45 Minuten (Stoppuhr). Du gewinnst ‚Routine' und bist im ‚Ernstfall' sicher viel abgeklärter!

1. Test

Comprehension test:

The Tailor family

The Taylors live in Dartford, a large town near London. Mr Taylor works in South-East London where he got a job at Vision Windows. Mrs Taylor is a secretary, but she doesn‘t go to her office every day. She’s got enough housework to do at home.

The Taylors have got a new detached house, with a garage and a huge garden around it. The house is very near the school. Their children are Helen and Sam. Helen is twelve, but Sam is only seven. There is a playground behind the school, and the children spend the whole afternoon there.

But last week everything was different.

Mrs Taylor was ill and stayed in bed. Bud luck for her! She had a dreadful headache and her husband phoned for the doctor.

When the children came home from school at half past three they wanted to help their mother. Helen washed up in the kitchen, tidied the living-room with the vacuum cleaner, and made tea.

Sam laid the table and did the shopping. He wrote a long list before he rode to the supermarket on his bike. He took his calculator with him. Do you know why? He wanted to see if the cashier at the checkout made a mistake.

There weren’t many customers in the supermarket so he was back home soon.

1 Are the following sentences true or false? Check them with the text.

	true	*false*
a) Mrs Taylor has got a part-time job.		
b) The children spend most of their spare time on the playground.		
c) The playground is far from the school.		
d) Mrs Taylor stayed in bed because she had bad luck.		
e) The children were lazy.		
f) The shopping took Sam a long time.		

2 Now correct the false sentences.

. . . .

. . . .

. . . .

. . . .

3 Can you complete Sam's shopping list?

cherries • potatoes • cigarettes • chocolate • bread • peas • milk • marmalade

a) three packets of . . . .
b) a bag of . . . .
c) a jar of . . . .
d) a bottle of . . . .
e) two pounds of . . . .
f) a tin of . . . .
g) a loaf of . . . .
h) a bar of . . . .

Which are the synonyms? – Write down the words only. 4

a) a **large** town ....

b) a **huge** garden ....

c) a **dreadful** headache ....

d) she **tidied** ....

Which word is the opposite? 5

a) a **new** house ....

b) **behind** the school ....

c) everything was **different** ....

d) she was **ill** ....

e) a **long** list ....

6 Find a word in the text.

a) She types letters. She is a . . . .

b) You clean the floor with it. It is a . . . .

c) He or she takes your money in a shop. He / She is the . . . .

d) It is a room where you cook. It is a . . . .

e) He helps people when they are ill. He is a . . . .

f) You add numbers on it. It is a . . . .

g) When you buy something in a shop you are the . . . .

7 One week later. Mrs Taylor writes a letter to her mother. Choose the correct word and fill in:

ago • any • any • for • lots of • ones • some • some • soon • still.

Dear Mum,

I'm . . . . in bed. I've been ill . . . . over a week now. I hope I'll feel better . . . .
The doctor came two days . . . . and he gave me . . . . pills. There isn't . . . . food left and Sam must buy . . . . things.
Yesterday he didn't get . . . . pears but he bought . . . . apples. I like the sweet . . . . very much.
I hope you are well.

Lots of love,

Angela

Fill in the correct form of the words in brackets. Add words where neccessary. 8

a) Mr Taylor . . . . (live) in Dartford, but he . . . . (not / work) there. Dartford is near London but it is . . . . (small) the capital.

b) The Taylors . . . . (move) to Dartford last year because Mr Taylor . . . . (not / find) a job in his home town.

c) They . . . . (be) in their new house . . . . ten months now.

d) Helen . . . . (enter) school in Dartford last September, but Sam . . . . (not / go) to school then because he . . . . (be) only four years old. He is five years . . . . (young) his sister.

e) Helen . . . . (be) in the new school . . . . last September. She . . . . (not / do) many tests yet, but she . . . . (do) some soon.

f) Mr Taylor . . . . (have) his old Astra . . . . 1987. He . . . . (buy) a new car next summer.

g) He is fond . . . . (take) trips at the weekends.

h) He is thinking . . . . (go) to Kent.

i) His wife is looking forward . . . . (see) a lot of old villages.

2. Test

Comprehension test:

Cats

Last Whitsun (Pfingsten) Emily Redman got a black cat from her parents. She named her little friend 'Smokey' and loved her very much. During her holidays they were playing together all day. Now school has begun again and it is sometimes very boring for Smokey to stay at home while Emily is in school.

One morning Emily decides to take her cat in her schoolbag to school. In Geography, Emily's first lesson, she lets Smokey sleep on the empty chair beside her. The second lesson is History. The cat keeps quiet all the time.

After break follows Biology. When Mrs Jennings, the teacher, has entered the classroom, she puts a small box on her desk. Then she shows the children a video about animals and everyone watches with great interest. After the film some boys are curious (neugierig) as to the contents (Inhalt) of the box. Mrs Jennings says that there is a small grey animal in it, which likes to live in houses and which loves to eat cheese.

When she sees that the pupils have no idea Mrs Jennings opens the box. The pupils in the class cry loudly and jump on their chairs when they see a mouse come out of the box.

The noise wakes Smokey up. When she sees the mouse run about the classroom, she tries to catch it. The mouse is very scared and therefore jumps into one of the girls' schoolbags, and soon Mrs Jennings can put it back into the box.

When the teacher sees Smokey sitting on her desk she smiles and says: "Where mice are, there will always be a cat, too."

True or false? 1

	true	false
a) Last Whitsun Emily bought a black cat.		
b) Smokey hated being alone at home.		
c) Geography was after break.		
d) Mrs Jennings teaches Biology.		
e) She has brought a little box with her.		
f) The children knew from the start what was in the box.		
g) Mrs Jennings jumped on the desk when she saw the mouse.		
h) Smokey slept until she heard a noise.		
i) The teacher was very angry when she saw that there was a cat in the classroom.		

Find opposites. 2

a) Emily has got a **black** cat, but her friend Gary has got a . . . . cat.

b) Emily **loves** Smokey, but she . . . . mice.

c) Geography is . . . ., but Maths is **boring**.

d) Smokey **always** tries to catch mice, but Simon . . . . does.

e) Mrs Jennings has **entered** the classroom; the headmaster has . . . . it.

3 Complete the conversation.

It's four o'clock, and Mrs Jennings is coming out of school with Emily.

a) Emily: (bietet Mrs Jennings an, ihre Katze zu halten)

. . . .

b) Mrs Jennings: (nimmt dankend an und fügt hinzu, dass Smokey ein sehr nettes Tier sei)

. . . .

. . . .

c) Emily: (stimmt zu und sagt, dass sie viele Mäuse fange)

. . . .

d) Mrs Jennings: (drückt ihr Entsetzen aus)

. . . .

e) Emily: (widerspricht ihr und sagt, dass es nicht gut sei, wenn es zu viele Mäuse gebe)

. . . .

f) Mrs Jennings: (möchte wissen, wo Smokey schlafe)

. . . .

g) Emily: (sagt, sie schlafe in der Küche)

. . . .

h) Mrs Jennings: (findet das toll)

. . . .

i) Emily: (sagt, dass Smokey viel Käse fresse)

. . . .

j) Mrs Jennings: (verabschiedet sich von Emily)

. . . .

k) Emily: (verabschiedet sich von Mrs Jennings)

. . . .

Fill in 'one' or 'ones'. 4

a) Emily has got a black cat; her cousin has got a grey . . . .

b) Garry likes big dogs, but Emily prefers small . . . .

c) A mouse is a tiny animal, an elephant is a huge . . . .

Write complete if-clauses. 5

a) If Emily came home from school early, she . . . . (play) with her cat.

b) Emily will get bad marks in Biology if she . . . . (not / learn) more.

c) If Emily goes to a party, she . . . . (take) Smokey with her.

d) Emily . . . . (not / learn) much if she plays with her cat all day.

6 Fill in the correct form of the verbs in brackets.

a) Emily . . . . (have) a cat of her own since Whitsun.

b) Last weekend the Redmans . . . . (go) climbing in Wales.

c) Emily . . . . (leave) Smokey at her aunt's before she . . . . (travel) to Wales.

d) There she . . . . (be) unhappy with her cat.

e) . . . . (play) with Smokey is great fun for her.

f) Smokey loves . . . . (sleep) under Emily's bed.

g) Next September Smokey . . . . (have) little kittens.

h) Emily . . . . (give) one of the kittens to her friend Steve.

i) Let us see what Smokey . . . . (do) at the moment.

j) She . . . . (run) after Spike, the Redman's dog.

k) Spike often . . . . (eat) from Emily's meals.

l) Spike . . . . (be) with the Redmans for five years now.

m) Spike . . . . (not, catch) mice – he likes Chappy.

n) Smokey . . . . (want) to catch a mouse yesterday but the mouse . . . . (be) too quick for her.

3. Test

Dictation. 1

From Britain's history.

In Celtic times winter was a very dangerous time. It was the season of witches[1] and evil spirits[2]. Although people were much afraid, they tried to frighten them away with great fires, especially on Halloween.

Traces[3] of ghosts and monsters can still be found today – but nowadays it's only young people who are dressed up for celebrating their Halloween parties.

Traditionally, tricks and treats is an American custom[4] which, unfortunately, has become quite dangerous. Today the tricks are often no longer just jam at your door bell or a dead mouse in your letter box, but serious damage. Sometimes people are hurt and on some occasions[5] the police have to be called.

More acceptable are the tricks on April Fool's Day. Once a local newspaper hoped to be successful with an exciting advertisement about a famous pop star who would play in the city hall. But except for a few school children most readers realized that it was just an April joke.

1 witch – *Hexe*
2 evil spirits – *böse Geister*
3 trace – *Spur*
4 custom – *Brauch*
5 occasion – *Gelegenheit*

Give the opposites. 2

a) The opposite of dangerous is . . . .

b) The opposite of serious is . . . .

c) The opposite of exciting is . . . .

d) The opposite of to shout is . . . .

3 Explain in a complete sentence.

a) Explain 'monster' in a complete sentence.

....

....

b) Explain in a complete sentence 'an American custom'.

....

....

c) Explain 'a witch' in a complete sentence.

....

....

4 Paraphrase the following words.

a) They were **defeated**

....

b) Some tricks are **acceptable**

....

c) to **frighten** them **away**

....

d) **except for** a few school children

....

Adjectives or adverbs? 5

What a nice evening for Rachel!

"Hi, Rachel, are you .... (nice) dressed tonight. Why do you look so .... (sad)? Show us a .... (happy) face."

"I'm sorry, but I can't look .... (happy). I feel .... (awful, sad). First everything seemed .... (great) until .... (sudden) David appeared. He was talking .... (quiet) to Lucy, and shortly afterwards the two .... (quick) went away."

"David had .... (faithful) promised me never to do anything like that. It is .... (real, unbelievable). I was .... (absolute, sure) that David .... (real) meant it."

6 Reflexive pronoun or *each other?*

Stuart and Claire wanted to buy .... a poster for their room. For more than an hour they talked with .... over which poster to take. But unfortunately they couldn't agree with .... So they decided to buy two posters. They like their posters and enjoy .... very much when they sit on their couch.

7 Translate into English.

a) Erinnerst du dich noch, Dawn, wie wir uns das erste Mal getroffen haben?

b) Ja natürlich, Patrick. Es war am 1. April, und du fühltest dich nicht wohl. Du hattest zu wenig geschlafen.

c) Richtig. Ich konnte mir nicht vorstellen, dass die Party am Abend vorher bis nach Mitternacht dauern würde.

d) Es muss sehr lustig gewesen sein.

e) Ja sicher, ich sagte mir: ‚Wenn du so früh gehen würdest, wärst du ein wirklicher Dummkopf.'

4. Test

Dictation. 1

London

Every day thousands of people travel to the city centre by bus or underground. Many of them are commuters[1] who live outside the British capital – in the suburbs and villages. Although about half a million people work in the square mile around St Paul's Cathedral, hardly anyone lives there.

It's this area where you find the city's most famous streets. They are crowded with cars and tourists who visit London at all times of the year. They come to see The Tower of London and the Crown Jewels, the Houses of Parliament and Big Ben, Trafalgar Square with Nelson's Column, and the other sights. Some people come to see the famous Thames Barrier; they go on a riverboat trip or watch a video about London's past. There used to be terrible floods and lots of people were drowned. Now everything is better, the high flood barriers have been built.

Most visitors do not go to London's shabby areas, such as East End, where the population is poor. Here are the immigrants'[2] houses and flats, because the rents are not so expensive. A lot of people there are without a regular job and without hope.

1 commuter – *Pendler*
2 immigrant – *Einwanderer*

Give the opposites. 2

a) The opposite of poor is . . . .

b) The opposite of to sell is . . . .

c) It is not expensive means it is . . . .

3 Give synonyms.

a) to destroy ....

b) terrible ....

c) **crowded** with cars ....

4 Define in a complete sentence.

a) A pub is ....

....

b) Rent is ....

....

c) A commuter is ....

....

5 Questions about Britain.

Answer in complete sentences.

a) Which of London's sights would you visit? Give a reason for your answer.

....

....

b) Give some information about the Thames Flood Barrier.

....

....

c) What is the difference between Northern Ireland and the Republic of Ireland?

....

....

Modal verbs. 6

Fill in the correct word and mind the tense.

a) Little Debbie (braucht nicht) . . . . clean her room. But when I was ten years old I (musste) . . . . tidy it.

b) At Christmas I always visited my grandparents. It was great. I (durfte) . . . . stay up till eleven o'clock.

c) (Musstest du) . . . . go shopping when you were a child?

Put the verbs into the passive. 7

Mind the tenses.

a) Our kitchen window (break) . . . . yesterday.

b) Today the great floods (keep) . . . . back by the Thames Barrier.

c) The photos of my brother (take) . . . . while we were in Ireland.

d) The new by-pass (not, open) . . . . yet.

e) Everyone hopes that it (open) . . . . soon.

Ask for the underlined words. 8

a) The streets of London are crowded with <u>cars</u>.

. . . .

b) Lots of people have to travel to London every day <u>because they work there.</u>

. . . .

c) A new road around the suburb will be built <u>next year</u>.

. . . .

9 Say it in English.

a) Viele Besucher, die jedes Jahr nach London kommen, besuchen die Baker Street. Sie wollen das Haus eines Mannes sehen, der eigentlich nur eine Idee des Schriftstellers A. C. Doyle war.

b) Die spannenden Abenteuer des Mannes, der als Sherlock Holmes bekannt wurde, sind von Millionen Menschen gelesen worden.

c) Die meisten der Geschichten sind ins Deutsche übersetzt worden.

d) Sogar Filme sind gemacht worden. Einige von ihnen sind sehr erfolgreich gewesen.

a) ....

....

....

b) ....

....

....

....

c) ....

....

d) ....

....

Lernbereich GRAMMATIK (S. 8–58)

1. Schreibe die Pluralformen.

a) taxis, buses, men, women, offices, lorries **b)** children, bikes, teachers **c)** classes, pupils, boys, girls, parties, weekends.

2. Setze *one* oder *ones* ein.

a) one, ones, one **b)** ones, ones, ones, one **c)** one, ones.

3. Sage es auf Englisch.

a) I need new sports shoes. My old ones are ugly. **b)** Clare tried on five dresses and she bought a blue one and two green ones. **c)** These oranges are expensive. I'd like (to have) the cheap ones.

4. Vervollständige die Stätze. (Verwende s-Genitiv.)

a) a two hours' rest **b)** the newsagent's, this month's magazine. **c)** today's paper **d)** the baker's, the chemist's **e)** today's weather forecast **f)** aunt's **g)** London's Underground **h)** Britain's history.

5. Vervollständige die Sätze. (Substantive im Singular.)

a) furniture, it **b)** knowledge, is **c)** progress **d)** homework, it, much, homework **e)** information, is, it **f)** news, is **g)** politics.

6. Übersetze. (Substantive im Plural.)

a) Look, my sister is wearing a new pair of glasses. **b)** She uses the scissors to cut the paper. **c)** Are those Andy's pyjamas? **d)** Andy doesn't wear trousers in summer, only shorts. **e)** He needs a new pair of jeans. **f)** His father buys a pair of trousers and two pairs of jeans. **g)** Andy's friend lives in the outskirts of Manchester. **h)** The boys made a lot of noise. They ran up and down the stairs.

7. Setze die fehlenden Pronomen ein.

a) Theirs **b)** mine **c)** his **d)** yours **e)** yours **f)** my, hers **g)** ours **h)** my, mine **i)** yours **j)** yours, ours.

8. Setze die richtige Form von *oneself* ein.

a) herself **b)** itself **c)** themselves **d)** himself **e)** themselves **f)** yourselves **g)** himself **h)** ourselves **i)** yourselves.

9. Setze die richtige Form von *oneself* ein.

a) yourself **b)** himself **c)** myself **d)** himself **e)** herself **f)** herself **g)** themselves **h)** itself **i)** ourselves.

10. Übersetze. Setze, wenn notwendig, die richtige Form von *oneself* ein.

a) Katie joined a youth club two weeks ago. **b)** At the first meeting she introduced herself to all the boys and girls. **c)** The group meets every Friday evening. **d)** They amuse themselves with dancing and playing. **e)** Katie can't remember having met such nice people before. **f)** She feels very at home in the club. **g)** Last weekend the young people met at the club.* **h)** Katie wondered how many people would come. **i)** Katie and her girl-friend did all the work for the party themselves. **j)** The guests amused themselves and helped themselves to the food. **k)** The neighbours didn't complain because they like listening to loud rock music themselves. **l)** Katie imagines organizing a party again next week. **m)** Her girl-friend won't refuse to help her.

* **in** the club – im Klub (als Gruppe), **at** the club – im Klub (als Gebäude)

11. Setze das richtige reflexive oder reziproke Pronomen ein.

a) each other **b)** each other **c)** herself **d)** themselves **e)** each other **f)** herself **g)** each other.

12. Setze *some* oder *any* und ihre Zusammensetzungen ein.

a) something, some **b)** some, anything **c)** somewhere, someone **d)** anything **e)** somewhere **f)** someone **g)** someone, anywhere **h)** something **i)** anything.

13. Setze die richtige Form der Adjektive ein.

a) cleverer, cleverest **b)** boring, most boring **c)** good, better than, best **d)** old, oldest, older than **e)** bad, worst **f)** beautiful, most beautiful.

14. Sage es auf Englisch. (Bilde Vergleiche.)

a) Our house is not as big as yours. **b)** My father is older than yours. **c)** An Opel is not as fast as a Jaguar. **d)** A Porsche is the fastest of all. **e)** A Porsche costs less than a Jaguar, but more than an Opel. **f)** My bike is as good as yours. **g)** I can drive faster than you. **h)** The more I train, the farther I can jump. **i)** My brother can jump farthest of all pupils.

15. Verbessere die Fehler.

a) John is older **than** his cousin. **b)** Martha is **more intelligent** than her sister. **c)** Keith is **worse** in English than Bob. **d)** But he is not **as** bad as John.

16. Setze die richtige Form des Adverbs ein.

a) quietly, loudly **b)** well **c)** wildly, madly **d)** in a friendly way, politely, angrily, quickly **e)** noisily.

17. Adjektiv oder Adverb?

a) quickly, slowly **b)** impolite **c)** rude, rudely **d)** in a friendly way, angrily **e)** quiet, quietly **f)** terrible, terribly loudly, horribly.

18. Schreibe den Komparativ und Superlativ der Adverbien.

a) harder, hardest **b)** more happily, most happily **c)** worse, worst **d)** earlier, earliest **e)** more wonderfully, most wonderfully **f)** more strongly, most strongly.

19. Verbessere die Fehler.

a) Susan sang **more** beautifully than Martha. **b)** Roger drives as **badly** as John. **c)** Bob drives **worst** of all. **d)** Mrs Ward drives more **carefully** than her husband. **e)** Peter reads **less** than his brother.

20. Setze die richtige Form ein (Adjektiv oder Adverb).

a) easy, easily **b)** easy, difficult **c)** quick, quickly **d)** nervously, nervous **e)** nervous, perfectly **f)** tired **g)** strange, seriously, hard.

21. Verwende das *simple past* und seine Verneinung.
a) laughed, didn't laugh **b)** came, didn't come **c)** saw, didn't see **d)** caught, didn't catch **e)** bought, didn't buy **f)** drew, didn't draw **g)** repeated, didn't repeat **h)** drove, didn't drive, drove **i)** relaxed, didn't relax **j)** sold, didn't sell **k)** knew, didn't know **l)** liked, didn't like.

22. Stelle Fragen und gib Antworten im *simple past.*
a) did … write, wrote **b)** did … come, came **c)** did … see, saw **d)** did … go, went **e)** did … ring, rang **f)** were, was **g)** did … choose, chose **h)** did … eat, ate **i)** did … post, posted **j)** did … lose, lost **k)** did … call, called **l)** did … pay, paid **m)** did … meet, met **n)** did … say, said **o)** did … steal, stole **p)** did … swim, swam **q)** did … ask, asked.

23. Es geschah gestern. (Verwende das *simple past.*)
a) came **b)** asked, did … leave **c)** answered, left, went **d)** had, talked **e)** watched, read **f)** did not sit, sat, was **g)** drank, ate, did not have **h)** said, wanted, left **i)** gave **j)** drove, lost, could, was.

24. Verwende das *present perfect.*
a) have not cleaned **b)** has just bought **c)** has finished **d)** have opened **e)** has copied **f)** has read **g)** has learnt **h)** has not slept **i)** has left **j)** has broken.

25. Übersetze. (Verwende *present perfect.*)
a) Have you already read the book? **b)** I haven't had time yet. **c)** Have you often watched detective thrillers on TV? **d)** I haven't often watched TV. **e)** Have you ever read a book by Agatha Christie? **f)** I have never heard the name. **g)** Have you ever been to Madame Tussaud's? **h)** I have been there twice, but I haven't visited the Chamber of Horrors yet.

26. Vervollständige die Sätze. (Verwende *present perfect.*)
a) has been … for, has not written … since **b)** has been … since, has been … for **c)** has known … for, have been … since **d)** has been … for, has been … since **e)** has not done … since, has not been … for **f)** has not seen … for, has had … since.

27. *Present perfect* oder *simple past*?
a) Did … enjoy, did, did not dance, was, played, have never heard **b)** Have you … been, have not been, was **c)** did you see, have not seen, saw.

28. Verwende *present perfect progressive.*
a) has Bob been waiting, has been waiting for **b)** have your friends been staying, have been staying, since **c)** have you been going, have been going ... for **d)** have you and Alan been playing, have been playing for **e)** has Geoff been studying, has been studying, for **f)** has it been raining, has been raining, since **g)** has this girl been crying, has been crying for.

29. Vervollständige den Dialog.
a) have you had **b)** have had, for **c)** Have you ever thought **d)** have always wanted, have liked, since **e)** have you seen **f)** have been, have been coming, for **g)** have been enjoying **h)** have always chosen (mehrfach unterbrochene Handlung!).

(S. 34–41)

30. Übersetze. (Vermischte Zeiten.)

a) Mr Ward has been living in Macclesfield for many years. b) His friend, Mr Müller, visited him last summer and they had a nice time in England. c) Mr Müller has been learning English for three years now. d) Mr Ward and his family have seen a lot of sights in the North of England, but they haven't been to York. Last weekend they visited Durham. e) How long has Mr Ward's son Jerry been playing in the football team? – He has been playing in it for one year. f) Mr Ward has been trying for days to call his friend, but he has never reached him. He was on holiday in Italy. g) Mr Ward was on holiday in Austria two years ago and after that he visited his friend in Bavaria. h) Mr Ward has been working in a car factory for two years. Before that he worked in a garage. i) How long has he been a mechanic? – He has been a mechanic for ten years.

31. Vervollständige die Sätze. (*Simple past* oder *past progressive.*)

a) was cooking, came, were you doing, was shopping b) was waiting, arrived, was waiting, wanted, came, were still talking c) left, was shining, hurried, was getting d) were walking, was raining.

32. Bilde Sätze. (Verwende *simple past* und *past perfect.*)

a) After he had arrived at the airport he took the bus to town. b) After he had arrived at the house Mr and Mrs Potter welcomed him. c) They visited a gallery in the afternoon after they had had a long and good breakfast. d) After they had gone on a boat trip they had a drink at the pub in the evening. e) They went to a concert in the evening after they had taken a walk along the river. f) The Potters gave a party after they had bought a lot to drink and eat. g) After Mr Garner had packed his suitcase he said good-bye to the Potters. h) After he had spent a day in Frankfurt he went home.

33. Verwende *past perfect* und *simple past.*

a) had left, did not know, was b) had lost, asked c) had told, found d) arrived, had had e) had stopped, jumped f) had taken, did not have g) had got, saw, could not h) met, had not seen i) had asked, gave.

34. Vervollständige die Sätze, verwende *will-future* oder *going to-future.*

a) am going to buy b) will be, will be c) are you going to do, are going to spend, will visit, will return d) is going to study e) will probably not come, am going to meet f) will help.

35. Bilde Sätze.

a) Peter is coming to see his friend tomorrow. b) Mrs Ward is taking the children to the zoo on Sunday c) They are having breakfast at 9 o'clock. d) Is Mr Ward staying at home tonight? e) He is travelling to London on Sunday. f) Mr Ward is going to a concert in the evening. g) They are playing Mozart. h) Mr Ward is taking a train to get to London. i) He is coming back on Monday morning. j) He is staying at a hotel on Sunday night.

36. Setze ein Gerund in die Lücken.

a) travelling / to travel b) flying c) walking, going d) staying, looking e) Going f) looking g) travelling h) talking.

37. Schreibe einen Satz und verwende ein Gerund und, wenn notwendig, die richtige Präposition.

a) Mr Clifford was fond of travelling to Australia. b) He had difficulty (in) finding out the cheapest flight c) At last he succeeded in getting a flight in September. d) He was not interested in flying with a small airline. **e)** Mr Clifford was afraid of missing his plane. **f)** He was tired of waiting at the airport for a very long time. **g)** He thought of staying in Australia for two months. **h)** He had a chance of coming back in October. **i)** He was looking forward to seeing his wife soon.

38. Verwende das Passiv.

a) is owned by Mr Green. **b)** A lot of cars must be repaired. **c)** The engines should be checked. **d)** All the work is done by Mr Green himself. **e)** Not all types of cars can be repaired by Mr Green. **f)** Buses mustn't be driven by him. **g)** The bills are written by Mr Green. **h)** The bills are seldom paid on time by the customers.

39. Vervollständige die Sätze. Verwende das Passiv.

a) was knocked down **b)** was blocked **c)** were taken **d)** was called **e)** was operated on **f)** was sent **g)** was visited **h)** was questioned **i)** was repaired **j)** was sent **k)** was not paid.

40. Verbessere die Fehler.

a) The taxi was **driven** by Mr Garner. **b)** The accident **was** not seen **by** the police. **c)** Mr Garner was **sent** to hospital. **d) The woman was operated on by the doctor.**

41. Bilde Sätze im Passiv.

a) A mess has been made in the classroom by the pupils. **b)** Paper has been thrown around all over the floor. **c)** Some chairs have been broken by the boys. **d)** One boy has been caught by the form teacher. **e)** A picture has been knocked off the wall. **f)** Two girls have been injured by a piece of chalk. **g)** A boy has been hit by a book. **h)** Bad things have been written on the blackboard. **i)** Mike's book has been torn to pieces. **j)** The headmaster has been called by the form teacher.

42. Bilde Sätze. Verwende das Passiv.

a) The walls will be painted. **b)** The rooms will be decorated. **c)** A new garage will be built. **d)** The roof will be repaired. **e)** The floors will be cleaned. **f)** A new kitchen will be bought. **g)** Friends will be invited.

43. Sage es auf Englisch.

a) My bike has been stolen. **b)** My watch was repaired yesterday. **c)** The new cinema will be opened in a week. **d)** The match was lost by our team. **e)** The next match must be won. **f)** The new player can't be paid.

44. Setze must – mustn't – needn't ein.

a) must, needn't, mustn't **b)** must, mustn't **c)** must, needn't **d)** mustn't, must, needn't **e)** needn't, must, needn't.

45. Sage es auf Englisch.

a) Mr Grey mustn't park here because the place must be kept clear. **b)** Mr White needn't hurry because he needn't be at the office at 8 o'clock. **c)** Mr Potter must be at home at 6 o'clock and he mustn't be late.

46. Verwende andere Zeiten der Modalverben.

a) had to get up, will have to get up **b)** did not have to help, will not have to help **c)** was not allowed to, will not be allowed to **d)** will be allowed to use, was allowed to **e)** will be able to play, was able to play.

47. Bilde Fragen. Frage nach den unterstrichenen Teilen.

a) What is Peter reading? **b)** What has he never read before? **c)** What is very interesting? **d)** Where did Robin Hood live? **e)** Who fought against the Sheriff of Nottingham? **f)** Why could the Sheriff not catch them? **g)** When did Robin and his men go to Nottingham?

48. Frage nach den unterstrichenen Teilen.

a) What is Mr Grant interested in? **b)** What did he hear about one day? **c)** What did he read? **d)** What was Mr Grant looking forward to? **e)** Where did he make a journey to last summer? **f)** What was he waiting for? **g)** Where did dark clouds come from? **h)** Where did an enormous creature suddenly come out of? **i)** What was Mr Grant very much afraid of? **j)** Where did he wake up?

49. Setze *who, which/that* oder *whose* ein.

a) who **b)** which/that **c)** which/that **d)** who **e)** which / that **f)** which / that **g)** whose) who.

50. Verbessere die Fehler.

a) Jim **who** is … **b)** The boat **which /that** **c) who** **d) whose.**

51. Setze *who, which* oder *that* ein und lasse das Pronomen weg, falls möglich.

a) which/that **b)** – **c)** – **d)** who **e)** which/that **f)** – **g)** who **h)** who.

52. Verbinde die beiden Sätze. Verwende Relativsätze und lasse das Pronomen weg.

a) Do you like the boats the spectators are looking at? **b)** The boats the teams are sitting in are expensive. **c)** The "dark blue" team we were talking about is sitting in the boat. **d)** Is that the Oxford team the reporter is speaking to? **e)** The teams the crowd is cheering at are at the start. **f)** The coach the Cambridge team is listening to is very good. **g)** The result I told you about was the same last year.

53. Übersetze ins Englische.

a) The team whose coach is American trains very often. **b)** That is the boat which / that belongs to Oxford. **c)** The boat which / that the university pays for is expensive. **d)** Jim has a friend who studies at Cambridge.

54. Bilde Sätze.

a) If the children hurry, they will catch the train. **b)** If it rains, they will not stay outside. **c)** If the boys and girls go by train, they can travel together. **d)** If the train is not crowded, everyone will have a seat. **e)** If the children are hungry, they will eat sandwiches. **f)** If they are fit, they can climb mountains. **g)** The boys will not get wet if they take their waterproofs. **h)** If they go on a tour, they must start early in the morning.

55. Vervollständige die Konversation.

a) had, had, would gamble **b)** would you go, won, won, would travel **c)** would you like, had, would cross **d)** could you, found, would book **e)** would come, had, would be, could.

56. Vervollständige die Sätze.

a) wanted **b)** will be **c)** must go **d)** could see **e)** cannot come, tell **f)** were **g)** will meet.

57. Sage es auf Englisch. Verwende die direkte Rede.

a) Can I meet you at the airport if you come by plane? **b)** I will come by car if my holidays are long enough **c)** I would visit the Highlands if I found the most beautiful route. **d)** You should go to a hotel if you don't like camping. **e)** You could go to the Isle of Skye if you had enough time.

58. Bilde Sätze mit der richtigen Wortstellung.

a) (In summer) Geoff often takes holidays in Wales in summer. **b)** He usually goes to pubs in the evening **c)** Geoff sometimes likes to visit the National Gallery in Aberystwyth. **d)** The Welsh usually speak English but they never forget their Welsh language. **e)** Geoff always tries to understand Welsh.

59. Beantworte die Fragen.

a) Janet sent Mr Bates a letter. **b)** The postman gave the letter to Peter. **c)** Janet told her friend an adventure. **d)** Mr Bates offered a cigarette to the postman. **e)** Robert showed his sister the pictures. **f)** Mr Cooper passed his wife her glasses. **g)** Monica teaches her German.

60. Bilde Sätze.

a) a tree to the picture. **b)** a letter to Mr Bates **c)** the accident to her girl-friend **d)** that problem to me **e)** himself to Mrs White **f)** tea to coffee **g)** nothing to her.

61. Verbessere die Fehler.

a) Geoff explained the problem to Mr Potter **b)** Sarah added the words to the list. **c)** Mr Potter showed it to his wife. **d)** Mr Evans introduced himself to the class. **e)** John described the way to me.

(S. 54–58)

Lernbereich
RECHTSCHREIBUNG (S. 61–79)

1. Kennst du London?
a) 4 b) 9 c) 3 d) 5 e) 2 f) 1 g) 8 h) 7 i) 10 j) 6.

2. Verwende große Anfangsbuchstaben.
a) Buckingham Palace, Her Majesty the Queen b) City, Great Britain c) Downing Street, British Prime Minister d) Trocadero Centre, Piccadilly Circus e) House of Commons, House of Lords f) August g) Thames Barrier h) William the Conqueror, Christmas Eve, Christmas Day, New Year's Day.

3. Mache ein Wort aus zwei.
a) ice-skating b) roller-skate c) wash-basin d) well-known e) alarm-clock f) frying-pan g) bedroom h) motorbike i) classroom j) earthquake k) keyboard l) surname m) family name n) cassette recorder o) leap year (Schaltjahr) p) shop assistant q) dining room r) drama club.

4. Setze zwei oder drei Wörter zusammen.
a) youth centre b) newsstand c) sleeping bag d) foreign language e) crossroads f) letter box g) daughter-in-law h) five-pound.

5. Schreibe die Zahlen aus.
a) twenty-one b) ninety-four c) a hundred and one d) two hundred and twenty-eight e) one thousand, one hundred and eleven f) thirtieth g) thirty-first h) ninety-ninth i) hundred and first j) two hundred and thirty-fourth.

6. Beachte den Apostroph.
a) Paul's b) girl's, She's, She's c) Who's, He's, He's not / He isn't d) children's. He's, London's history.

7. Ergänze -s oder -es.
a) radios b) leaves c) bushes d) knives e) calves f) cliffs g) beats h) pushes i) teaches j) watches k) misses l) talks.

8. ys oder ies?
a) ferries b) parties c) diaries d) jerseys e) monkeys f) valleys g) stories h) hobbies i) replies j) tidies k) stays l) studies m) enjoys n) hurries o) plays p) copies.

9. y oder i?
a) studied b) stayed c) carried d) hurried e) trying f) playing g) busiest h) happily.

10. Zwei Konsonanten?
a) sitting b) swimming c) shopping d) cutting e) dropped f) planning g) skidded h) robber i) thinner j) traveller k) runner l) fittest m) answered.

11. Setze ll oder l in die Lücken ein.
b) successful, almost c) till, also d) full, until e) although, till f) useful, full g) travellers, travel h) all together, altogether.

12. Bleibt das -e oder nicht?
a) surprised, writing b) leaving, practising c) being, dancing, swimming.

13. Wähle das richtige Wort aus.
a) by b) farther (far *weit,* farther *weiter*) c) hole d) lain e) sale f) thrown g) through h) weak i) wear j) whose.

14. Setze die richtigen Wörter ein.
a) write, ride, right b) there, They're, They're, their c) although, also d) want, won't e) really, rarely f) know, no, now.

15. Finde die fehlenden Wörter.
a) island b) cupboard c) evening d) calf e) chalk f) Parliament g) column h) foreign.

16. Finde die 12 Wörter mit einem stummen Laut.
answer, climb, hour, interest, knife, listen, mustn't, neighbour, often, sandwich, talk, whose.

17. Schwierige Wörter mit dem Laut [e].
a) red b) pleasure c) said d) many e) lemon f) weapon g) leisure h) says.

18. Schwierige Wörter mit dem Laut [i:].
a) tease b) believe c) cheese d) these e) fever f) receive g) ceiling h) police.

19. Schwierige Wörter mit dem Laut [u:].
a) true b) food c) lose d) choose e) canoe f) ruler g) move h) juice.

20. Schwierige Wörter mit dem Laut [ei].
a) cake b) train c) today d) table e) weigh f) stationer g) Spain h) wake.

21. Übersetze.
a) grammar, active, passive, present perfect, future, infinitive, participle, subject, object b) doctor, detective, architect, captain, secretary, mechanic c) coffee, cocoa, lemonade, tea d) physics, chemistry, biology, mathematics / maths, geography, music e) Geography, Africa, America, Asia, Australia, Ireland, Scotland, temperature, climate f) supermarket, marmalade, sugar, English chocolate, cigarettes, tobacco.

22. Übersetze.
a) machine b) October c) toilet d) Parliament e) address f) marmalade g) copy h) thousand (HOLIDAYS) i) yoghurt j) microphone k) trumpet l) detective m) housewife n) chocolate o) carrot p) rocket (HOMEWORK).

23. Finde 12 Fehler und verbessere sie.
week, Mrs Clay's, carried – skidded, (fell) off, too – There (were) – assistant, immediately knocked – you're – (faster) than.

Lernbereich
WORTSCHATZ (S. 82–109)

1. Setze die richtigen Wörter ein.
a) coat, glove, boots, sweater, shirt, trousers, costume **b)** screen, joystick, symbol, copy, plug, printer, lead, order **c)** pens, pencil, satchel, biro, book, ruler.

2. Kleidung und Computer. Bilde zwei Gruppen aus je 12 Wörtern.
a) to change, denim, fashion, fashionable, to fit, jumper, to put on, scarf, to sew, to take off, to wear, well-dressed **b)** breakdown, central unit, to click on, to connect, to copy, disk, keyboard, mouse, order, to press, to print, to save.

3. Vervollständige den Stundenplan.
a) Assembly **b)** break **c)** lunch **d)** History **e)** Geography **f)** Religious Education **g)** Science **h)** Maths **i)** Music **j)** P.E. / Physical Education **k)** English **l)** Home Economics **m)** Art **n)** French **o)** games.

4. Vervollständige die Tabelle.
d) donkey, David, detective, diving, Denmark, daisy **e)** eagle, Edward, electrician, Eire elm (Ulme) **f)** fox, Fred, fireman, football, France, flower **g)** goat, George, guide, gymnastics / golf, Germany / Great Britain, grapefruit **h)** hippopotamus, Henry, headmaster / headmistress, horse riding, Holland, holly.

5. Welches Wort passt?
a) Take, Bring **b)** takes, brings **c)** bring, take **d)** boiling, make **e)** cook **f)** cook **g)** boil **h)** ride **i)** run **j)** goes **k)** drives **l)** watched / saw **m)** look **n)** see **o)** hear **p)** listen to.

6. Finde das passende Verb.
a) lay **b)** grow **c)** light **d)** catch **e)** have **f)** make **g)** give (a lift = im Auto mitnehmen) **h)** take.

7. Welches Substantiv gehört zu welchem Verb?
b) 1 **c)** 3 **d)** 2 (ein Formular ausfüllen) **e)** 5 **f)** 7 **g)** 6 **h)** 8.

8. Finde Begriffe für die Personen.
a) conjurer / conjuror **b)** teacher **c)** reporter **d)** dealer **e)** driver **f)** painter **g)** inventor **h)** baker **i)** postman / postwoman **j)** businessman / businesswoman **k)** footballer **l)** singer.

9. Finde die Substantive.
a) statement **b)** expression **c)** painting **d)** spelling **e)** crossing **f)** drawing **g)** meaning **h)** swimming **i)** shopping **j)** drink **k)** telephone **l)** movement **m)** beginning **n)** end (Ende) oder ending (Endung, Schluss) **o)** visit **p)** information.

10. Einige schwierige Substantive.
a) entrance **b)** sale **c)** pronunciation **d)** thought **e)** advice **f)** description **g)** flight **h)** pleasure.

11. Finde die Adjektive.

a) crowded **b)** tidy **c)** friendly **d)** correct **e)** lucky **f)** beautiful **g)** locked **h)** changeable **i)** cloudy **j)** powerful **k)** following **l)** married **m)** rainy **n)** sunny **o)** successful **p)** wonderful.

12. Vervollständige die Tabelle.

b) lover, love, lovely **c)** user, use, useful / useless **d)** beginner, beginning **e)** writer, writing **f)** visitor, visit **g)** robber, robbery **h)** listener, listening **i)** builder, building **j)** painter, painting **k)** life, lively **l)** success, successful **m)** youngster, youth **n)** difference **o)** fashionable **p)** dangerous.

13. Menschen und ihre Berufe.

b) 6 **c)** 1 **d)** 9 **e)** 10 **f)** 2 **g)** 5 **h)** 3 **i)** 7 **j)** 8.

14. Fahrzeuge.

a) … for long distances. **b)** … very small bus. **c)** … up the hill. **d)** … furniture and beds in it. **e)** … for carrying goods. **f)** … for camping. **g)** … that carries people or cars across a river or lake.

15. Gebäude.

a) … with no upstairs. **b)** … stands alone and has a garden around it. **c)** … joined at one side to another house (Doppelhaushälfte) **d)** … a large building with lots of flats and offices. **e)** … stands in a row of houses (Reihenhaus).

16. Räume.

a) … a large room in a school where you and your classmates have your meals. **b)** … a big room in a youth hostel where a lot of people sleep. **c)** … a room in the house where you sleep. **d)** … a hall where you do exercises for the body. **e)** … a workshop where cars are repaired (Werkstatt).

17. Finde Synonyme.

a) mend **b)** start **c)** leave **d)** great **e)** cycle **f)** happy **g)** right **h)** awful **i)** enter **j)** ruin.

18. Setze Wörter ein, die das Gleiche bezeichnen wie die fett gedruckten.

a) liked **b)** saw **c)** free **d)** great **e)** best.

19. Erkläre die fett gedruckten Wörter.

a) 3 **b)** 4 **c)** 1 **d)** 2 **e)** 6 **f)** 7 **g)** 5 **h)** 9 **i)** 8.

20. Füge Wörter und Erklärungen zusammen.

b) 10 **c)** 12 **d)** 9 **e)** 8 **f)** 7 **g)** 6 **h)** 5 **i)** 1 **j)** 2 **k)** 3 **l)** 4.

21. Finde das Gegenteil.

a) short **b)** stupid **c)** happy **d)** poor **e)** interesting **f)** quiet **g)** often **h)** wet **i)** remember **j)** cheap **k)** heavy **l)** find **m)** difficult **n)** end **o)** angry – **opposite meaning.**

22. Vervollständige den Text mit *opposites.*

a) hate **b)** whisper **c)** buy **d)** lies **e)** win (we will win!) **f)** close / shut **g)** push **h)** exit **i)** keep **j)** nothing **k)** funny **l)** alone / by myself **m)** different.

23. Setze die weibliche oder männliche Form ein.
a) daughter **b)** husband **c)** aunt **d)** wives **e)** woman **f)** daughter-in-law **g)** women **h)** queen **i)** waitress **j)** policewoman (Polizistin) **k)** princess **l)** stewardess.

24. Schreibe die *opposites*.
a) bad **b)** safe **c)** worse (bad, -, worst!) **d)** first **e)** worst **f)** high **g)** negative **h)** serious **i)** outside **j)** before **k)** for **l)** alone **m)** without **n)** behind **o)** down **p)** on.

25. Bilde *opposites* mit Vorsilben.
a) unfriendly **b)** unusual **c)** impatient **d)** to disagree **e)** to unpack **f)** uninteresting **g)** uncomfortable **h)** unlucky **i)** irregular.

26. Welches Wort im Text sagt dir, dass ...?
a) next to Tower Bridge **b)** Tower closed: 24th-26th December **c)** by Underground: The Circle or District lines **d)** there is no sadder spot on the earth (sad = traurig) **e)** you are advised to leave at least two hours for your visit.

27. „Falsche Freunde". Übersetze ins Englische und Deutsche.
a) hall, Fußboden **b)** skirt, Felsen **c)** mark, Notiz / Anmerkung **d)** coffee, Café **e)** way, Kunst **f)** to take a seat, stattfinden **g)** city centre, Großstadt **h)** bench, Ufer / Bank **i)** crisps, Chips / Pommes frites **j)** so / therefore, auch.

28. „Falsche Freunde". Übersetze ins Deutsche.
a) Wo **b)** werden **c)** Glocke / Klingel **d)** Miete **e)** Teller **f)** (ich) frage mich **g)** örtlich / im Ort (nicht: Kneipenmannschaft!) **h)** Schlange **i)** Plätzchen / Keks **j)** Ufer.

29. Wirf sie nicht durcheinander.
a) because (weil) **b)** although (obwohl) **c)** if (wenn / falls) **d)** so (deshalb) **e)** till (bis) **f)** while (während) **g)** but (aber) **h)** as soon as (sobald als) **i)** still (noch).

30. Schreibe die Zahlen aus.
a) thirty-one **b)** twenty-eight / twenty-nine **c)** twelve **d)** fifty-two **e)** three hundred and sixty-five **f)** three hundred and sixty-six **g)** one hundred **h)** one hundred **i)** twelve **j)** three.

31. Schreibe das Datum.
a) May 14th 1995 **b)** April 1st 1997 **c)** December 2nd 1995 **d)** August 3rd 1990 **e)** October 10th 1996.

32. Zeitangaben. Setze die richtige Präposition ein, falls notwendig.
a) at, at **b)** from ... to, until **c)** on **d)** on, on, in **e)** in, ...

33. Setze die richtige Präposition ein.
a) to, by, at, opposite, by, on **b)** to, for, by.

34. Du willst dich bedanken.
a) thanks (a lot), That's all right **b)** Thank you, Not at all.

35. Sage es auf Englisch.

a) Thanks for your help, Jason. – That's all right. **b)** Thank you very much, Mrs Wilson. The book is really interesting. – Don't mention it. **c)** It was nice of you to give me a lift in your car, Mr Brooks. Thank you very much. – That's all right. Don't mention it. – You're welcome.

36. Du brauchst Hilfe.

d) – **b)** – **c)** – **f)** – **h)** – **e)** – **a)** – **g)**

37. Sage es auf Englisch.

a) Can I have another cup of tea, Jane? – Yes, of course. **b)** Would you explain the homework once again, Mr Brook? – Yes, of course. Which exercise is it? **c)** Could you post this letter for me? – I'm sorry, I can't. I'm in a hurry. **d)** Please help me, Andy. The box is very heavy. – I'm afraid, I can't at the moment. I'm waiting for my mother.

38. Sage, dass es dir leidtut.

a) (I've forgotten) my homework. I'm so sorry. – (That's) all right. Please show me the exercise tomorrow. **b)** I'm sorry, I'm late, Miss Potter. I missed the bus. – It doesn't matter. **c)** Pardon? I didn't understand the / that word, Mr Circle. Could you please repeat the sentence? **d)** Excuse me, may I have the key for the classroom?

39. Menschen beschreiben.

a) long, fair, blue, tall, thin, jeans, sweater, almost **b)** short, fat, fair, long, brown, beard, glasses, about.

40. Meinungen.

a) ... what you think of German soccer? **b)** ... the German team are favourites for the European Championship. **c)** ... can't agree and adds he feels that Holland are the better team. **d)** ... says he isn't so sure about it. He thinks Holland is no longer as good as two years ago.

41. Was du in bestimmten Situationen sagen kannst.

a) 9 **b)** 10 **c)** 5 **d)** 2 **e)** 6 **f)** 4 **g)** 1 **h)** 7 **i)** 3 **j)** 11 **k)** 12 **l)** 8.

42. Finde die fünf Fehler und verbessere sie.

a) got (become = werden!), taken (to take photos) **b)** in the afternoon **c)** Not at all / It's a pleasure / You're welcome **d)** What colour is your new car?

Lernbereich PRÜFUNGSTRAINING

Test 1 (S. 111–115)

1. Sind die folgenden Sätze richtig?
a) T b) T c) F d) F e) F f) F.

2. Korrigiere die falschen Sätze.
c) It's near the school **d)** She was ill **e)** They did a lot of things **f)** There weren't many customers.

3. Kannst du Sams Einkaufsliste vervollständigen?
a) cigarettes **b)** potatoes **c)** marmalade **d)** milk **e)** cherries **f)** peas **g)** bread **h)** chocolate.

4. Welches sind die Synonyme?
a) big **b)** enormous **c)** terrible **d)** cleaned.

5. Welches Wort bedeutet das Gegenteil?
a) old **b)** in front of **c)** the same **d)** healthy / well **e)** short.

6. Finde ein Wort im Text.
a) secretary **b)** vacuum cleaner **c)** cashier **d)** kitchen **e)** doctor **f)** calculator **g)** customer.

7. Wähle das richtige Wort und setze es ein.
still, for, soon, ago, lots of, any, some, any, some, ones.

8. Setze die richtige Form der Wörter in Klammern ein. Ergänze Wörter, wo es notwendig ist.
a) lives, does not, smaller than **b)** moved, did not find **c)** have been, for **d)** entered, did not go, was, younger than **e)** has been, since, has not done, will do **f)** has had, since, will buy / is going to buy **g)** of taking **h)** of going **i)** to seeing.

Test 2 (S. 116–120)

1. Richtig oder falsch?
a) F b) T c) F d) T e) T f) F g) F h) T i) F.

2. Finde das Gegenteil.
a) white **b)** hates **c)** interesting **d)** never **e)** left.

3. Vervollständige die Unterhaltung.
a) Would you like to hold my cat? **b)** Yes, I'd like to. Smokey is a very nice pet. **c)** Yes, she is. She catches a lot of mice. **d)** How awful! **e)** I don't think it is. It's no good if there are too many mice. **f)** Where does Smokey sleep? **g)** She sleeps in the kitchen. **h)** Oh, that's wonderful. **i)** Smokey eats a lot of cheese. **j)** Goodbye, Emily. **k)** Goodbye Mrs Jennings.

4. Setze *one* oder *ones* ein.
a) one **b)** ones **c)** one.

5. Schreibe vollständige if-Sätze.
a) would play **b)** does not learn **c)** will take **d)** will not / won't learn.

6. Setze die richtige Form der Verben in Klammern ein.
a) has had **b)** went **c)** (had) left, travelled **d)** was **e)** Playing **f)** sleeping **g)** will have **h)** is going to give / will give **i)** is doing **j)** is running **k)** eats **l)** has been **m)** doesn't catch **n)** wanted, was.

Test 3 (S. 121–124)

2. Gib das Gegenteil an.
a) safe **b)** funny **c)** boring / dull **d)** to whisper.

3. Erkläre in vollständigen Sätzen.
a) A monster is a dangerous creature which is not human. **b)** It is a tradition in the U.S.A. **c)** A witch is a woman who can do magic.

4. Umschreibe die folgenden Wörter.
a) They lost a game / war. **b)** They are reasonable / not too extreme. **c)** They make them leave because they're afraid. **d)** apart from a few school children.

5. Adjektiv oder Adverb.
nicely, sad, happy, happy, awfully, sad, great, suddenly, quietly, quickly, faithfully, really, unbelievable, absolutely sure, really.

6. Reflexivpronomen oder *each other*?
themselves, each, other, each other, themselves.

7. Übersetze ins Englische.
a) Do you still remember, Dawn, how we met for the first time? **b)** Yes, of course, Patrick. It was on April 1, and you weren't feeling well. You had had too little sleep. **c)** Right / That's right. I couldn't imagine that the party the night before would last until after midnight. **d)** It must have been great. **e)** Yes, of course. I said to myself 'You really would be stupid to go / if you went so early'.

Test 4 (S. 125–128)

2. Gib das Gegenteil an.
a) rich **b)** buy **c)** cheap / inexpensive.

3. Gib die Synonyme an.
a) to ruin **b)** awful **c)** full.

4. Definiere in einem vollständigen Satz.
a) … a house / place where you can have a drink and meet friends. **b)** … the money you've got to pay for your flat. **c)** … someone who travels quite a distance from home to work every day.

5. Fragen über Großbritannien.

a) I would visit the Tower of London and Rock Circus. I could see the Crown Jewels and also the great rock stars. **b)** They built the Thames Flood Barrier because there used to be terrible floods and lots of people died. Everyone hopes that it is better now. **c)** Northern Ireland is part of Great Britain. The Republic of Ireland is an independent state, called Eire.

6. Modale Hilfsverben.

a) needn't, had to **b)** was allowed to **c)** Did you have to.

7. Setze die Verben ins Passiv.

a) was broken **b)** are kept **c)** were taken **d)** hasn't been opened **e)** will be opened.

8. Frage nach den unterstrichenen Teilen.

a) What are they crowded with? **b)** Why do they have **to travel** to London every day? **c)** When will it be built?

9. Sage es auf Englisch.

a) Many visitors who come to London every year visit Baker Street. They want to see the home of a man who was actually only an idea of the author A.C. Doyle. **b)** The thrilling adventures of the man who became known as Sherlock Holmes have been read by millions of people. **c)** Most of the stories have been translated into German. **d)** Even films have been made. Some of them have been very successful.

(S. 126–128)

Inhalt

Vorwort

Mit dem zweiten Teil von *Englisch Übungsbuch 7./8. Klasse* begeben wir uns inhaltlich in die USA. Die Übungen und Beispiele sind auf die USA bezogen und vermitteln auch verschiedene landeskundliche Informationen. Folglich werden auch alle Wörter in der amerikanischen Schreibweise erscheinen, so findet man *neighbor* anstelle von *neighbour*, aber auch *streetcar* anstelle von *tram.* Die britische Schreibweise oder das entsprechende Wort aus dem britischen Englisch (BE) haben wir meist in Klammern dahinter gesetzt.

Im Lernbereich GRAMMATIK werden zahlreiche Wiederholungsübungen angeboten, um den bisher behandelten Stoff ins Gedächtnis zurückzurufen. Die Zeiten erscheinen in einem Überblick und auch die Bedingungssätze, die häufig zu Fehlern führen, werden eingehend wiederholt und um den neuen Typ 3 ergänzt. Vielfältige Übungsformen und übersichtliche Darstellungen helfen, den Überblick zu behalten und den Stoff eingehend zu üben. Die Übungen sind dabei in inhaltliche Zusammenhänge eingebunden und trainieren gleichzeitig die Fähigkeit, sich zu verschiedenen Sachverhalten zu äußern und Aussagen anderer richtig zu verstehen.

Der Lernbereich RECHTSCHREIBUNG behandelt Wörter, die leicht verwechselt werden oder im Plural oder der dritten Person Singular eine abweichende Schreibweise haben. Besonders leicht kommt es zu Fehlern bei Wörtern, die zwar gleich ausgesprochen, aber unterschiedlich geschrieben werden, darum können sie hier auch besonders gründlich geübt werden.

Im Lernbereich WORTSCHATZ steht natürlich der Unterschied zwischen dem britischen und amerikanischen Englisch im Vordergrund. Behandelt werden Unterschiede in der Schreibung, die leicht zu merken sind. Schwieriger wird es, wenn beide Sprachen unterschiedliche Wörter verwenden. Doch die Zahl dieser Unterschiede ist überschaubar und lässt sich leicht behalten.

Jedes Kapitel kann einzeln für sich bearbeitet werden. Somit besteht die Möglichkeit, individuelle Schwerpunkte zu setzen. In den Inhaltsverzeichnissen ist das Übungsangebot ausführlich dargelegt.

Der Lösungsteil im Anhang erlaubt auch hier wieder die eigenständige Überprüfung der Ergebnisse.

Lernbereich GRAMMATIK

1 Substantiv – Artikel

Fachausdrücke

Englisch:	Deutsch:	Beispiel:
adjective	Adjektiv, Eigenschaftswort	
positive	Positiv, Grundform des Adjektivs	big, intelligent
comparative	Komparativ (1. Steigerungsform)	bigger, more intelligent
superlative	Superlative (2. Steigerungsform)	biggest, most intelligent
adverb	Adverb, Umstandswort	
- of definite time	- der bestimmten Zeit	yesterday
- of indefinite time	- der unbestimmten Zeit	now, still, already
- of degree	- des Grades	very, quite, fairly
- of frequency	- der Häufigkeit	sometimes, always, twice
- of manner	- der Art und Weise	easily, fast, quickly
- of place	- des Ortes	here, inside
adverbial (phrase)	adverbiale Bestimmung	at the door, years ago, in 1997
article	Artikel	
definite article	bestimmter Artikel	the
indefinite article	unbestimmter Artikel	a, an
auxiliary (verb)	Hilfsverb	
defective auxiliary	unvollständiges Hilfsverb	can - could; may - might
modal auxiliary	modales Hilfsverb	can - may, should, must
backshift of tenses	Rückverschiebung der Zeitformen des Verbs bei indirekter Rede	
by-agent	Täter, Verursacher einer Handlung	The jewel was stolen **by the thief.**
clause	Satz, Satzteil	If you are thirsty …
if-clause	wenn-Teil im Bedingungssatz	
main clause	Hauptsatz	
relative clause	Relativsatz	The man who opened the door…
subordinate clause	Nebensatz	
conditional sentence/clause	Bedingungssatz	If it gets hot, he will open the door.

conjunctions	Konjunktionen	as soon as, after, when
demonstrative determiner	Demonstrativbegleiter	**this** book, **that** car
infinitive	Infinitiv, Grundform des Verbs	to clean, to swim
irregular plural	unregelmäßige Pluralform	thief - thieves
irregular verb	unregelmäßiges Verb	do - did - done
of-phrase	Darstellen von Besitz-, Bezugsverhältnissen	James is a friend of mine. A bottle of lemonade ...
ordinal number	Ordnungszahl	(the) first
passive	Passiv	was built, will be taken
past participle	Partizip Perfekt (3. Form des Verbs)	written, rung, taken
phrasal verb	Verb mit Präposition	to talk about, to throw away
progressive forms	Verlaufsformen des Verbs	I am / was / have been reading
pronoun	Pronomen	
general pronoun	allgemeines Pronomen („man“)	One should know when to stop.
indefinite pronoun	unbestimmtes Pronomen	someone, anything
personal pronoun	Personalpronomen, -begleiter	I, you, she, we
possessive adjective / possessive determiner	Possessivpronomen, -begleiter (adjektivisch gebraucht)	my, your, her, our
possessive pronoun	Possessivpronomen (substantivisch gebraucht)	mine, yours, hers, ours
prop word	Stützwort	one, ones
question word	Fragewort	where, when, who, how
reflexive pronoun	Reflexivpronomen	myself, herself, themselves
reported speech	indirekte Rede	He said that...
s-genitive	s-Genitiv	Whose is this book? Is it **Carl's?**
tense	Zeit(form)	

1 Substantiv – Artikel

1 Whose is it?

Revision

Peter's car is in the garage.
Mr Morgan bought my parents' house.
Professor Higgins's (Higgins') house is in Evanston.
The children's and the gentlemen's departments are on the first floor.
Al Capone was Chicago's most famous criminal.

The roof of this building needs repairing.
The leaves of the tree will turn yellow and red in fall (BE: autumn).

Besitz- und Bezugsverhältnisse werden bei Personen, Tieren und geografischen Begriffen durch den s-Genitiv, bei Sachen durch die of-phrase ausgedrückt.

Verbinde die Wörter der linken Spalte mit den Sätzen der rechten Spalte, indem du den s-Genitiv oder die of-phrase gebrauchst.

a) President Clinton	Their toys are spread all over the floor in the kindergarten.
b) America	Its park cannot be visited by the public.
c) the children	The British army was defeated by his soldiers in 1781.
d) John F. Kennedy	His wife is called Hillary Rodham.
e) the skyscraper	Their right to vote did not yet exist in the 19th century.
f) Baron von Steuben	Its biggest city is New York.
g) the White House	His most famous saying was, „Ich bin ein Berliner."
h) the women	Its elevator (BE: lift) is out of order.
i) the dog	His name is still remembered by most Americans.
j) George Washington	People do not like its biscuits.

Example:

a) President Clinton's wife is called Hillary Rodham.

Use the s-genitive 2

Whose book is this? - I guess it is Mary'**s**.

My dog has swallowed a chicken bone. And now he is at the vet'**s**.

I think it is time for me to go to the hairdresser'**s**.

Bei eindeutigen Besitz- oder Bezugsverhältnissen **entfällt** das **Bezugswort** nach dem s-Genitiv. Dies trifft dann zu, wenn das Bezugswort unmittelbar vorausgeht oder Institutionen und Geschäftsräume bezeichnet werden.

Rodney Howard is a neighbor **of** my grandfather'**s**.

Jonathan is a cousin **of mine**.

Die Strukturen	**Substantiv**	+	**of**	+	**s-Genitiv**
und	**Substantiv**	+	**of**	+	**Possessivpronomen** *(mine, yours, his, hers, its, ours, yours, theirs)*

werden ebenfalls ohne Bezugswort gebraucht.

Du möchtest ausdrücken, dass

a) du Zahnschmerzen hast und zum Zahnarzt gehen musst.

b) du beim Fleischer ein Pfund Würste kaufen möchtest.

c) dein Freund einer der Söhne des Bürgermeisters ist.

d) du die Ferien bei deiner Tante und deinem Onkel verbringen wirst.

e) du beim Bäcker Brot kaufen willst.

f) Dr. Braine ein Bruder deines Französischlehrers ist.

g) Susan eine Enkelin der Smiths und eine ihrer Nachbarinnen ist.

3 Use a possessive pronoun instead of the s-genitive.

Aunt Cathrin is a sister of **my mother's.**

Aunt Cathrin is a sister of hers.

a) This mobile home belongs to a friend of **my parents.**

. . . .

b) You have just met a daughter of **the Browns.**

. . . .

c) You have just met a daughter of **Mr Brown('s).**

. . . .

d) You have just met a daughter of **Mrs Brown('s).**

. . . .

4 Odd man out - the definite article

Schaue dir die vier Wörter in jeder Zeile an. Eines von ihnen passt nicht zu den andern dreien. Trage den Buchstaben, der in Klammern steht, in die Lücke des unten stehenden Satzes ein.

house	(k)	happiness	(a)	tree	(m)	desk	(w)
cat	(l)	village	(p)	life	(b)	street	(o)
telephone	(j)	pen	(n)	book	(y)	joy	(s)
flower	(z)	death	(t)	cowboy	(x)	leaf	(d)
pioneer	(e)	elephant	(q)	fear	(r)	cabin	(u)
truck	(f)	leisure	(a)	pueblo	(r)	airport	(s)
mountain	(s)	bear	(o)	tension	(c)	cemetery	(a)
anger	(t)	tower	(c)	Indian	(u)	feather	(k)

The odd men are ☐ ☐ ☐ ☐ ☐ ☐ ☐ ☐ nouns.

Life is wonderful. ***Das** Leben ist herrlich.*

The author knows how to keep up tension. *Der Autor weiß, wie man **die** Spannung aufrechterhält*

Gold is a very precious metal.

Abstrakte Begriffe und **Stoffbezeichnungen** werden im Englischen **ohne** den bestimmten **Artikel** gebraucht, wenn sie nicht näher bestimmt sind.

Choose the right letter 5

Trage den ersten Buchstaben hinter der Lücke in das Kästchen ein, wenn du den bestimmten Artikel gebrauchst, den zweiten, wenn du ihn nicht gebrauchst.

a) ....(p/g) life of the first settlers in America was extremely hard.

b) The young man was severely punished for..............(e/z) crime he had committed in Idaho.

c) The USA exports..............(l/o) corn to many countries all over the world.

d) ....(g/p) water can be more dangerous than..............(w/l) fire.

e) ....(e/k) wheat which Russia bought from France was very expensive.

f) Metals like..............(e/m) iron and copper are still needed in industry.

g) ....(a/f) copper which had been imported from the Third World Countries greatly influenced the Dow Jones Index.

h) ....(n/t) gold which was found in California caused the gold rush in the 19th century.

Lösung: ☐ ☐ ☐ ☐ ☐ ☐ + ☐ ☐ ☐

6 Fill in the definite article if necessary.

People und **man** werden je nach Bedeutung mit oder ohne den bestimmten Artikel gebraucht.

people	=	die Leute, die Menschen, man
the people	=	das Volk
the peoples	=	die Völker
man	=	der Mensch (allgemein), die Menschheit
the man	=	der Mann
the men	=	die Männer

most / most of + plural noun und *half the / half of + noun* werden ohne den bestimmten Artikel gebraucht.
Deutsch: **die** meisten, **die** Hälfte

a) .... people in big cities are often more lonely than .... people in small villages.

b) .... man is the most intelligent living being.

c) .... Roman people was highly cultivated at the time of the birth of Christ.

d) .... people in America enjoy fast food.

e) .... man must learn how to save energy.

f) For the second time Bill Clinton was elected President by .... American people.

g) In Colorado we met a group of Indians; .... most of them still live on reservations.

h) More than .... half of the population in Chicago are black.

i) The police are looking for .... man who saw the accident yesterday.

j) .... people in this area suffer from a lot of diseases because .... man was unable to foresee the dangers of pollution and overcrowding.

Decide whether the definite article is necessary or not. 7

Juan lives in **San Diego**.
Chicago is the biggest city on **Lake Michigan**.
Mount Rainier in **Washington** is 4392 m high.
Fifth Avenue is one of the most famous streets in New York.
From the top of **Sears Tower** you can have a magnificent view over Chicago.

Eigennamen, geografische Begriffe, Straßen- und Gebäudenamen, Institutionen sowie **Wochentage und Monatsnamen im Singular** stehen, wenn keine nähere Bestimmung folgt, **ohne** den bestimmten Artikel.
Namen von **Flüssen, Meeren, Gebirgen und Schiffen** werden dagegen **mit** dem bestimmten Artikel gebraucht: the Mississippi River, the Atlantic Ocean, the Mayflower.

a) .... Yosemite, ... Yellowstone, ... Mesa Verde and .... Everglades are National Parks worth visiting in .... USA.

b) .... July of 1995 was the hottest month since temperatures had been registered in Illinois.

c) .... Sir Edmund Hillary was the first man to climb .... Mount Everest; he reached the top of .... mountain in 1953.

d) .... Rocky Mountains and .... Appalachians stretch from .... North to .... South and divide .... America into different regions.

e) Many musicals set out to conquer the world from .... Broadway.

f) .... Lake Superior, ... Lake Michigan, ... Lake Huron, ... Lake Erie and .... Lake Ontario are on the borderline between .... United States of America and .... Canada.

g) I will always remember .... Saturday of our first date.

h) Before the Pilgrim Fathers came to .... America they went from .... England to .... Netherlands.

8 Fill in the definite article where suitable.

In Germany **school** starts earlier than in America.
(**school** = der Unterricht)
The school is one of the oldest buildings in our town.
(**the school** = das Schulgebäude)

Bildungseinrichtungen, politische, religiöse und kirchliche Institutionen werden nur dann mit dem bestimmten Artikel gebraucht, wenn sie näher bestimmt sind oder das Gebäude an sich bezeichnen.

A panel discussion (Podiumsdiskussion) on .... education

College Lecturer: I think that .... education is a lifelong process .... education which our children are offered at the moment cannot catch up with the necessities of our modern world. I suggest .... school should start earlier – at the age of four, for example.

Father: I would not like my little daughter to go to .... school so early. .... school is too far away, ... kindergarten is much nearer.

Schoolteacher: I often watch young kids who go to .... church on .... Sunday morning with their parents. They can't go to .... church, which is in the center of the town, on their own; it's too dangerous, and .... school is even farther away.

College Lecturer: All these are minor problems which can easily be solved if the kids don't walk to .... school but go by .... bus. .... bus to .... George Washington School leaves next to .... Roman Catholic church.

Mother: I hope .... Congress will not decide in favor (BE: favour) of an earlier school entrance age. Perhaps we ought to organize a demonstration in front of .... Capitol in .... Washington, D.C..

Schoolteacher: Even with .... education starting at an earlier age we will not enable more students to get into .... college than we do now. There'll still be financial problems to cope with.

Tanslate the following sentences. Mind the article. 9

a) Most people cannot stand being criticized by others.

b) Man will have to think about the effects of the throw-away mentality.

c) Mr Blake will be the man to improve the economic situation of our firm.

d) There are a lot of people unemployed in this industrial area; half of them will never get a job again because they are unqualified or just too old.

e) After the accident at the nuclear power station most scientists were taken to hospital for check-ups. The nearest hospital soon could not accept any more patients.

f) School starts earlier than church, but the church is farther away than the school. So we have to get up early, even on Sundays.

The indefinite article - put the nouns into the right column. 10

Last year Mr O'Brien bought **a** house and **a** new car.

For the fruit salad you need **a** banana, **a** pear, **a** peach, **an** apple and **an** orange.

Tonight's last train arrived **an** hour ago.

Many people do not believe in the idea of **a** United Europe.

Vor **Konsonanten** lautet der unbestimmte Artikel **a / ə /, vor Vokalen an / ə n /**. Welche der beiden Formen gebraucht wird, hängt dabei von der Aussprache, nicht von der Schreibung ab.

a /ə/	an / ən /
a computer	an adult
a modern painting	an old man
a yellow schoolbus	an iron bar
a US citizen	an unusual event
a united country	an unavoidable mistake
a European country	an endless war
a soap opera	an SOS call
a fire department	an FBI agent
a long-distance call	an LP
a rocket	an RAF officer
a hound /haʊnd/	an hour/aʊə(r) /
a hotel	an honest offer
a handkerchief	an honorable man
a hostage (Geisel)	an heir (Erbe / Erbin)

Schlage in deinem Wörterbuch nach, wenn du die Aussprache nicht mehr weißt!

tepee, OPEC agreement, unhappy girl, unforgettable performance, rear light, emergency, university degree, T-shirt, Yankee, vacation, uncomfortable seat, earthquake, unicorn, unsinkable ship, interstate highway, unit, oven, unpleasant event, warehouse, essential element

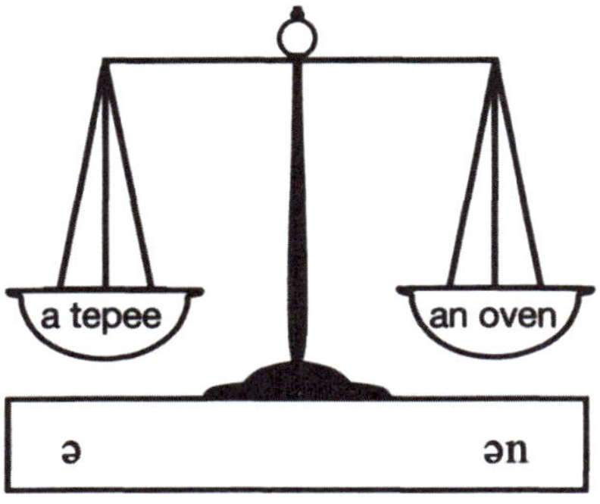

Jobs, nationalities and beliefs with the indefinite article. Fill in the gaps where necessary.

11

Bob MacMahon is **an** executive officer and his sister is **a** lawyer.
... ist Verwaltungsbeamter ... ist Rechtsanwältin.

Neil O'Brien is **an** Irishman.
... ist Ire.
Häufig wird in diesem Fall auch das Adjektiv verwendet: Neil O'Brien is Irish.

John F. Kenney was **a** Catholic.
... war Katholik / katholisch.

Ivan Olinsky is *a* socialist.
... ist Sozialist.

Die Zugehörigkeit zu **Berufsgruppen, Nationalitäten, Religionen und politischen Parteien** wird - im Gegensatz zum Deutschen - **mit dem unbestimmten Artikel** ausgedrückt.

In 1996 Bill Clinton was re-elected President of the United States.
Jack Ribew has been mayor of Bradford, Kentucky, since 1994.

Bestimmte (einmalige) **Titelbezeichnungen** stehen - wie im Deutschen - ohne Artikel.

Introducing oneself - a TV discussion on environmental awareness.

The participants in an international TV discussion on ecological questions introduce themselves to the audience.

a) My name is William Brooming. As .... Englishman from the Liverpool industrial area I am especially interested in the problems of air pollution. I work as .... engineer in .... big chemical plant. From 1986 to 1995 I was .... chairman of the RSPP (Royal Society for the Prevention of Pollution).

b) I am Jack Ribew. I have been .... mayor of Bradford, Kentucky, for two years now. My father was .... Irishman from Blarney. He was .... farmer in Ireland. I used to be .... sales manager before I became .... mayor of Bradford. I am .... Roman Catholic and therefore worried about the moral and ethical aspects of pollution.

c) I'm called Juan Rodriguez. I am Spaniard from Seville. I was trained as .... chemical engineer and I have been .... managing director of Chemtec Ltd. since 1992. As my wife is nurse in one of Seville's biggest hospitals I have been dealing with both the chemical and medical aspects of ecology.

d) I am Herbert Bülow. I am .... clergyman, ... Protestant. Though I am .... German I live and work in Austria. I am married to .... social worker in Vienna. My wife is .... Catholic. She is .... Frenchwoman from Rouen. I think no matter if you are .... Protestant, ... Catholic, ... Jew, or .... Muslim, the protection of the environment should be a concern of all of us.

e) My name is Svetlana Borkhorov. I am .... housewife and .... mother of four young children from Chernobyl. My husband, who was .... scientist at the atomic power station, died after the Chernobyl disaster of 1986. I am .... atheist and .... Communist, but I am of the opinion that ecology cannot be a question of political or religious convictions.

f) Ich spreche leider nicht Englisch. Mein Name ist Günther Bannwarth. Ich bin Psychologe und Präsident des Deutschen Umweltschutzvereins (DUV e.V.). Ich bin Katholik und als Liberaler Mitglied der F.D.P.. Meine Frau ist Engländerin. Als Ärztin ist sie die Umweltbeauftragte (environmental health officer) der Stadt Duisburg.

What will the simultaneous translator say? Translate part f).

Special offers - the indefinite article with numbers and expressions of time and quantity. 12

These marshmallows cost 95 cents **a** pound.
...je/pro Pfund.

How much is this whiskey (BE: whisky)? - It is $ 30 **a** bottle.
...je/pro/die Flasche.

Though retired he still works twenty-five hours **a** week.
... pro/die Woche.

Der unbestimmte Artikel steht bei **Maß- und Zeitangaben**, die im Deutschen durch „je“ oder „pro“ bezeichnet werden.

Beachte: a hundred (hundert); **a** thousand (tausend).

To go shopping or not to go shopping?

GOODLIFE FOOD CORPORATION Ltd.

THIS WEEK'S SPECIAL OFFERS

POTATOES (top quality, imported from Europe)	$ 1.307kg
ORANGES (Florida Queen)	$ 2.45/pound
PINEAPPLE (Hawaiian Star)	$ 2.10/piece
STRAWBERRIES (Red Crown)	$ 11.30/basket
WHITE WINE ('Californian Auslese')	
Two Bottles in Presentation Box	$ 18.45/box
WHISKEY (Jim Beam)	$ 25.40/bottle
DIET COKE	$ 0.65/can
FLOWERS (Valentine's Pride)	$ 12.85/bunch
Vacation Offer (First Class Hotel in Jacksonville, Florida)	**$ 935.00/prs./week**

Monday morning at the breakfast table. The McAllisters are talking about this week's shopping. As Grandma Linda cannot find her glasses her husband Geoffrey reads out the special offers advertised in „The Des Moines Post".

Linda: Any special offers this week, dear?

Geoffrey: Oh yes. Quite a lot. GOODLIFE'S seem to be rather cheap this week. What do we need?

Linda: What about vegetables? Anything special?

Geoffrey: Not really. Just potatoes. They are $ 1.30 a kilo.

Linda: We need some fruit.

Geoffrey: I see. An apple .... day keeps the doctor away. But there are no apples advertised today.

The oranges cost ...., the pineapples are offered at .... and their strawberries are ....

Linda: We have run out of beverages (Getränke).

Geoffrey: They offer two bottles of white wine at ...., the whiskey is .... and Diet Coke will be ....

Linda: Tomorrow will be February 14. We need a small gift for Aunt Agatha.

Geoffrey: We could get some flowers. Valentine's Pride they are called and they are ....

Linda: Anything else we might get?

Geoffrey: Forget all about shopping. Let's fly to Jacksonville, Florida. They offer a vacation for... .That means: No shopping, no heavy bags to carry, no Aunt Agatha tomorrow.

Scrambled sentences - put the words into the right order. 13

Fiona is quite a nice girl. *... ein recht nettes Mädchen.*

Jill was half an hour late. *... kam eine halbe Stunde zu spät.*

Bei den Ausdrücken ***half, quite, what, such, rather, many*** (manch ein) wird - im Gegensatz zum Deutschen - der unbestimmte Artikel nachgestellt, desgleichen in den Verbindungen ***too + adjective***
however + adjective
so + adjective
sowie in einigen feststehenden Wendungen.

too great a loss	–	*ein zu großer Verlust*
so bad an experience	–	*eine so schlechte Erfahrung*
to have a headache	–	*Kopfweh haben*
to be in a hurry	–	*in Eile sein*
to take a seat	–	*Platz nehmen*
to have a drink	–	*etwas trinken*
to take an interest in	–	*sich für etwas interessieren*
to speak in a low / loud voice	–	*leise / laut sprechen*
to go for a swim / a ride	–	*schwimmen / reiten gehen*
on an average	–	*im Durchschnitt*
at a loss	–	*mit Verlust*

a) new - within - a - Jack - built - O'Brien - farmhouse - year - his - half

. . . .

b) own - TV - average - and - on - cars - an - sets - Americans - two - three

Americans . . . . two cars . . . .

c) was – for – he – quite – moving – many – an – settler – West – a – adventure – to

Moving to the West . . . .

. . . .

d) to – hurry – car – was – loss – his – as – had – at – in – a – Terry – a – sell – he

As he was . . . . Terry had to sell . . . .

. . . .

e) my – however – it – wife – dress – a – will – expensive – buy – is / may be

However . . . . my wife will . . . .

. . . .

f) Barbara – first – ride – drink – went – they – near – Howard – went – for – the – and – for – pool – after – a – that – and – had – a – finally – swim – they – a

First Barbara and Howard . . . . ride, after . . . . swim,

and finally . . . . drink . . . . pool.

14 Translate the following sentences.

a) Das war ein zu schrecklicher Unfall. Ich kann ihn nicht vergessen.

b) Marilyn Monroe war eine recht begabte Schauspielerin.

c) „Ich habe Magenschmerzen", sagte Lewis leise.

d) Das ist eine so aufregende Geschichte. Die Zeitungen und das Fernsehen interessieren sich schon dafür.

Who is he? 15

Fill in the definite or indefinite article, or leave it out if necessary.

Have you ever heard of Samuel Langhorne Clemens? He lived in .... United States of .... America about .... hundred years ago (1835 - 1910), and he was .... American writer and .... humorist. Even .... people in America do not know his real name, but .... most of them know quite lot about his life and career because they all have read such .... famous novel as „The Adventures of Tom Sawyer“. And while reading so fascinating .... story as „The Adventures of Huckleberry Finn“ many .... American or German schoolboys may dream of traveling (BE: travelling) down .... Mississippi River. But you must not forget that .... life in those days was hard for black people in .... South of America, especially .... life of a runaway slave like Huck's friend Jim. In spite of .... hardships described „Huck Finn“ is quite .... amusing and funny story.

Now I hope you will have taken .... interest in reading these two novels written by too popular .... author as not to be known by his pen-name:

Lösungswort: ☐ ☐ ☐ ☐   ☐ ☐ ☐ ☐ ☐

2 Pronomen

16 Fill in the suitable pronoun.

Achte in den folgenden Beispielsätzen neben den Personalpronomen besonders auf den unterschiedlichen Gebrauch des adjektivischen Possessivpronomens (possessive adjective/possessive determiner) und des substantivischen Possessivpronomens (possessive pronoun):

I parked **my** car next to Tom's car.

His car is red, **mine** is blue.

Where are the Smiths? Isn't that green Chevrolet **their** car?

No, that is our Chevrolet, sorry. **Ours** is dark green, **theirs** is light green.

Personalpronomen *(personal pronouns)*	Possessivpronomen	
	possessive adjectives	possessive pronouns
I	my	mine
you	your	yours
he	his	his
she	her	hers
it	its	its
we	our	ours
you	your	yours
they	their	theirs

- Die *possessive adjectives my, your, his, her, its, our, your, their* stehen immer **vor einem Substantiv**.
- Die *possessive pronouns mine, yours, his, hers, its, ours, yours, theirs* beziehen sich auf ein **vorangehendes Substantiv**, das nicht wiederholt wird. Sie stehen **allein**, d.h. ohne ein Substantiv.

On the beach

Fill in the correct personal pronouns and possessive pronouns / possessive determiners.

a) Barry: Did you see Tom's new bike? .... saddle alone cost more than .... whole bike.

b) Mark: It's not .... bike .... is broken and so he took .... sister's - and I think .... doesn't even know that .... has got it now. Listen, Jack and I just had .... lunch. Have you had .... ?

c) Barry: Not yet - and I'm not hungry at the moment. Daisy, will Christine be around today? I haven't seen .... for ages.

d) Daisy: No, she won't .... parents are celebrating .... wedding anniversary today and the family will spend the whole week at .... holiday home in Santa Monica. It's really hot today, isn't it?. I don't want a sunburn. Before .... skin starts to turn red I should use some sun-tan lotion.

e) Barry: If you can't find .... , you can take ....

f) Daisy: Thanks, that's very nice of .... Rachel, may I borrow .... *Boys 'n Girls* magazine again?

g) Rachel: It's not .... , it's Barry's magazine. You have to look in .... bag, it must be in........ left side-pocket, I think. On page 15 there is an article about *Faithless*.

h) Daisy: I know. They are really fantastic .... last video was a scream, wasn't it?

i) Mark: I don't think so. I like *Bon Jovi* better .... are not only .... brother's favorite band, but also ....

j) Daisy: Don't be silly. .... brother and .... have got no taste. All the girls in .... class are fans of *Faithless* and in the *Boys 'n Girls* charts .... new single is number one.

k) Rachel: Oh stop it, you two. I am trying to read a letter from Ben. He is staying in Boston with .... aunt, and next month he could visit .... and .... family. There's enough room in .... house. And of course - Daisy is right.

l) Mark: Hey, Barry! Help me. Are you on side or on .... ?

m) Barry: I'm on neither side - neither on .... , nor on .... I'd like to go swimming now. I forgot my flippers (*Schwimmflossen*). Whose are these?

n) Mark: Look, there's an *M* on them so they are .... The blue ones are Stephen's and the red ones are Sandra's, but .... are too small for you, bigfoot. Stephen's flippers should fit. So take .... or .... instead.

17 Mind the reflexive pronoun.

① **I** can see **myself** in the mirror.

② **Clare** knows Chicago so well because she has been there **herself**.

③ The **dog** was scratching **itself** behind the ear.

④ Are **you** still hungry, boys? There are sandwiches on the table. Help **yourselves**!

⑤ The **children** made the model planes **themselves**.

⑥ Can **we** make **ourselves** useful in the kitchen?

⑦ Paul, **you** shouldn't write a letter to Mary. **You** should talk to her **yourself**.

- Ein Reflexivpronomen wird verwendet, wenn das Subjekt (*I, Clare, the children ...*) und das Objekt (*myself, herself, themselves ...*) dieselbe Person oder Sache bezeichnen.
- Reflexivpronomen können auch eingesetzt werden, um ein Substantiv besonders hervorzuheben (Sätze ②, ⑤, ⑦). Man nennt es dann verstärkendes Pronomen (*emphasizing pronoun*).
- Die Reflexivpronomen haben im Plural eine abweichende Schreibweise: *ourselves, yourselves, themselves*.

Translate:

First translate sentences ① to ⑦ above then continue with sentences ⑧ to ⑩.

⑧ Do you **remember** me? We **met** in Dallas last summer!

⑨ Wayne stayed in bed yesterday because he didn't **feel** well.

⑩ Sally **wondered** how much money she had spent last week.

Wie die Sätze 8 bis 10 zeigen, sind viele Verben im Deutschen **reflexiv**, im Englischen dagegen **nicht reflexiv**.

Do some more translation practice! 18

Folgende Verben, die im Deutschen reflexiv gebraucht werden, im Englischen aber nicht, solltest du dir merken:

to change	-	*sich ändern, sich umziehen*	**to meet**	-	*sich treffen*
to complain	-	*sich beschweren*	**to move**	-	*sich bewegen*
to feel	-	*sich fühlen*	**to open**	-	*sich öffnen*
to happen	-	*sich ereignen*	**to refuse**	-	*sich weigern*
to hide	-	*sich verstecken*	**to remember**	-	*sich erinnern*
to hurry	-	*sich beeilen*	**to sit down**	-	*sich setzen*
to imagine	-	*sich vorstellen*	**to wonder**	-	*sich fragen*
to join	-	*sich anschließen, beitreten*			

American Football

a) Letzte Woche schlössen sich Dave und Luke dem American Football Club ihrer Schule an.

b) Sie mögen American Football selbst (an sich) sehr gerne, aber es ist auch wichtig für sie, in ihrer Schulmannschaft zu spielen.

c) Zuerst stellen sie sich dem Trainer (*coach*) und der Mannschaft vor.

d) Luke zeigt einen alten Football-Helm (*football helmet*), den sein Vater vor vielen Jahren selbst benutzte.

e) Dave zieht sich sehr sorgfältig seine Schutzkleidung (*padded clothes*) an.

f) Beide wollen sich gegen Verletzungen (*injuries*) schützen - *American Football* kann sehr gefährlich sein.

g) Luke trainiert (*to train*) häufig alleine und er fragt sich, wann er in der Mannschaft spielen wird (*to be on the team*).

h) Dave und Luke fühlen sich im Klub sehr glücklich. Sie können es sich nicht vorstellen, ohne *American Football* zu leben.

19 Get to know some English proverbs - general / indefinite pronouns.

Das allgemeine / unpersönliche und das unbestimmte Pronomen treten in verschiedenen Formen auf:

① **One** is never too old to learn.

② **We** soon believe what we want to believe.

③ **Someone** tried to steal my car. (*Jemand / Man hat versucht, mein Auto zu stehlen.*)

④ **You** can never tell. (*Man kann nie wissen.*)

⑤ In America **they** (people) celebrate *Thanksgiving Day* in every state.

- Das allgemeine / unpersönliche Pronomen (*general pronoun*) ***one*** bezeichnet keine bestimmte, sondern eine „allgemeine" Person. Es entspricht deshalb dem deutschen ***man*** (①).
- Das allgemeine / unpersönliche Pronomen ***one*** kommt häufig in Sprichwörtern, Redensarten und Floskeln vor.
- An die Stelle von ***one*** können auch ***we, you, they, people*** oder auch ***someone*** treten. Es kommt darauf an, ob sich der Sprecher in die Aussage mit einschließt oder nicht und ob von einzelnen unbekannten Personen oder einer größeren Gruppe gesprochen wird (② bis ⑤).

English proverbs

Bilde Sprichwörter aus den Satzteilen der linken und der rechten Spalte. Setze die Buchstaben in Klammern in die Kästchen ein.

1. As you make your bed	(N)	a)	in two places at once.	(L)
2. One is as old	(W)	b)	and drink the milk.	(S)
3. One cannot be	(R)	c)	so you must lie in it.	(E)
4. One should love	(E)	d)	as one feels.	(O)
5. You cannot sell the cow	(N)	e)	one's neighbor as oneself.	(A)

Lösungswort: ☐ ☐ ☐ ☐ ☐ ☐ ☐ ☐ ☐ ☐

3 Adverbien

Funktionen und Arten von Adverbien (*function and classification of adverbs*)

Adverbien bestimmen ein Wort, einen Satzteil oder einen ganzen Satz näher.

① ein Verb: The man **ran quickly** into the shop.

② ein Adjektiv: She is **seriously ill.**

③ ein Adverb: Tim speaks English **surprisingly well.**

④ ein Substantiv: When it comes to baseball, John is **quite an expert.**

Adverbien lassen sich entsprechend ihrer Bedeutung und Aufgabe in einem Satz in verschiedene Arten unterteilen:

- **Adverbien der bestimmten Zeit (*adverbs of definite time*):**
  today, yesterday
- **Adverbien der unbestimmten Zeit (*adverbs of indefinite time*):**
  now, yet, still, already, before, afterwards
- **Adverbien des Ortes (*adverbs of place*):**
  here, everywhere, down, inside
- **Adverbien der Art und Weise (*adverbs of manner*):**
  quickly, beautifully, slowly, hard, fast, easily
- **Adverbien des Grades (*adverbs of degree*):**
  very, fairly, quite, too, absolutely, rather
- **Adverbien der Häufigkeit (*adverbs of frequency*):**
  always, twice, daily, sometimes, mostly, generally, seldom

20 A mountain of adverbs and adverbials!

There is a whole mountain of adverbs below - adverbs of different kinds. Put the adverbs into the correct containers.

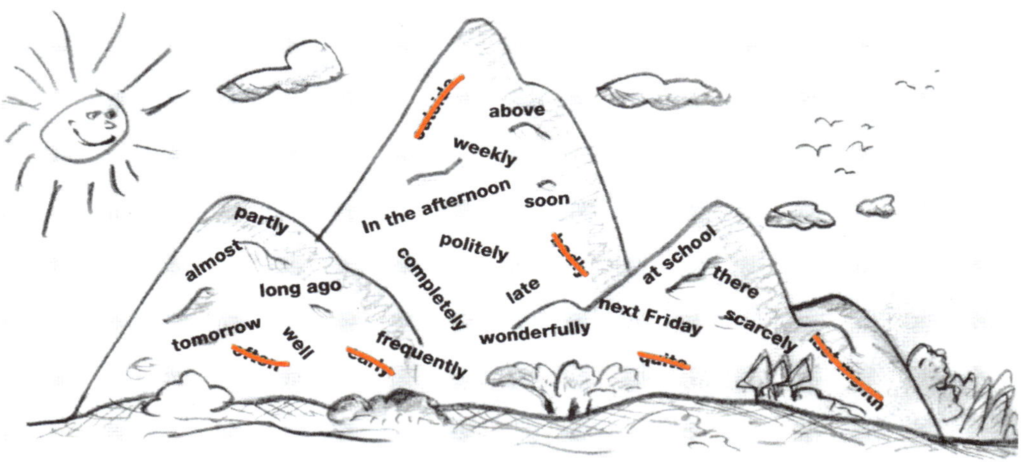

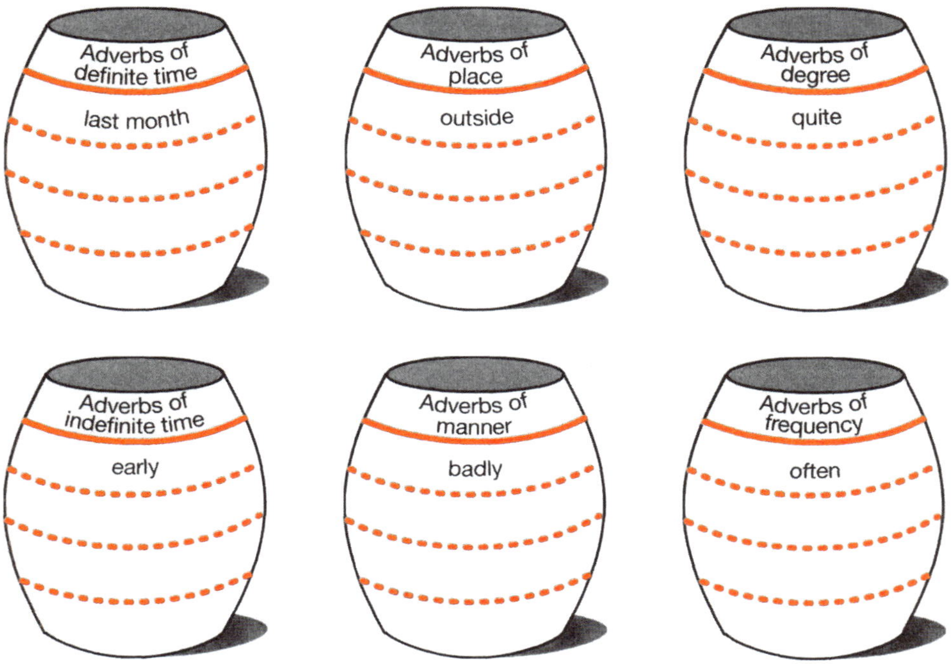

Revision

Adjective or adverb? 21

Die Bildung von Adverbien (*formation of adverbs*)

In einigen wenigen Fällen werden Adverbien aus dem **Partizip Präsens** oder dem **Partizip Perfekt** und der Endung **-ly** gebildet.

① **Partizip Präsens + *ly*** → **Adverb**

surprising + *ly* → surprisingly

Surprisingly, there were only two passengers on the train to Boston.

② **Partizip Perfekt + *ly*** → **Adverb**

excited + *ly* → excitedly

Barbara opened her birthday presents **excitedly**.

In der Regel aber gilt:

Du bildest das Adverb aus dem entsprechenden **Adjektiv** und der Endung **-*ly***:

① **Adjektiv + *ly*** →	**Adverb**
The teacher asked an **easy** question.	Tony answered the question **easily**.
John is a **slow** thinker.	John thinks **slowly**.
Mrs Miller is a **wonderful** piano player.	Mrs Miller plays the piano **wonderfully**.

- Adjektive (Eigenschaftswörter) und Adverbien (Umstandswörter) unterscheiden sich im Englischen schon allein durch die Form: **Adjektiv + *ly* = Adverb**.
- Mit dem **Adjektiv** beschreibst du, **wie** jemand oder etwas **ist**.
- Mit dem **Adverb** beschreibst du, **wie** jemand etwas **macht**.

At the supermarket

Fill in the missing adjective or adverb. Use the words given in brackets.

a) Suzie arrived at the supermarket after a .... (short) walk from her new house.

b) Her mom (BE: mum) was very .... (busy) so she had asked her to run down the street .... (quick) to the supermarket to buy a few things for a .... (delicious) dinner.

c) The doors of the supermarket opened .... (slow) and Suzie went inside, ... (careful) thinking about the things to buy.

d) She found the .... (different) vegetables and the frozen meat .... (easy), but then things turned out .... (different) from what she had expected.

e) Where were the spices (Gewürze)? She stood .... (helpless) in front of an .... (enormous) shelf and looked .... (angry) at the other customers who were walking .... (busy). They seemed to find everything .... (quick).

f) Suddenly she heard the .... (soft) voice of a shop-assistant: „Can I help you? You seem to be a bit .... (helpless) at the moment."

g) Suzie nodded .... (quiet) and .... (short) afterwards she had all the things she needed.

h) When she wanted to pay she saw an .... (endless) queue of people in front of the cash-desks. The queue was moving .... (incredible; slow). Some customers waited .... (patient - geduldig), others complained .... (terrible; loud). „Just my kind of luck", Suzie thought .... (unhappy).

Find out more about adverbs. 22

Wichtige Besonderheiten bei der Bildung von Adverbien

- Endet das Adjektiv auf **-y**, wird dieses **y** beim Adverb zu **i**, auf das dann die Endung **-ly** folgt:
  angry → angri**ly** easy → easi**ly**
- Endet das Adjektiv auf **Konsonant und -le**, dann entfällt beim Adverb dieses **-le** und wird durch die Endung **-ly** ersetzt.
  possi**ble** → possi**bly** terri**ble** → terri**bly**
  sim**ple** → sim**ply** sensi**ble** → sensi**bly**
- Endet das Adjektiv auf **Vokal und -le**, dann bleibt dieses **-le** erhalten.
  pale (*bleich*) → palely **aber: whole → wholly**
  sole (*allein*) → solely
- Endet das Adjektiv auf **-ic**, dann wird das Adverb mit **-ally** gebildet:
  automatic → automatically fantastic → fantastically
  aber: public → publicly
- Einige wenige Adverbien haben die gleiche Form wie das Adjektiv und dazu noch ein **weiteres** Adverb mit der Endung **-ly**, das allerdings eine andere Bedeutung hat:

Adjektiv / Adverb			Adverb auf – ly		
deep	-	*tief*	deeply	-	*zutiefst, tief*
fair	-	*ehrlich*	fairly	-	*ziemlich, ehrlich*
hard	-	*schwer, schwierig*	hardly	-	*kaum*
high	-	*hoch, laut*	highly	-	*höchst, sehr*
just	-	*gerade*	justly	-	*gerecht, mit Recht*
late	-	*spät*	lately	-	*kürzlich, neulich*
near	-	*nahe*	nearly	-	*beinahe*

- **Adjektive auf -ly** haben ein **gleichlautendes Adverb** oder sie bilden das **Adverb** durch eine **Umschreibung**:

  gleichlautend: early, weekly, daily, monthly, nightly, enough, fast, long, much, less, little

  Adverb durch Umschreibung:
  friendly → in a friendly way (*freundlich*)
  difficult → with difficulty (*schwerlich*)
  timely → in time (*rechtzeitig*)
  cowardly → like a coward (*feige*)

Make adverbs!

When making the adverbs, keep the rules above in mind.

a) polite	____________	j) full	____________
b) fanatic	____________	k) fast	____________
c) monthly	____________	l) heavy	____________
d) extreme	____________	m) complete	____________
e) horrible	____________	n) daily	____________
f) comfortable	____________	o) sensible	____________
g) economical	____________	p) exclusive	____________
h) true	____________	q) friendly	____________
i) early	____________	r) whole	____________

23 Translate.

Und noch eine Besonderheit: Zustandsverben

Nach einigen Verben, die eine Eigenschaft oder einen Zustand ausdrücken, steht ein **Adjektiv** und kein **Adverb**. Folgende **Zustandsverben** solltest du dir merken:

be	- *sein*	**seem**	- *scheinen*
become / get	- *werden*	**smell**	- *riechen*
feel	- *sich fühlen*	**sound**	- *klingen*
look	- *aussehen*	**taste**	- *schmecken*

The birthday party

Translate the following sentences. Be sure to mind the rule above and to use the adjective or adverb correctly.

a) Als Betty auf der Geburtstagsparty eintraf, fühlte sie sich zuerst (*at first*) nervös.

When Betty arrived . . . .

b) Sie öffnete vorsichtig die Tür und schaute sich schnell um (*to look around*).

She opened the door . . . .

c) Alle ihre Freunde waren da und sahen glücklich aus.

All her friends . . . .

d) Betty begrüßte Chris und Helen. Die Mädchen antworteten höflich.

Betty said hello . . . .

e) Die Party wurde schnell sehr fröhlich (*lively*). Betty tanzte mit Peter, dann mit Harry.

The party . . . .

f) Harry sagte: „Du tanzt perfekt! Ich hole dir schnell ein Glas Limonade und ein Stück Pizza. Die Pizza schmeckt fantastisch“.

Harry said: „You dance . . . .

. . . .

24 Comparative and superlative of adverbs

Revision

Die Steigerung von Adverbien (*comparison of adverbs*)

Bei der Steigerung von Adverbien solltest du dir einige Regeln merken:

- Die einsilbigen Adverbien und *early* werden mit **-er** und **-est**, alle Adverbien auf **-ly** mit **more** und **most** gesteigert:

Grundstufe (Positiv):	hard	quickly
Komparativ:	hard**er**	**more** quickly
Superlativ:	hard**est**	**most** quickly

- Die Steigerungsformen einiger unregelmäßiger Adverbien solltest du dir genau einprägen:

Positiv:	**well**	**badly**	**much / a lot**	**a little**
Komparativ:	better	worse	more	less
Superlativ:	best	worst	most	least

Write the comparative and the superlative forms of the following adverbs.

a) rapidly	b)	c) ....
....	....	worse
....	most easily	....
d)	e)	f) ....
more heavily	earlier	....
....	....	best

Spot and correct the mistakes! 25

The following sentences are wrong. Correct the mistakes using the proper comparative or superlative form of the adverb.

a) Josh ate his dinner more quicklier than Steve.

b) Uncle James reads littler than his brother Henry.

c) Tony plays tennis as bad as Bill.

d) Jason plays tennis badliest of all.

e) A tiger fights more aggressive than a cheetah.

Place the adverbs correctly. 26

Die Stellung von Adverbien und adverbialen Bestimmungen im Satz (*position of adverbs and adverbial phrases in sentences*)

Grundsätzlich können Adverbien und adverbiale Bestimmungen an drei Positionen im Satz auftauchen: am Satzanfang, in der Satzmitte und am Satzende.

(ADVERB) – Subjekt – (ADVERB) – Prädikat – Objekt – (ADVERB)

- Adverbien stehen im Englischen (anders als im Deutschen!) **nie** zwischen Prädikat (Verb) und direktem Objekt:
  He opened the door **quickly**.
  *Er öffnete **schnell** die Tür.*
- Wenn sich Adverbien auf das Verb des Satzes oder auf den ganzen Satz beziehen, dann stehen sie vor dem Prädikat:
  I **always** spend my holidays at the seaside.
- Wenn das Prädikat eines Satzes aus Hilfsverb und Verb besteht, dann steht das Adverb zwischen Hilfsverb und Verb:
  We **have never** been in New York.
- Wenn ein Adverb besonders betont werden soll, dann steht es am Satzende:
  He answered her question **immediately**.
- Wenn mehrere adverbiale Bestimmungen in einem Satz vorkommen, dann lautet die Reihenfolge: Adverb der Art und Weise (1) - Adverb des Ortes (2) - Adverb der Zeit (3):
  He **quickly** (1) ran to **the swimming pool** (2) **early in the morning** (3).

Adverbien der Art und Weise (adverbs of manner)

Adverbien der Art und Weise (adverbs of manner) stehen meist:

- **hinter** einem **Verb**, das sie näher bestimmen, bzw. am **Satzende**:
  They drove **carelessly**.
- **vor** einem **Adjektiv**, das sie näher bestimmen:
  Tom is **absolutely** crazy.
- vor einem weiteren **Adverb**, das näher bestimmt wird:
  She plays the piano **wonderfully well**.

Diana's first driving lesson

Write a complete sentence with the words given. Be sure to place the adverb of manner correctly.

Example:

Diana / the car / the door / of / slowly / opened
Diana opened the door of the car slowly.

a) She / sat down / the engine / carefully / started / and / quickly

b) Smoothly / ran / Diana / and / the engine / extremely / was / pleased with herself

c) How / quickly / the car / wonderfully / drove / down the street!

d) „too fast / drive / Miss Wilson / don't" / the driving instructor's / voice / soft / politely / warned

e) Reduced / Diana / the speed / immediately / of the car

27 Adverbs of time and place - find the right word order.

Adverb der Zeit	Subjekt	Verb	Objekt	Adverb des Ortes	Adverb(ien) der Zeit
①	I	met	my uncle		last week.
②	Mr Carlson	starts	work	at his office	at 8.30 every day.
③	The children	played		near the river	yesterday.
④ Next year	we	won't spend	Easter	at home.	

- **Adverbien der Zeit** und **Adverbien des Ortes** (*adverbs of time and adverbs of place*) stehen meist am Ende des Satzes (Satz ① bis ③). Nur wenn eine Zeit- oder Ortsangabe **besonders betont** werden soll, steht sie am Satzanfang (Satz ④).
- Treten Adverbien der Zeit und Adverbien des Ortes gleichzeitig in einem Satz auf, dann gilt im Gegensatz zum Deutschen: Das Adverb des **Ortes** steht **vor** dem Adverb der **Zeit**.
- Treten mehrere Adverbien der Zeit oder des Ortes am Satzende auf, dann steht die genaue Zeitangabe / Ortsangabe (1) meist an erster Stelle vor der weniger genauen (2):
  She told him to visit her **at ten o'clock** (1) **on Friday** (2).

A short holiday for the Gruenbaums

Some adverbs of time and place are not in their proper position. Use numbers to „rewrite" the sentences.

Example:

[1] Mr and Mrs Gruenbaum and their daughters Sarah and Rebecca [4] last week [2] went on a short hiking trip [3] through Yosemite National Park.

a) [ ] at the camping-site [ ] they arrived [ ] on Monday morning [ ] at 10.30.

b) [ ] at the visitors' center [ ] immediately [ ] they checked [ ] the hiking routes.

c) [ ] they decided [ ] on the next day [ ] to do the hike [ ] up the *Ghost River Canyon*.

d) [ ] on Tuesday [ ] in *Yosemite National Park* [ ] hiked [ ] the Gruenbaums [ ] for twelve hours.

e) [ ] to the camping-site [ ] they came back [ ] late [ ] after a difficult and exhausting (*anstrengend*) trip [ ] in the evening.

f) [ ] they visited [ ] the next day [ ] the *Yosemite National Park Museum* [ ] in the morning.

9) [ ] afterwards [ ] the whole afternoon [ ] they relaxed [ ] at the swimming pool.

h) [ ] early [ ] on Thursday LJ the Gruenbaums [ ] drove back [ ] to San Francisco [ ] in the morning.

28 Adverbs of frequency and degree

Subjekt	Hilfsverb	Adverb der Häufigkeiz / des Grades	Verb	Objekt by-agent	Adverb der Häufigkeit
① The crop	was	almost	destroyed	by the rain.	
② They	can	hardly	practice	their English	twice a week.
③ You	mustn't		interrupt	me	so often.
④ Tony		occasionally	visits	his stepfather.	

- In den meisten Fällen stehen Adverbien der Häufigkeit und Adverbien des Grades (*adverbs of frequency and adverbs of degree*) in der **Satzmitte** (Satz ①, ② und ④). Nur wenn sie **besonders betont** werden sollen, rücken sie an den Satzanfang.
- Für Adverbien der Häufigkeit gilt: Zumeist stehen sie wie die Adverbien der Zeit am **Satzende** (Satz ② und ③). Nur in seltenen Fällen der besonderen Betonung findet man sie am Satzanfang.

Dave und Luke: their first American Football match

Complete the following sentences. Insert (einfügen) the adverbs of degree and frequency correctly.

Example:

The school football team played. + **last Thursday / well / at Dave's and Luke's high school**

The school football team played well at Dave's and Luke's high school last Thursday.

a) The team didn't play. + **badly / last summer**

b) The team practiced (BE: practised). + **extremely / during the summer / on the playing field / hard**

c) Luke ran in his first match for the team. + **incredibly / fast**

d) He could get through the defense (BE: defence). + **often / quickly / in the first quarter**

e) Luke scored two touchdowns. + **easily / in the beginning**

f) Dave didn't play. + **surprisingly / successfully**

g) After the match he left the field because he was disappointed. + **slowly / rather**

And finally - get ready for some translation practice. 29

Translate the following sentences. Remember to place the adverbs of frequency and degree correctly.

a) Jacqueline vergaß vollständig, Brot, Käse und Wein zu kaufen.

b) Nach dem Termin beim Zahnarzt (appointment at the dentist's) konnte Raymond kaum sprechen.

c) Ich gehe sonntags immer zur Kirche.

d) Auf Partys raucht Thomas manchmal eine Zigarre (cigar).

e) Ich putze meine Wohnung einmal pro Woche oder zumindest (at least) dreimal in jedem Monat.

f) Der Arzt riet Mr Jennings, die Medizin viermal täglich (viermal jeden Tag) einzunehmen (to take the medicine).

g) Die Übung ist beinahe beendet.

h) Jetzt bist du ein ziemlicher Experte im Gebrauch (in using) von Adverbien.

4 Verben und Zeitformen

Revision

Übersicht über den Gebrauch der Zeiten (tenses) im Englischen:

Mr Hales **is** American. He lives in Philadelphia.
simple present - **Dauerzustand**

Mr Hales reads the newspaper **every morning after breakfast.**
simple present - **regelmäßige, gewohnheitsmäßige Handlung**

Mr Hales **is reading** the newspaper. So don't disturb him.
present progressive - **Handlung, die im Augenblick des Sprechens gerade abläuft - keine Entsprechung im Deutschen.**

Yesterday Mr Hales **read** the newspaper **after lunch.**
simple past - **Handlung, die zu einem bestimmten Zeitpunkt der Vergangenheit abgeschlossen wurde.**
Im Deutschen gibt es zwei Übersetzungsmöglichkeiten:
*Gestern **las** Mr Hales die Zeitung nach dem Mittagessen* (Präteritum).
*Gestern **hat** Mr Hales die Zeitung nach dem Mittagessen **gelesen*** (Perfekt).

Mr Hales **was reading** the newspaper **when the phone rang.**
past progressive - **Handlung, die zu einem bestimmten Zeitpunkt der Vergangenheit im Gange war, als eine zweite Handlung einsetzte.**

Mr Hales **has already** read the newspaper. **So you can throw it away.**
present perfect - **Handlung in der Vergangenheit, die zwar abgeschlossen ist, deren Ergebnis aber in der Gegenwart noch spürbar ist.**

Mr Hales **has been reading** the newspaper **for two hours now.**
present perfect progressive **Handlung, die in der Vergangenheit begann und gegenwärtig noch andauert.**
Beachte: *Mr Hales **liest** seit zwei Stunden Zeitung.*

Mr Hales **will read** the newspaper **tomorrow morning after breakfast.**
will-future - **(gewohnheitsmäßige) Handlung in der Zukunft**

Mr Hales **will have read** the newspaper by **9 o'clock tomorrow morning.**
future perfect - **Handlung, die zu einem bestimmten Zeitpunkt in der Zukunft abgeschlossen sein wird.**

Mr Hales is on his way to the living room. He is **going to read** the newspaper.
going to-future - **Absicht, die verwirklicht werden wird.**

Mr Hales **would** now **read** the newspaper, **but it has not yet arrived.**
conditional I - **Absicht, die (in der Zukunft) unter bestimmten Bedingungen verwirklicht werden würde.**

Mr Hales **would have read** the newspaper, **but he could not find it.**
conditional II - **Absicht, die in der Vergangenheit unter bestimmten Bedingungen verwirklicht worden wäre.**

Choose the right tense. 30

Bob and Neil meet at the bus stop. Complete their dialog by filling in the correct tense of the verbs.

Bob: Hello, Neil. I .... (to see) you for quite a long time.

Neil: Hi, Bob, Well, I .... (to go) on holiday (AE: vacation) last month.

Bob: Oh, ... (to do) you? Where .... (to go)?

Neil: Well, at the beginning of the summer holidays my father .... (to have) to fly to the USA on a business trip. You know, he .... (to be) the manager of an electronic firm for fifteen years and he .... (to work) together with a lot of American corporations since 1985.

Bob: you .... (to fly) to New York?

Neil: No, we .... (to do). We .... (to go) from London (Heathrow Airport) to Cincinnati, Ohio.

Bob: I .... (to see). How long .... it .... (to take) you to go there?

Neil: About seven hours.

Bob: That .... (to be) quite a long time, ... (to be) it?

Neil: Oh, no, it .... (to be). Not really. While we .... (to fly) across the Atlantic Ocean, they .... (to serve) meals and drinks and they .... (to show) a film. So time .... (to pass) quickly.

Bob: .... (to stay) you .... in Ohio all the time?

Neil: Oh, my bus .... (to come). I'll tell you when we meet again next week at school. I'm off. Bye.

31 Translate the following sentences.

a) Chicago ist eine der größten Städte in den USA.

b) Paul Bradley arbeitet seit fünf Jahren als Polizist in New York.

c) Im Jahre 1492 hat Columbus Amerika entdeckt.

d) Mrs Elliot hat den Zug verpasst. Der nächste Zug fährt heute Abend um 8.13. Deshalb wird sie ein Taxi nehmen.

e) Mrs Batson has been living in Seattle for twenty years. Now she is going to move to California where it will be warmer.

f) Mr Hillerman is going to buy a new car. He has had his old car since 1992. He then bought it secondhand from his neighbor (BE: neighbour).

32 Fill in the correct tense.

Do you remember Neil and Bob talking about Neil's trip to America?
Well, here they meet again.

Complete their dialog (BE: dialogue) by filling in the correct tense of the verbs in brackets.

Bob: Hi, Neil. Now, what about Cincinnati and Ohio? Did you stay there all the time?

Neil: No, we .... (to do). You see, my uncle .... (to live) in Cincinnati for almost twenty years. He .... (to go) there when he .... (to be) a young man and .... (to marry) an American girl in 1973. They .... (to come) back to Germany in 1989 and .... (to stay) a couple of weeks with my family. But their children, Richard and Sarah, ... (not to be) to Europe so far. I .... (hope) they .... (to come) next year.

Anyway, while my father .... (to do) his business tour, my uncle and my aunt .... (to show) me around the area quite a bit.

Bob: you .... (to see) any Indians at all?

Neil: Of course not. Not all Americans .... (to be) either Indians or cowboys. We .... (to go) north and .... (to have) a look at the Niagara Falls. Gigantic. They .... (to be visited) .... by millions of tourists from all over the world every year. Richard and Sarah .... (not to be) there either.

Bob: you .... (to go) to Chicago as well?

Neil: Oh, yes, we .... (to do). We .... (to spend) almost a week there. It (to be) great.

Bob: Great? .... (to be) it not dangerous to live in Chicago? I mean, gangsters, Al Capone?

Neil: Oh, no, not at all. For years Chicago .... (not to have) a higher crime rate than other big cities in America. But tell me, ... you .... (to be) to America?

Bob: No, I .... (to have). But I .... (to think), I .... (to go) there soon. Must be interesting.

Link sentences together using the past perfect simple. 33

Bildung:	**had**	**+**	**past participle**
	had	+	opened
	had	+	done
	had	+	seen
	had	+	been
	had	+	had
After Jane	**had**		**seen** that horrible film on TV, she **was** nervous.

Das *past perfect* beschreibt ein Ereignis, das vor einem anderen Ereignis in der Vergangenheit abgelaufen ist. Nebensätze, die eine Vorzeitigkeit ausdrücken, werden häufig durch die Konjunktionen (*conjunctions*) *after*, as soon as (sobald), *when* und dergleichen eingeleitet.

Harry Biggs in New York. One thing after the other. Combine the following sentences.

to buy a map of New York

to walk up Broadway

to visit the Rockefeller Center (BE: centre)

to look around Central Park

to have lunch at a fast food restaurant

to go up the Empire State Building by elevator (BE: lift)

to take a lot of photos

to go on a boat trip on the East River

to visit the Statue of Liberty

to walk around Chinatown

to have dinner in Little Italy

After he **had bought** a map of New York, Harry Biggs **walked** up Broadway.

After he **had walked** up ... he **visited** ...

When ...

34 Form sentences by using the *past perfect progressive* + *for/since*.

Past Perfect Progressive

He had been driving on the highway for hours, when suddenly his car broke down.

Bildung: had + been + ing-form past tense

Das past perfect progressive betont Verlauf und Dauer eines Vorgangs oder einer Handlung, die noch andauert, wenn zu einem bestimmten Zeitpunkt in der Vergangenheit ein neuer Vorgang oder eine neue Handlung eintritt.

Fire in a skyscraper in Denver

What had these people been doing when the fire broke out at 10.15? Look at the example and go on making sentences.

A secretary	had been typing	letters for two hours,...
A doctor	to examine patients	since
A detective	to question a suspicious person	since
A window cleaner	to clean windows	for
A lawyer	to dictate letters	since
A businessman	to sit in the front of the computer	for
A musician	to rehearse songs	since
A journalist	to write reports	for
A housewife	to do the laundry	for
A waitress	to serve meals	since

... when the fire broke out at 10.15.

5 Infinitivkonstruktionen

35 Compare the use of the infinitive in English and German.

- **Wir unterscheiden im Englischen Infinitivkonstruktionen mit *to* und Infinitivkonstruktionen ohne *to*:**
  ① The doctor began **to examine** the patient carefully.
  ② The patient didn't **take** his medicine correctly.
- **In vielen Fällen wird der Infinitiv im Englischen so verwendet, wie wir es vom Deutschen her gewohnt sind.**

Translation exercise

Bill and Craig are both fourteen years old and go to high school. During their lunch break they talk about different things. **Translate!**

Bill: What a morning! Most of my math exercises were wrong and the teacher told mit **to do** them again.

Craig: Do you have **to work** on them after school?

Bill: Yes, and there is nobody **to help** me.

Craig: So you can't **play** tennis with me, right?

Bill: 'm afraid not. Homework comes first - and Dad told me **to wash** his car and **to cut** the grass in the garden. Bad luck. Where is John? I want **to have** my comics back. Did you **meet** him yesterday?

Craig: No, I didn't. But I saw him today. He missed the bus and asked his mom **to drive** him to school. I saw him **arrive** in his mother's car. He was in a hurry so he forgot **to give** me your comics.

Bill: John seems **to forget** quite a lot of things. Two days ago he wanted to play baseball with us. But he forgot **to bring** his bat and so he couldn't **play**. His mistake.

Craig: Right. Did you **hear** the bell? It's time **to go** to our classroom. Chemistry - it's interesting to see all those experiments, but don't **ask** me **to explain** them. Sometimes I just don't **understand** one word.

36 Look at the verbs followed by an infinitive with *to*.

Es gibt im Englischen eine ganze Reihe von Verben, an welche direkt ein Infinitiv mit to angeschlossen werden kann:

Verbs followed directly by an infinitive with *to*			
agree	arrange	attempt	choose
consent	decide	determine	expect
forget	hesitate	hope	learn
manage	offer	prepare	promise
refuse	remember	seem	start
try	want	wish	

Christopher Columbus

Complete the following sentences with the verbs given below.

agree • consent • decide (2x) • hesitate • hope • manage • offer • prepare • promise • refuse • try • want • seem

a) When Columbus .... sail west he .... find a new route to India.

b) The king and queen of Spain .... give him some ships and they .... pay for the expedition.

c) Columbus .... accept the offer and .... do his best for Spain.

d) The ships sailed for weeks. They .... sail through many storms but the ocean .... have no end.

e) Finally the sailors .... go any further. They .... return to Spain immediately.

f) Columbus .... obey because he believed in his plans. He .... change the sailors' opinion.

g) The sailors .... give Columbus another three days.

h) Nothing happened at first. When the sailors .... return they finally saw the coast of a Caribbean island on October 12,1492.

37 Translate.

	Subjekt	Verb	Objekt	Infinitiv mit to
①	She	asked	him	to close the door.
②	Kate	wanted	her sister	to buy some bread.
③	The policeman	warned	the children	not to cross the road.
④	Mr Smith	expects	his son	to become a doctor.
⑤	Helen's parents	permitted	her	to go to the party.

An den Beispielsätzen fällt Folgendes auf:

- Die englischen wie die deutschen Sätze haben denselben Aufbau: Subjekt - Verb - Objekt - Infinitiv mit *to*.
- Bei der Übersetzung vom Englischen ins Deutsche gibt es zwei Möglichkeiten: Wir können eine Infinitivkonstruktion verwenden oder einen Nebensatz mit *dass* bilden.
- In den englischen Beispielsätzen benötigen alle Verben ein Objekt, bevor der Infinitiv mit *to* angefügt werden kann.

Translate the sentences ① to ⑤. Some sentences are quite easy, others are more difficult. Give it a try!

① (!) Sie ....

② (!) Kate ....

③ Der Polizeibeamte ....

④ (!) Mr Smith ....

⑤ Helens Eltern ....

Folgende Verbgruppen solltest du dir merken! Bei ihnen tritt die Konstruktion Verb - Objekt + Infinitiv mit *to* häufig auf:

- **Verben des Aufforderns, Befehlens und Zulassens:** *advise, allow, ask,* order, permit, tell, warn, would like
- **Verben des Wünschens, Wollens, Nichtwünschens und Nichtwollens:** *expect, intend, prefer, want, wish*

Make sentences. 38

Read each sentence carefully. Then write a second sentence or question in the simple past from the words given.

a) „Don't forget to buy some lemonade", Tom said to me.
Tom / remind / me / buy some lemonade

b) Mrs Miller told Jane about Christine's birthday present. Bad luck for Christine!
Christine / want / it / be a surprise

c) Herbie really liked Louise.
He / ask / Louise / marry him

d) Yesterday I saw your son in a night club.
You / allow / your son / go there **?**

e) Mr and Mrs Reilly didn't want to spend the summer vacation alone.
They / invite / the Parkers / stay with them

f) The roads were covered with snow and ice.
The radio / warn / the drivers / drive slowly

g) The Chicago Bulls played against the New York Yankees last Friday.
You / expect / the Chicago Bulls I win **?**

Translate the following sentences. 39

The Pilgrims in Massachusetts

a) When the Pilgrims (Puritaner, eine Religionsgemeinschaft aus England; dt. eigentlich *Pilger*) decided to leave England they chose Virginia for their new home.

b) They expected the journey on the *Mayflower* to be long and rough.

c) A storm drove the *Mayflower* far north, away from Virginia. The captain offered the Pilgrims to take them down south again.

d) The Pilgrims ordered the captain to sail to the coast and asked him to let them leave the ship.

e) Soon the Pilgrims met Indians who allowed them to settle on their land.

f) The Indians helped the Puritans to survive (überleben) the first hard winter in America.

g) In the spring they advised them to grow corn (BE: maize) and permitted them to hunt with them.

h) In the autumn the Puritans had a good harvest. They thanked God and invited the Indians to celebrate (feiern) „Thanksgiving" (Erntedankfest) with them.

40 Connect the sentences and translate.

① It wasn’t easy for him to carry all his suitcases.
*Es war nicht einfach **für** ihn, alle seine Koffer zu tragen.*

② Mrs Jones bought a newspaper for her husband to read on the train.
Mrs Jones kaufte eine Zeitung, die ihr Ehemann im Zug lesen konnte.

- In vielen Fällen kann ***for*** mit ***für*** übersetzt werden. (①)
- Manchmal ist es inhaltlich und stilistisch notwendig, die ***for + infinitive*** - Konstruktion im Deutschen in ein **Hauptsatz - Nebensatz - Gefüge** zu verwandeln, (②)

Make sentences and translate them afterwards. If you connect the sentences correctly, the solution will give you the name of America’s biggest mountain range.

a) We missed the plane to Washington and there was no other flight	(R)		them to understand.	(U)
b) It is important	(C)		the visitors to see.	(S)
c) 5.30 in the morning is too early	(Y)	**for**	us to hear the doorbell.	(I)
d) They wanted to help the old man, but he talked too quickly	(O)		teenagers to meet.	(T)
e) In many towns in America there is no place	(N)		young people to get a good education.	(K)
f) Leave the door of the sitting-room open	(A)		me to get up.	(M)
g) In Disneyland there are so many things	(N)		us to arrive on time.	(O)

Lösungswort: ☐☐☐☐☐ ☐☐☐☐☐☐☐☐☐

Make sentences using the infinitive with *to* and question words. 41

① Tom **explained** (to me) **how to do** the exercise.

② We haven't **decided where to go** for the weekend.

③ Gary **doesn't know whether to go** to the party or not.

④ She **told** me **when to phone** her aunt.

- Die Konstruktion aus **Verb + Fragewort + Infinitiv** mit *to* ist nur mit bestimmten Verben möglich. Du solltest dir merken: *ask - decide - explain - forget - know - remember - show - tell - understand*
- Als Fragewörter (*question words*) werden häufig eingesetzt: *what - where - how - when - whether*

New in Philadelphia (Part I)

Justina Neubauer has moved from Karlsruhe to Philadelphia. Her first days are quite difficult because she has to find out so many different things.

Make sentences with the information given. Be sure to use verb + question word + infinitive with *to*.

Example: Justina / not to know / where / get / map of Philadelphia
Justina **doesn't know where to get** a map of Philadelphia.

a) She / not to know / where / find / taxi at the airport

b) In her new apartment (BE: flat) / she / not to understand / how / switch on / dishwasher

c) Later a friendly neighbor / show her / how / use / ticket machine for bus tickets

d) At the bank / Justina / ask / when / pick up / new credit card

e) A man in the street / tell her / where / find / good supermarket

f) In the supermarket / Justina / decide / what / buy / for the next few days

g) In the evening / she / cannot decide / whether / cook / some spaghetti or some soup

h) For the next day / she / plan to find out / when / best call (BE: ring/phone) / her relatives in Karlsruhe

42 Complete the sentences.

New in Philadelphia (Part II)

To organize her daily life in Philadelphia, Justina Neubauer has to ask for a lot of information. Complete each question, using the following verbs and question words:

rent • find • wear • order • pay • switch off • take •
when • how (2x) • which • what • where (2x)

a) Can you tell me ...where to find... the public library?

b) Do you know .... a Chinese meal?

c) May I ask you .... a bike?

d) Do you remember .... the electricity bills?

e) Would you please show me .... the air-conditioning?

f) Do you remember .... bus .... to the city center?

g) Can you help me to decide................................on my first day at work?

43 Complete the sentences using the infinitive with *to* after superlatives and ordinal numbers.

1 Father is always **the last to get up** on Sundays.

2 Donna was **the only one to have** no mistakes in her test.

3 **The first man to walk** on the moon was Neil Armstrong.

4 If the roads are covered with ice, **the worst thing to be done** is to drive fast.

5 **The highest building to be seen** in New York is the Empire State Building.

- The first und the last können alleine stehen (① und ③). The only muss dagegen mit dem Stützwort one / ones verbunden werden (③).
- Bei der Übersetzung der Konstruktion Infinitiv mit to nach Ordnungszahlen und Superlativen gebrauchen wir im Deutschen einen Relativsatz.
- Die Konstruktion Infinitiv mit to nach Ordnungszahlen und Superlativen kann sowohl im Aktiv (① bis ③) als auch im Passiv (④ und ⑤) verwendet werden.

American Records

Complete the sentences with an infinitive with to in the active or in the passive voice.

a) The only boxer .... (become) world champion three times was Muhammad Ali.

b) The longest river .... (find) in the USA is the Mississippi.

c) The first American woman .... (launch = abschießen, befördern) into space was Sally K. Ride.

d) The most expensive American city .... (live) in is New York.

e) The biggest hamburger ever .... (eat) was made in Seymour, Wisconsin.

The infinitive with to in subordinate clauses - make sentences. 44

① CD Stephen King's new thriller is **the book to buy**.
... the book (which) you should buy.

② For grammar problems in English your English teacher is **the person to ask**.
... the person (who) you could / should ask.

③ The suitcase is too heavy for me. I need **somebody to help** me with it.
... somebody who can help me with it.

Häufig haben wir im Englischen in den vorangegangenen Übungen Infinitivkonstruktionen mit *to* anstelle von Nebensätzen (*subordinate clauses*) verwendet. In den folgenden Beispielen und Übungen lernst du eine Möglichkeit kennen, wie ein Infinitiv mit *to* einen Relativsatz (*relative clause*) mit modalem Hilfsverb (*modal auxiliary*) ersetzen kann.

New in Philadelphia (Part III)

Justina Neubauer has made friends with Sharon Smith - a very friendly neighbor. Sharon can give Justina a lot of good advice.

Complete the sentences with the words given. Use an infinitive with *to* or *make a subordinate relative clause with a modal auxiliary*.

Example: For problems with the fridge / Tina / apartment 12b / woman / ask

For problems with the fridge Tina in apartment 12b is the woman **to ask**.

For problems with the fridge Tina in apartment 12b is the woman **you can ask**.

a) If you want to buy some cheap furniture / shop / 159 Willbury Road / place / go

b) Film / see / this week / the latest with Arnold Schwarzenegger

c) Do you want to go on vacation in fall? Cape Cod / nice place / spend a few days

d) To have a good time on Saturday night / *O'Henry's Cocktail Bar* / place / be

e) Problems with the washing machine? / Mr Porter next door / man / help

f) And if you need someone to talk to in the middle of the night: My number / number / call

45 The infinitive with feel, hear, see, notice, watch - connect the sentences.

Subjekt	Verb der Wahrnehmung	direktes Objekt	Infinitiv ohne *to*	
① The Indians	watched	the settlers	**arrive**	at their hunting grounds.
② They	saw	them	**build**	farmhouses and stables.
③ The Indians	heard	white hunters	**shoot**	deer and buffalo.
④ They	felt	cold winds	**blow**	through the forests.

- Nach **Verben des Wahrnehmens und des Beobachtens** kann der Infinitiv ohne *to* verwendet werden: *feel, hear, notice, see, watch*.
- Der Infinitiv ohne *to* drückt hier aus: Der Vorgang, das Geschehen ist abgeschlossen oder es wird ein Vorgang, Geschehen aus einer Folge von Ereignissen geschildert.

In a Navajo village

At the Grand Canyon National Park the Navajo Indians show visitors something of their everyday life and their old culture and traditions.

Make sentences. If you connect the sentences correctly, the solution will give you the name of the river flowing through *Grand Canyon National Park*.

1. The visitors see	walk through the shops.	(R)
2. They hear Navajo men	play traditional games.	(O)
3. They watch Navajo women	touch their faces.	(D)
4. The Navajo people notice	sell beautiful Indian bracelets.	(A)
5. The Indians watch the tourists	the Indians make pots and baskets.	(C)

6. The visitors notice some Indian shops	cook traditional meals.	(L)
7. The tourists feel the hot wind	the tourists pinch (klauen) souvenirs without paying.	(O)
8. They watch Navajo children	sing old battle songs.	(O)

Lösungswort:

1	2	3	4	5	6	7	8

The infinitive without to after *can, must, may*. Translate. 46

Read carefully what Tony and Carol are saying:

a) Tony: **May** I use your pen, please?

b) Carol: Sure, you **can have** it for a while, but you **mustn't lose** it. By the way - didn't you take Kevin's pen yesterday?

c) Tony: Yes, I did. I **must tell** you that I can't find it anywhere. But - you **needn't tell** Kevin, O.K.?

d) Carol: I won't let him know, but you **had better look** for the pen.

e) Tony: I'm tired of looking for that stupid thing. I **would rather buy** him a new one.

f) Carol: I **would sooner wait** a few days. It **may turn up** somewhere.

- Nach modalen **Hilfsverben** (*modal auxiliaries*) wie *can, must, may, mustn't, needn't* kann direkt ein Infinitiv ohne *to* folgen.
- Nach Ausdrücken wie
  - I / he / she *had better* – Ich / Er / Sie *sollte lieber / besser ...*
  - I / he / she *had rather* – Ich / Er / Sie *möchte / würde lieber ...*
  - I / he / she *would sooner* – Ich / Er / Sie *möchte / würde eher ...*

  steht im Englischen ein Infinitiv ohne *to*.

Translate the dialog between Tony and Carol.

47 Translate the dialog.

Use a modal auxiliary or one of the following expressions: *had better / would rather / would sooner*

a) Jack: Hausaufgaben machen! Ich würde lieber draußen Fußball spielen. Kann ich noch ein Glas Limonade haben?

b) Jill: Sicher. Aber du solltest nicht zu viel trinken. Dir könnte übel werden (to get sick).

c) Jack: Du brauchst dir keine Sorgen zu machen (to worry). Kannst du mir dein Hausheft geben?

d) Jill: An deiner Stelle (If I were / was you) würde ich die Aufgaben eher für mich allein machen (to do the exercises on one's own).

e) Jack: Mathe ist immer sehr schwierig. Ich kann viele Dinge nicht verstehen.

f) Jill: Du darfst nicht so schnell aufgeben (to give up).

g) Jack: Ich hasse Algebra-Übungen. Da würde ich eher den ganzen Nachmittag im Garten arbeiten. Dürfen wir in der Klassenarbeit Taschenrechner (pocket calculators) benutzen?

h) Jill: Nein, das dürfen wir natürlich nicht! Aus diesem Grund (That's why) solltest du dich jetzt lieber auf deine Übungsaufgaben konzentrieren (to concentrate on one's exercises).

48 The infinitive without to after *make* and *let*.

Subjekt	make let	direktes Objekt	Infinitiv ohne *to*		deutsche Bedeutung
① The Boss	**makes**	his workers	**work**	hard at the car factory.	*lassen*
② His managers	**make**	them	**wear**	helmets for safety.	*dafür sorgen*
③ They	**let**	their boss	**know**	the production figures.	*lassen*
④ the Boss	**lets**	his workers	**buy**	cars at special prices.	*erlauben*

Bestimmt ist dir an diesen Beispielen aufgefallen, dass das deutsche Verb „lassen" in zwei gegensätzlichen Bedeutungen verwendet werden kann:

Im Englischen verwendet man ***make* + Infinitiv ohne *to*** um auszudrücken, dass jemand zu etwas gebracht, veranlasst oder gar gezwungen werden soll, etwas zu tun, oder dass jemand veranlasst, dass etwas geschieht.

Wird etwas erlaubt oder zugelassen, dann steht im Englischen ***let* + Infinitiv ohne *to***.

Commercials, commercials!

Use *make* and the information given in the pictures to write a sentence.

Example:

Snow-White and your shirts look as white as snow!

Snow-White I look / your shirts / white as snow

***Snow-White* makes your shirts look as white as snow.**

Sharkies - and you can jump higher than Michael Jordan.

Sharkies I jump higher / than / Michael Jordan

. . . .

Barko-Barko: your dog will run faster than any cat in the neighborhood.

Barko-Barko I your dog / run faster / than / the cats in the neighborhood

. . . .

Cars go better with *Supergas*.

Supergas / your car / go better

. . . .

Hairy Harry – and your hair grows like weeds (Unkraut).

Hairy Harry / your hair / grow like weeds

. . . .

Daniel's dreary (depressing) day !

Use *let* and the information given in the pictures to write a sentence.

Example:

alarm clock / not to sleep / longer than 6.30 a.m.

Daniel's alarm clock doesn't let him sleep longer than 6.30 a.m.

. . . .

The bus / Daniel / wait / for half an hour in the rain

. . . .

Geoffrey / Daniel / not to copy / maths homework

. . . .

Daniel's mother / not to practice / the drums in the afternoon

. . . .

Later Shirley / carry / Daniel / all the heavy shopping bags

. . . .

Man at the entrance to the club / Daniel and Shirley / not to enter / the *Techno-Factory*

. . . .

6 Das Passiv

Revision

① Some settlers founded **Boston** in 1630

② **Boston** was founded in 1630.

Bildung: Das Passiv wird mit einer Form von to be und dem past participle (3. Form des Verbs) gebildet.

Gebrauch: Der Passivsatz ② stellt eine Handlung, ein Ereignis aus einer anderen Sicht als der Aktivsatz ① dar.

- Im Passivsatz wird der „Täter", der Verursacher einer Handlung meist nicht genannt, weil er **unbekannt** ist oder weil er als **unwichtig** angesehen wird.
- Der Passivsatz stellt das Ergebnis der Handlung in den Vordergrund: Das Objekt des Aktivsatzes wird zum Subjekt des Passivsatzes.

Mark the passive forms. 49

Read the text carefully, mark all the verb forms in the passive voice and list them below.

Burglary!

Last night a shop window at Miller's Department Store, Eisenhower Avenue was broken. Four CD players, seven portable telephones and two color TV sets were taken away by the thieves.

Three young men were seen driving away from the scene of crime. A piece of broken glass was stained with blood - one of the criminals must be injured. Also, a black stocking mask (Strumpfmaske) has been found.

The thieves, however, have not been arrested by the police yet.

Revision

Die Zeitformen des Passiv (*the passive forms of the verb*)

Die folgende Tabelle zeigt dir am Beispiel des unregelmäßigen Verbs to take (*took - taken*) die verschiedenen Zeitformen im Passiv:

tense of the verb	active voice	passive voice form of *to be* + *past participle*
simple present	take / takes	am /are / is taken
present progressive	am / is / are taking	am / are / is being taken
simple past	took	was / were taken
past progressive	was / were taking	was / were being taken
present perfect	have / has taken	have / has been taken
past perfect	had taken	had been taken
will - future	will take	will be taken
going to - future	am / are / is going to take	am / are / is going to be taken
conditional	would take	would be taken

- Die Verwendung der Zeitformen in Passivsätzen folgt den gleichen Regeln wie in Aktivsätzen.
- Bei den **Verlaufsformen** (*progressive forms*) sind nur *present progressive* und *past progressive* üblich. Es werden Vorgänge und Ereignisse beschrieben, die noch nicht beendet sind bzw. waren oder die gerade noch ablaufen bzw. abliefen.
  The house is being cleaned at the moment
  While the speeches were being delivered the protesters shouted.
- **Passivsätze mit Hilfsverben** sind auch möglich:
  The car must be sold next week.
  The windows should have been closed.
  The thieves cannot be found.
  A copy of the book may be taken without payment.

50 Use the passive. Mind the correct tense.

The first day at work

Martha Miller has just started to work as a secretary for Megabyte, a new computer firm in Sun Valley, California. After her first day she tells her boyfriend Ryan Jones about the things she has found out.

Use the *simple present* and the verbs / modal auxiliary verbs given in the brackets to complete the sentences in the passive voice.

a) Wages at Megabyte . . . . (pay) every week.

b) At the cafeteria little snacks . . . . (may / buy) from 9 o'clock to 5 o'clock.

c) Used computers and software items . . . . (sell) every Thursday afternoon.

d) A new computer chip . . . . (design). But that is top secret!

What people don't like

Complete the following sentences with being and the past participle of one of the verbs.

ask • bite • hurt • invite • leave • pollute • use

Example: Terry doesn't like his bike **being used** by his brother.

a) Jack doesn't like . . . . stupid questions.

b) The Carlsons don't like the neighbors coming to their parties without . . . .

c) Many people don't want to see nature . . . . by factories.

d) Aunt Mary doesn't like her dentist. She is afraid of . . . .

e) Little Kevin wants his parents to stay at home. He doesn't like . . . . alone in the house.

f) Uncle George doesn't like Waldo, the Yorkshire terrier. He is afraid of . . . . by the dog.

At the garage

Mr Mortimer Hudson is 78. He owns a Ford Model T, the first car built with the help of an assembly line (Fließband) in 1908. Every now and then his vintage car (Oldtimer) has to spend a day at a garage.

Use the *simple past* to make sentences in the passive voice from the information given.

Example: door locks / to oil / carefully
The door locks were oiled carefully.

a) brakes and lights / to check / thoroughly / and / air and oil filters / to replace

. . . .

b) all the windows / to clean / and / air pressure of tires (BE: tyres) / to increase

. . . .

b) spark plugs (BE: sparking plugs) (Zündkerzen) / to change / and / hubcaps (Radkappen) and bumpers (Stoßstange) / to polish

. . . .

d) some rust / to remove / some parts / to paint

. . . .

Cowboys

Being a cowboy in America's Wild West is every boy's dream. Having watched all those westerns on TV we know precisely what living as a cowboy is like, don't you think?

Transform the following active sentences into passive sentences. Use the *present progressive* and the *past progressive*

Example: Cowboys are riding horses.
Horses are being ridden.

a) They were branding the cows.

. . . .

b) They are drinking whiskey at the saloon.

. . . .

c) Cowboys are singing folk songs at the camp fire.

. . . .

d) They are eating ham and beans for breakfast.

. . . .

An old ghost town

A ghost town in the Wild West can be a very sad sight.

Say what has happened. Use the *present perfect* and the information given below to make sentences in the passive voice

Example: tree near old saloon / to hit / by lightning
The tree near the old saloon has been hit by lightning.

a) door of saloon / to steal

. . . .

b) windows of several houses / to break / by storms

. . . .

c) wheels of stage-coach (Postkutsche) / to damage

. . . .

d) stable near sheriff's office / to burn down / and / many houses / to pull down (abreißen)

. . . .

New at UCLA

Lorna and Gladys are students at **UCLA** - the **U**niversity of **C**alifornia at **L**os **A**ngeles. Lorna has only just arrived, so her room-mate (Mitbewohnerin des Zimmers im Studentenwohnheim) has to answer a lot of questions.

Can you do Gladys' job? Make questions in the passive voice using the *will-future*.

Example: When will the lectures be given? (from 8.30 a.m. to 6.30 p.m.)
The lectures will be given from 8.30 a.m. to 6.30 p.m..

a) When will the debate about feminism be held? (in about two weeks)

. . . .

b) Where will new methods in education be discussed? (at the Roosevelt Study Center)

. . . .

c) When will the discussion on agricultural problems be started? (tomorrow)

. . . .

d) Who will be teaching political economy? (Professor Rutherford-Keynes)

. . . .

A new house

Mr and Mrs Wellington have just bought a new house. Well, an old new house, actually. A lot of things have to be changed or repaired.

Make passive sentences to say what will be done. Use *will-future* for the sentences marked (W) and *going to-future* for the sentences marked (G).

Example: walls / to paint **(G)**
The walls are going to be painted.

a) new carpet in bedroom / to put down **(W)**

. . . .

b) new garage / to build **(G)**

. . . .

c) telephone / to connect **(W)**

. . . .

d) lights / to check **(G)**

. . . .

Mixed tenses

Use the verbs in the brackets to complete the following passive sentences.

a) I can't find the tea spoons. Where . . . . .they. . . . .

. . . .? (keep)

b) When Mr Brown returned to his car he . . . .(give) a ticket by the traffic warden.

c) His name is Theodore, but he . . . .(may + call) Teddy by his friends.

d) After the vet had examined the dogs, they . . . .(to take) to his surgery.

e) If the driver hadn't been so careful, he . . . .(injure) in the accident.

Translate by using the passive. 51

All of a sudden you meet an old friend whom you haven't seen for a long time. You tell him in English that...

Example: eure alte Schule abgerissen wurde.
Our old school has been pulled down.

a) dein Auto gestern gestohlen worden ist.

. . . .

b) ein italienisches Restaurant nächste Woche eröffnet werden wird.

. . . .

c) deinem Fußballverein eine zweite Chance (a second chance) gegeben werden sollte.

. . . .

d) das neue Rathaus (town hall) nicht gebaut werden kann.

. . . .

by-agent: to use or not to use ... ? 52

Das Passiv mit *by-agent* (*the passive with by-agent*)

Soll im Passivsatz der „Täter“ oder Verursacher einer Handlung genannt werden, dann geschieht dies mit dem sogenannten *by-agent*.

① Several buildings in town have been damaged **by** a hurricane.

② Yellow Submarine wasn't written **by** the *Rolling Stones*. It was written **by** the *Beatles*.

③ The boy was nearly run over **by** a car.

④ The North American continent was crossed **by** the Lewis and Clark Expedition.

- Durch den *by-agent* erhält der „Täter" oder Verursacher einer Handlung im Passivsatz mehr Gewicht.
- Bei wichtigen Persönlichkeiten (Autoren, Entdecker, Komponisten usw.) ist es notwendig, einen *by-agent* im Passivsatz zu verwenden (Sätze ② und ④). Der *by-agent* ist immer notwendig, wenn der **Verursacher** einer Handlung betont werden soll.

Transform the following sentences from the active into the passive voice. Be careful! Sometimes the *by-agent* is necessary, sometimes you won't need it.

a) Someone had stolen my tennis racket before I went back to the tennis court.

. . . .

b) Albert Einstein discovered the *Theory of Relativity*.

. . . .

c) You can buy some cake at the supermarket.

. . . .

d) They built the *Empire State Building* in 1931.

. . . .

e) Somebody left the door of the gym (Sporthalle) open yesterday.

. . . .

f) American scientists discoverd the power of nuclear energy.

. . . .

g) They will write a class test on Wednesday.

. . . .

h) Bart and Lucy will return the books to the library tomorrow.

. . . .

Make passive sentences. Mind the phrasal verbs. 53

active voice	*passive voice*
She took **care of** her little sister.	Her little sister was taken **care of**.
They **kicked** Harry **out** of the team.	Harry was **kicked out** of the team.
They often **talk about** the TV show.	The TV show **is** often **talked about**.
James **has thrown** his old frisbee **away**.	The old frisbee **has been thrown away**.

- Kommt im Aktivsatz ein Verb mit Präposition (*phrasal verb*) vor, dann steht im Passivsatz die Präposition **direkt nach** dem Partizip Perfekt.

Transform the following sentences from the active into the passive voice. Be sure to place the *phrasal verbs* correctly and keep the *by-agent* in mind

a) Jimmy „Fist“ Murray had knocked out Pedro „Hammer“ Alvarez in round three.

. . . .

b) They closed down the cinema yesterday.

. . . .

c) The fire brigade is going to put out the fire quickly.

. . . .

d) Someone rang me up in the middle of the night.

. . . .

e) The farmers are bringing in the harvest now.

. . . .

7 Satzarten

54 Scrambled questions and answers.

Revision

Which question goes with which answer?
(G) —— (?)

(G) Can you help me with the dishes, please? I'm in a bit of a hurry.

(0) Did you see any Broadway productions when you were in the United States?

(G) Did you often go to the cinema when you were young?

(W) When and where will the next Olympic Games take place?

(S) Whose books are those over there on the desk in the library?

(I) Where does the new college professor live?

(G) Can anybody lend me two dollars, please? I'd like to have a cheeseburger in the cafeteria.

(O) Have you ever been to Detroit?

(H) They are Bill's. I guess he'll fetch them after lunch.

(N) No, I haven't. I don't think it's worth going there. It's just an industrial town.

(E) No, I can't. I'm sorry, but I must be off in a minute.

(A) No idea. Anyway, they won't be in America this time.

(E) Oh, no. I didn't. I was not really keen on films.

(R) No, we didn't. We didn't go to New York at all.

(T) Just come with me. We can have an egg sandwich at my place.

(N) In Oak Park. He bought a house there last month.

Put the pairs of letters in the brackets in the right order and you will get the name of a famous American.

Lösung: ☐☐☐☐☐☐ ☐☐☐☐☐☐☐☐☐☐

Ask questions to which the underlined parts of the sentence are the answers

55

		Mr Burns	takes	his car	to the garage	twice a year.
What	**does**	**Mr Burns**	**take**	?	to the garage	twice a year.
Where	**does**	**Mr Burns**	**take**	his car	?	twice a year.
How often	**does**	**Mr Burns**	**take**	his car	to the garage	?

Im Englischen muss die Grundstruktur der Wortstellung im Aussagesatz

Subjekt - Verb - Objekt

auch bei der Fragestellung beibehalten werden. Um dies zu erreichen, wird die Umschreibung mit „*to do*" gebraucht.

a) Helen Broady and her friends read the notes at school every morning.

What do ....?

Where do ....?

When do ....?

b) The taxi driver takes the passengers to the airport at five o'clock.

Who does the taxi driver ....?

Where ....?

When ....?

c) In 1620 the Mayflower carried 102 colonists to Cape Cod because they wanted to start a new life in America.

When ....?

Who ....?

How many colonists ....?

Where ....?

Why ....?

What ....?

Where ....?

56 More questions without *to do*.

Read the following dialog and the grammatical rules below. Underline the questions and mark the type of question A, B or C in ( ).

A tourist from France, Madame Pasquier, has just arrived at O'Hare International Airport in Chicago. She asks an American passenger questions about the Art Institute of Chicago.

Mme Pasquier: Excuse me, please. Are you English? ( )

Passenger: No, I'm not. I'm American.

Mme Pasquier: Oh, I see. Are you from Chicago? ( )

Passenger: Yes, I am.

Mme Pasquier: Have you ever been to the Art Institute of Chicago? ( )

Passenger: Oh, yes, I have. I have often been there.

Mme Pasquier: Can you tell me how to get there? ( )

Passenger: Oh, that's not difficult to find. Go to Grant Park and then you'll have to ask again.

Mme Pasquier: Could I walk there if the weather was fine? ( )

Passenger: No, you couldn't. It's too far. You'd better take a taxi or go by subway (BE: underground, tube).

Mme Pasquier: Where's the nearest subway station? ( )

Passenger: It's just over there. You can't miss it.

Mme Pasquier: When will the next train leave? ( )

Passenger: It will leave in a couple of minutes, I guess. But there are trains every ten minutes.

Mme Pasquier: Oh, by the way, who runs the Art Institute? ( )

Passenger: I think it's the City of Chicago, but I'm not quite sure.

Mme Pasquier: Hm, how many people go there every day? ( )

Passenger: I don't really know. Must be thousands.

Die Umschreibung mit *to do* wird nicht gebraucht, wenn das Verb ein Hilfsverb (*auxiliary*) (A) oder ein unvollständiges Hilfsverb (*defective auxiliary*) (B) ist.
In diesen Fällen werden - wie im Deutschen - Subjekt und Verb vertauscht.

S	–	v	→	V –	S	?
You		*are...*		*Are*	*you...*	?

Ohne Umschreibung mit to do werden auch Fragen gebildet, in denen das Fragewort (*question word*) Subjekt oder Teil des Subjekts ist (C).

S	→	V		
Who		*wrote*	*that novel*	?
How many people		*live*	*in Corpus Christi, Texas*	?

Find the proper questions. 57

CLEAN - CLEANER - CLEANFIX

STARLIGHT INC., the firm which produces the new household cleaner **CLEANFIX** wants to find out what housewives think of its newest product. They hold interviews.

Which questions does the interviewer, Mr Proper, ask Mrs Scrubber, a housewife from Wilmington, North Carolina?

Mr Proper: . . . . ?

Mrs Scrubber: Yes, I do. I use **CLEANFIX** regularly.

Mr Proper: . . . . ?

Mrs Scrubber: I use it in the kitchen, in the bathroom, everywhere.

Mr Proper: . . . . ?

Mrs Scrubber: Oh, yes, he does. My husband cleans his car and his bike with it.

Mr Proper: . . . . ?

Mrs Scrubber: My children? Well, they don't really clean anything with it. They use **CLEANFIX** for making bubbles.

Mr Proper: . . . . ?

Mrs Scrubber: Yes, I do. I allow them to play with **CLEANFIX** because I don't think it can do any harm.

Mr Proper: . . . . ?

Mrs Scrubber: In the bathroom? I use it twice a week, you see.

Mr Proper: . . . . ?

Mrs Scrubber: I always buy it at the little shop on the corner.

Mr Proper: . . . . ?

Mrs Scrubber: Well, yes. I think it is too expensive. It could be cheaper.

58 Use reported speech.

In der indirekten Rede wird wiedergegeben, was jemand gerade sagt oder früher gesagt hat.

direct speech	**direct speech**
Mr Becker **says**	Mr Becker **says**
„**I** like America.	(that) **he** likes America.
I came to Detroit five years ago.	(that) **he** came to Detroit five years ago
My children have been living with us for two years.	(that) **his** children have been living with **them** for two years.
We don't think **we** will ever go back to Germany."	**they** don't think **they**'ll ever go back to Germany.

Steht im Einleitungssatz present tense oder present perfect (*he says that, he has said that...*), so wird im Nebensatz (that-clause) keine Rückverschiebung der Zeit (*backshift of tenses*) durchgeführt. Personalpronomen und Possessivbegleiter werden jedoch verändert:

I	**→**	**he / she**	**my**	**→**	**his / her**	**me**	**→**	**him / her**
we	**→**	**they**	**our**	**→**	**their**	**us**	**→**	**them**

Vor *that* steht kein Komma; *that* kann auch weggelassen werden.

Das Deutsche gebraucht in der indirekten Rede den Konjunktiv.
Herr Becker sagt, er **liebe** Amerika.
er **sei** vor fünf Jahren nach Detroit **gekommen**.

On the occasion of his eightieth birthday next week Mr King is being interviewed by a newspaper reporter.

Reporter: „When were you born, Mr King?“

Mr King: „I was born in 1918. It will be my eightieth birthday next week.“

Reporter: „Where did your parents live then?“

Mr King: „They lived in Ohio. They had a small farm there and they were rather poor people.“

Reporter: „Did you have any brothers and sisters?“

Mr King: „Oh, yes. I had an elder brother and two younger sisters. My brother died some years ago. He had worked on my father's farm. My sisters are still alive. When they were young they moved to New Orleans and got married there. They have come here with their families for my birthday.“

Reporter: „What was life like when you were young?“

Mr King: „Life was hard, but quiet. There were not so many cars, no TV sets, no computers, no discos. We had to get up early and help our parents with their farm. Then we walked to school. It was a very small school and the teacher was very strict, but we learned (auch: learnt) a lot.“

Reporter: „What did you do after school?“

Mr King: „I became a carpenter. After I'd got married I moved to St. Louis. Here I opened my own business in 1941 and my family and I have been living here ever since.“

Reporter: „What would you do if you were young again?“

Mr King: „I wouldn't work as much as I did, I'd travel a lot, and I'd retire earlier to enjoy life more.“

The newpaper reporter takes notes. She writes:

Mr King says (that) he was born . . . .

(that) he . . . .

Complete her newpaper article in reported speech.

Reported speech with backshift of tenses
Indirekte Rede ***mit*** *Rückverschiebung der Zeitformen*

past tense	**backshift of tenses**
Mrs Grisham **said,**	„I **am** a Chicago police officer."
	present tense ↓ **past tense**
Mrs Grisham **said** (that)	she **was** a Chicago police officer.
Deutsch: Mrs Grisham sagte, sie **sei** Polizeibeamtin in Chicago.	
Mrs Grisham **said,**	„I **have** been living in Illinois for 20 years."
	present perfect progressive ↓ **past** perfect progressive
Mrs Grisham **said** (that)	she **had** been living in Illinois for 20 years.
Mrs Grisham **said,**	„I **arrived** at the museum after the fire **had broken** out.'
	past tense ↓ **past perfect** — **past perfect** ↓ **past perfect**
Mrs Grisham **said** (that)	she **had arrived** at the museum after the fire **had broken** out.
Mrs Grisham said,	„There **will** always **be** trouble in the poor quarters of the town."
	will-future ↓ **conditional**
Mrs Grisham **said** (that)	there **would** always **be** trouble in the poor quarters of the town.

Steht im Hauptsatz (He said that...) das Verb des Sagens und Denkens im past tense, so muss die Zeit im Nebensatz um eine „Stufe" zurückversetzt werden (*backshift of tenses*).

SYNOPSIS - (ÜBERBLICK)

Hauptsatz (*main clause*)	**Nebensatz** (*subordinate clause* = *that-clause*)		
past tense He said (that)...	**simple present** he writes	→	**simple past** he wrote
	present progressive he **is** writing	→	**past progressive** he **was** writing
	present perfect simple he **has** written	→	**past perfect simple** he **had** written
	present perfect progressive he **has** been writing	→	**past perfect progressive** he **had** been writing
	simple past he wrote	→	**past perfect simple** he **had** written
	past progressive he **was** writing	→	**past perfect progressive** he **had** been writing
	will-future he **will** write	→	**conditional** he **would** write

PRESENT → PAST

PRESENT PERFECT → PAST PERFECT

PAST → PAST PERFECT

PAST PERFECT → PAST PERFECT

WILL-FUTURE → CONDITIONAL

Expressions of time and place in reported speech
Zeit- und Ortsangaben in der indirekten Rede

today	⟶	that day
tonight	⟶	that night
now	⟶	then
this week	⟶	that week
yesterday	⟶	the day before
last night	⟶	the night before
last week	⟶	the week before
last year	⟶	the year before
two years ago	⟶	two years before
tomorrow	⟶	the following day / the next day
next week	⟶	the following week / the next week
next year	⟶	the following year / the next year
here	⟶	there
this / these	⟶	that / those

Bei der Umwandlung der direkten Rede in die indirekte Rede müssen in der Regel die Zeit- und Ortsangaben **verändert** werden.

Sie bleiben jedoch **unverändert**, wenn das Gesagte noch innerhalb des angegebenen Zeitraums oder an demselben Ort in der indirekten Rede wiedergegeben wird.

Beispiel: **In 1619** a Pilgrim Father promised his family, „We'll start an new and happier life in America **next year.**"

In **1619** a Pilgrim Father promised his family that they would start a new and happier life in America **the following year**.

Mr Fuller: „We'll get our new car **next week.**"

Mrs Fuller: „I beg your pardon, dear. What did you say?"

Mr Fuller: „I said that we'd get our new car **next week.**"

Transform the following sentences into reported speech; think of the adverbials of time. 59

a) Father said, „The children **have** been working hard **today**."
Two years ago Father said (that) the children ...

b) The police officer said, „The police **arrested** the suspect two days **ago**."
The police officer said (that) the police ...

c) The coach said, „The team **will** certainly win the baseball match **tomorrow**."
The coach said (that) the team ...

d) The engineer on the oil rig thought, „The supply ship **came** on Wednesday **last week**; so it **will be here** again on Tuesday **next week**."
The engineer on the oil rig thought (that)...

e) The director announced, „The performance **will** start at quarter past eight **tonight**."
The director announced (that) the performance ...

Step by Step 60

1. **Read the following sentences carefully and underline the words which you must change if you transform direct speech into reported speech.**
2. **Change the words according to the rules above and enter them into the columns below.**
3. **Transform the sentences. Use reported speech instead of direct speech.**

a) The ranger in the National Park explained, „<u>We</u> <u>opened</u> <u>this</u> exhibition only two years <u>ago</u>."

b) The sales representative said, „I will sell these items at a lower price today."

c) The ambulance men said, „Tonight we are going to take these injured people to different hospitals."

d) Last year the President said, „We will start our campaign against hunger in these underdeveloped countries next week."

e) On his arrival in California the gold prospector said, „After we had packed all these things on our wagons last year we followed the Santa Fe trail to the West."

pronoun	tense	adverb / adverbial	determiner
a) they	had opened	before	that

The ranger in the National Park explained that they had opened that exhibition only two hours before.

b) Continue ...

61 Spot the mistakes in the following sentences and enter the wrong and your corrected form of each sentence in the blanks below.

a) Mr Anderson said that he has bought his new house in 1986 as soon as he had saved enough money.

b) Last April my uncle in Philadelphia wrote that he has lived in America for fifteen years and that he would come to visit us in Europe next month.

c) In 1773 the Bostonians declared that they will not pay taxes any longer if they would not be represented in the English Parliament from now on.

d) Last month the President declared that the economic situation of the USA improved since 1992 and that I will publish the newest statistics tomorrow.

e) The Washington Post wrote in 1976 that it will inform our readers next week whether it has found out further details about this scandal (the Watergate Affair).

a) has bought –
had bought ✓

– wrong
✓ correct

b) ....
....

c) ....
....

d) ....
....

e) ....
....

Give a correct version of the whole sentence.

a) Mr Anderson said that . . . .

Transform the following sentences into reported speech. Think of changing the pronouns as well. 62

a) The foreign politician said in the interview, „The financial situation of my country is getting worse from day to day."
The politican said (that) the financial situation ...

b) The Indian woman said, „I have been living on the reservation since I was born. I don't really like the life which we live."
The Indian woman said (that) she ...

c) She added, „My grandfather was the chief of our tribe. He had been hunting buffalo in the prairies until the railroad came."
She added (that) her grandfather...

d) The teacher promised, „We will certainly go on an excursion to Yosemite National Park."
The teacher promised (that) they ...

e) The homeless woman said, „I had been working in this firm for fifteen years. I lost my job in 1993. I have been living in the streets ever since. I hope times will soon be better."
The homeless woman said (that) she ...

f) The mayor announced, „We will do everything to solve the problems of homeless and unemployed people."
The mayor announced (that) they ...

g) The winner of the Nobel Prize said, „I wrote my book in order to show the social injustices in my home country."
The winner of the Nobel Prize said (that) she ...

Transform the following sentences into reported speech. Think of changing the adverbs, too. 63

a) Jill said, „I will go downtown and do some shopping for the party next week."
Jill said (that)...

b) The weatherman reported, „There were heavy storms on the Atlantic coast last night and there won't be any sunshine in this part of the country before tomorrow."
The weatherman said (that)...

c) Mr and Mrs Howard said, „Last year we spent our holidays at Durango, Colorado, but next year we will go to Florida."
Mr and Mrs Howard said (that)...

d) When he woke up Alan thought, „Yesterday I had a terrible headache. I hope I'll feel better again today."
Alan thought (that)...

e) The captain said, „Last week we flew to Hong Kong. Tomorrow we will fly to Tokyo and next week we will fly to Singapore."
The captain said (that)...

f) The young man said, „I have been waiting here for two hours now and I have been reading this newspaper article over and over again. I am not going to wait any longer and I will certainly not come back tomorrow."
The young man said (that)...

g) The journalist wrote, „The social conditions in the slum areas of this city were extremely bad last year. I am sure they have not improved this year and they will be even worse next year."
The journalist said (that)...

64 Talking about oneself.

Five young people spend their vacation together. They talk about themselves, about their lives, their past, their future, their hopes.

Maren (16) from Chicago:

„I live at Evanston. My father has been a lecturer at the University of Illinois for three years and my mother has been working as a psychologist in a hospital for two years. My elder sister got married last month. She will move to Florida next week together with her husband. Two years ago I flew to Cologne on the Rhine on a students' exchange. My German had not been really good up to then, but it improved a lot while I was staying with a German family."

Enrico (17) from Albuquerque:

„I have been living with my mother since my parents got divorced in 1993. Mom has been working in a cafeteria since then. I have not met my father in the last few years. He is a truck driver and therefore he is often away. Some months ago I started to do a paper route (BE: round) every morning. This gives me some pocket money which I spend on books about computers. We live in a mobile home. I don't think we'll stay there in New Mexico. We will certainly move to Baltimore where my grandparents bought a house last year."

Stan (14) from Charleston, South Carolina:

„I'm from Charleston. My native town is the place where the Civil War began more than a hundred years ago. Tourists who come there will see many traces of our Old South - Fort Sumter, for example, or the Old Slave Market. My father is a lawyer. My mother died in a car accident when I was still very young. After graduation from high school I want to go to college in order to become a doctor. I was quite good at playing basketball in my school team until I broke my leg last year. I don't think I will ever be able to play again."

Jose (18) from San Diego:

„I don't really know who my parents are. I got lost or they left me behind after they had crossed the Mexican border illegally. Anyway, a trucker found me near the highway. He took me home, and I have been living with him, his wife and their two children ever since. I work as a car mechanic in a big garage for the time being, but I'm going to be a trucker as well later on. That will be more exciting."

Kathleen (15) from Dallas:

„My mom and my dad met at (the) Mesa Verde National Park eighteen years ago. Mom had been working there as a guide for tourists. She is Indian. Her family still lives near the Park. They don't want to move away from there. My parents have a big house in Dallas. My father has been in the oil business since we moved there in 1987. I don't think I will stay there for good (für immer)."

At home again, after six weeks, they tell their parents, their brothers and sisters, their friends about their new acquaintances and about their thoughts, hopes and plans.
What do they say? Use reported speech.

Maren said that she lived at Evanston. Her father had been a lecturer ...

Enrico from Albuquerque told us that ...

Stan said that ...

Write a report. 65

The reporter of the *Birmington News* has just phoned the local police station to get a report on what happened during the last twenty-four hours.

These are her notes:

a) serious street accident - two people injured - one driver obviously drunk - fled - police looking for a green car - front part damaged - yesterday

b) fire in the knitwear factory – broke out at 7.35 last night – fire brigade extinguished fire by midnight – no one hurt – perhaps short circuit (Kurzschluss) – perhaps arson (Brandstiftung).

c) burglary in house in Lincoln Street – window broken – owners on vacation – safe open – jewelry (BE: jewellery) and cash stolen - noise - neighbors called police

d) bank robber arrested – anonymous hint at house – house searched – money from last week's bank robbery found - man and woman arrested - woman perhaps not guilty

e) fourteen–year–old girl – missed for 10 days – found in a lonely hut near Willows' Lake – worried about school report – parents got her back – glad

Write down in direct speech what the policeman told the reporter:

Policeman: Yesterday there was a serious street accident. Two people were injured. One of the car drivers was obviously drunk. ...

In the conference of the editorial staff the journalist reports what the policeman told him a couple of minutes ago.

The police said that yesterday there had been a serious street accident. Two people had been injured. ...

66 Rewrite the text in direct speech.

During the meeting of the town council a minute-taker (Protokollführer) noted down what the members of the council said:

The mayor announced that it was not possible to build a new cultural center for concerts and theater (BE: theatre) performances. The town did not have enough money to realize such an expensive project.

Mr Whitman replied that the council had decided to build the center many years before and that there had been time enough to get the financial means (Mittel) ready.

Mrs Bentry argued that she agreed to the mayor's argument. She thought that a new school building for the junior high school would be more essential than a cultural center where especially young people would not go

Mrs Niemec answered that society was obliged (verpflichtet) to do something for young people in order to keep them off the street. She went on to say that it was a necessity to offer young people something to do during their spare time, above all in rural areas.

Mr Warren stated that sixteen-year-old boys and girls could not be bothered with cultural values. He said that those people would rather go to discos or enjoy sports events than boring theater performances.

. . . .

In the end the mayor said that he had been listening to different arguments for two and a half hours and he had discovered an hour before that the majority was against building the center. He said that he, too, thought that a new school building would be of the utmost urgency.

If you had been a member of the town council, what would you have said?

I would have said that . . . .

. . . .

. . . .

Write the text above in direct speech:

The mayor: „It is not possible to build ...

Translate. 67

Ein Fremdenführer in Savannah, Georgia, berichtet über den amerikanischen Bürgerkrieg vor einer Gruppe deutscher Touristen, von denen einige jedoch nicht Englisch sprechen. Kannst du die Rolle des Dolmetschers übernehmen? Beachte den Konjunktiv in der indirekten Rede im Deutschen.

Tourist Guide: By the 1850s in the North and the South of the USA were completely different from each other. The North was an industrial country whereas the South strongly depended on agriculture.

Du: Der Fremdenführer sagte, in den fünfziger Jahren habe sich der Norden der USA vollkommen vom Süden unterschieden. Der Norden sei ein Industrieland gewesen, während der Süden stark von der Landwirtschaft abhängig gewesen sei.

Tourist Guide: The Southerners owned Negro slaves who worked on their plantations. Slavery was, however, forbidden in the Northern states.

Du: Er sagte, die Südstaatler ....

....

Tourist Guide: In 1860, Abraham Lincoln, who had always been against slavery, became President. The Southern states then formed their own government because they feared that slavery would be abolished.

Du: Er sagte, im Jahre 1860 sei ....

....

Tourist Guide: So the Civil War began and many soldiers on both sides lost their lives. Finally, the North won the war and the slaves in the South were set free. President Lincoln was killed by a fanatical Southerner only a few days after the end of the war.

Du: Er sagte, deshalb habe der Bürgerkrieg ....

....

68 Questions in reported speech.

The Senator of Illinois asked me, „Do you like America?"
The Senator of Illinois asked me if / whether I liked America

Direkte Entscheidungsfragen, d.h. Fragen, die mit Ja oder Nein beantwortet werden können, werden nicht durch ein Fragewort eingeleitet.
Indirekte Entscheidungsfragen werden durch *if* oder whether (=ob) eingeleitet.

Nach **if = ob** kann auch *will* oder *would* gebraucht werden.

Frank asks me, „Will you be here tomorrow?"
→ Frank asks me if I will be here tomorrow.
Frank fragt mich, ob ich morgen hier sei.

Last year Frank asked me, „Will you be here tomorrow?"
→ Last year Frank asked me if I would be there the next day.
Letztes Jahr fragte mich Frank, ob ich am nächsten Tag dort sei.

The bank clerk asked Jane, „**How much** money do you want to draw from your account?"
⇨ The bank clerk asked Jane **how much** money **she wanted** to draw from her account.
Der Bankangestellte fragte Jane, wie viel Geld sie von ihrem Konto abheben wolle.

Direkte Fragen, die durch ein Fragewort eingeleitet werden, behalten das Fragewort in der indirekten Frage bei.

Die **Wortstellung** in der **indirekten Frage** entspricht der **Wortstellung** des **Aussagesatzes.** (Subject - Verb ...).

Im Übrigen gelten für die Umwandlung direkter Fragen in indirekte Fragen die für die indirekte Rede allgemein gültigen Regeln (*backshift of tenses, etc.*).

Which of the following transformations from direct questions to reported questions is correct? Enter the letter of your choice in the little boxes below. The solution denotes something which you are perhaps not too fond of.

Police Officer: „Why did you not stop at the traffic lights, Mr Warren?"

The Police Officer asked Mr Warren
a) why he did not stop at the traffic lights. (E)
b) whether he did not stop at the traffic lights. (L)
c) why he had not stopped at the traffic lights. (G)

Managing Director: „Were you late again yesterday, Miss Turner?"

An hour ago the managing director asked Miss Turner
a) if she was late again the day before. (C)
b) when she had been late again the day before. (M)
c) if she had been late again yesterday. (R)

Two years later the managing director asked Miss Turner
a) whether she had been late again the day before. (A)
b) if she was late again the day before. (G)
c) if she had been late again yesterday. (R)

Journalist: „What will your next novel be about, Mrs Price?"

A journalist wanted to know
a) what Mrs Price's next novel will be about. (K)
b) what Mrs Price's next novel was about. (T)
c) what Mrs Price's next novel would be about. (M)

A tourist in Lassen Volcanic National Park, California: „How many visitors came to the Park in 1995?"

A tourist in Lassen Volcanic National Park asked a ranger
a) how many tourists came to the Park in 1995. (U)
b) if many tourists have come to the Park in 1995. (H)
c) how many tourists had come to the Park in 1995. (M)

A passenger on a train: „When will we arrive at Oklahoma City?"

A passenger on a train asked the guard
a) when they will arrive at Oklahoma City. (I)
b) when they would arrive at Oklahoma City. (A)
c) when we would arrive at Oklahoma City. (B)

A guest in an Italian restaurant: „How long have you been working in Baltimore, Mario?"

A guest in an Italian restaurant asked Mario, the waiter
a) how long he has been working in Baltimore. (D)
b) how long he had been working in Baltimore. (R)
c) how long he had worked in Baltimore. (Z)

Lösung: ☐☐☐☐☐☐☐

69 Use reported speech for the translation.

Christopher Peele from Battle Creek, Michigan, and his German friend Kerstin Berger visit the excavations of a Roman bath in Southern Germany. An archaeologist explains the Roman remains (Überreste) to them. But Christopher does not speak German, so Kerstin must translate.

Now it is your turn. Take Kerstin's part. Use reported speech.

Archaeologist: Vor etwa 1900 Jahren gab es römische Siedlungen von Nordafrika bis Britannien.

Christopher: What does he say about Africa?

Kerstin: He says that about 1900 years ago there were Roman settlements from North Africa to Britain.

Archaeologist: Von einer Stadt zur anderen bauten die Römer gute, breite Straßen.

Christopher: What was „gut“?

Kerstin: He says that...

Archaeologist: So konnten die römischen Soldaten schnell von einem Ort zum anderen marschieren.

Christopher: I understand „Soldat“. Is that „soldier?“

Kerstin: Yes, it is. He says that...

Archaeologist: Aber die Römer lebten nicht nur in Städten und Militärlagern (military camps), sondern auch in kleinen Dörfern und in Bauernhäusern.

Christopher: What does he say about „military“?

Kerstin: He says that...

Archaeologist: Normalerweise gehörte ein Bad zu einem solchen Bauernhaus.

Christopher: What is bad?

Kerstin: Nothing is bad. He says that...

Archaeologist: Die römischen Bäder hatten eine Art Zentralheizung, die man hier sehen kann.

Kerstin: He says that...

Archaeologist: Die Römer kamen hierher in diese Bäder, um zu baden, aber auch um zu spielen, etwas zu trinken und um miteinander zu reden.

Kerstin: He says that...

After his return to Battle Creek Christopher tells his parents about his visit to the Roman excavations. What does he say?

The archaeologist said that about 1900 years ago there had been Roman settlements from North Africa to Britain.

Go on

Revision

70 Complete the conditional sentences.

if-clause: *simple present*	main clause: *will + infinitive*
If the bus comes at nine o'clock,	we will be home around ten o'clock,
If you are thirsty,	you will find some lemonade in the fridge,
If Peter gets a good grade,	he will be very happy.
leicht erfüllbare, wahrscheinliche Bedingung	**Folge für die Zukunft**

Complete the conditional sentences (type 1) with one of the verbs. Use simple present or will-future.

catch • eat • find • steal • go skiing

a) If you . . . . all that ice-cream, you will be ill.

b) If you leave your bike unlocked, someone . . . . it.

c) If the police . . . . the burglar, they will arrest him.

d) If Tim and Jane work hard for their exams, they . . . . a good job

e) We . . . . tomorrow, if it is not too cold.

71 Make conditional sentences (type 1).

An afternoon in town

a) the children / hurry up with their homework / have time to play

. . . .

b) sun / shine / they not stay / inside the house

. . . .

c) the boys and girls / have enough money / go downtown by bus

. . . .

d) the bus / be not crowded / everyone / have a seat

. . . .

e) the children / be hungry in town / eat a hamburger at a fast food restaurant

. . . .

f) the children / have more time / they / visit the zoo

. . . .

Complete the conversation. Use if-clauses (type 2). 72

if-clause: ***simple past***	**main clause:** ***would + infinitive*** **(*conditional 1*)**
If Jeremy was at home,	he would play table tennis with his brother.
If 1 had a lot of money,	I would buy a new CD player.
If the boxer won the fight,	he would be world champion.
schwer erfüllbare, sehr unwahrscheinliche Bedingung	**gedachte Folge für die Gegenwart oder die Zukunft**

A party on Saturday night?

Debbie and Jill live in the Midwestern state of Indiana, in a small town called Fort Dodge. They are sixteen and both attend the local high school. At the moment they are making plans for the weekend.

Complete their conversation - make conditional sentences (type 2). Use the verbs in brackets and make sure to use *simple past* in the if-clause and *would + infinitive* (*conditional I*) in the *main clause*.

a) Jill: If I . . . . (to make) fewer mistakes in my next math (BE: maths) test, I . . . . (to get) an „A“ in my school report.

b) Debbie: Oh, forget about school. What can we do at the weekend? If I . . . . (to own) a car, I . . . . (to drive) to Des Moines and go to a disco.

c) Jill: Yes, if... ! If I only . . . . (to have) some money left, I . . . . (to buy) a ticket for the Greyhound and visit my brother. He is a university student at Bloomington. But I have spent my money last week.

d) Debbie: No money - that is a problem. So we can't go to a disco. If my parents only . . . . (to allow) it, I . . . . (to invite) some friends to a party at our house. But mom and dad don't like parties at all - no chance.

e) Jill: Well, my parents are different. We can party at our house.

73 Translation practice: If I visited California ...

How about a holiday trip to the USA? A round trip through California perhaps? Translate the following German sentences into English. You will get conditional sentences (type 2). Don't forget the headline!

Wenn ich . . . .

a) Wenn ich genug Geld hätte, würde ich nächsten Sommer in die USA fliegen.

. . . .

b) Wenn ich eine Menge Zeit hätte, würde ich in Kalifornien herumreisen (to travel around).

. . . .

c) Wenn ich an Computern interessiert wäre (to be interested in), würde ich Silicon Valley besuchen.

. . . .

d) Ich würde einen Tag in einer alten Goldgräberstadt (town of the times of the gold rush) verbringen, wenn ich eine solche Stadt finden würde.

. . . .

e) Ich würde im Yosemite National Park zelten (to go camping), wenn ich einige Freunde treffen würde.

f) Wenn ich dort einen Bären sähe, würde ich mich sicherlich sehr fürchten.

Make conditional sentences (type 3). 74

Auf den folgenden Seiten wirst du nun einen neuen Typ von Bedingungssatz kennen lernen, der ganz einfach *conditional sentence type 3* genannt wird.

if-clause: *past perfect*	main clause: *conditional perfect* *would + have + past participle* (3. Form)
If we had left the hotel earlier	we would have arrived home sooner.
If she hadn't spent her money on candy	she would have had some money left.
If I had kown the answers in the test,	I would have got a better grade.
nicht erfüllbare, ganz und gar ausgeschlossene Bedingung	**nur gedachte Folge für die Vergangenheit**

- *If*-Sätze vom Typ 3 beziehen sich ausschließlich auf die Vergangenheit.
- Niemals would im *If*-Satz!

If...: Things could have been quite different, couldn't they?

Connect if-clauses (left) and main clauses (right) to get conditional sentences (type 3). Write down the complete conditional sentences and translate them into German.

If

the weather had been nice,	(1)	she would have given me a present,	(a)
John had seen the red traffic light	(2)	it would not have been stolen.	(b)
we had come home earlier,	(3)	it would have climbed up the tree quickly.	(c)
Susi had closed the door of the fridge,	(4)	I would have invited her to the party.	(d)
they had found the cinema,	(5)	Jane and Fred could have gone to the beach.	(e)
I had met Tanya	(6)	he would have stopped the car in time.	(f)
mother had remembered my birthday,	(7)	they could have bought a ticket for *Terminator I.*	(g)
the cat had seen the dog	(8)	the ice-cream would not have melted.	(h)
Mr Brown had locked his car,	(9)	we could have watched the news on TV.	(i)

Example: (1 - e) If the weather had been nice, Jane and Fred could have gone to the beach.
Wenn das Wetter schön gewesen wäre, hätten Jane und Fred an den Strand gehen können.

75 Complete the sentences.

Bad luck for James on Friday 13th

Use the verbs in brackets to make conditional sentences (type 3).

Remember: No *would* in the /f-clause!

Example: If James had **set the** alarm clock properly, he **would have woken up** earlier.

a) If he . . . (to get up) in time, he . . . (to have) enough time for breakfast.

b) If James . . . (to eat) his breakfast, he . . . (not to be) so hungry.

c) James . . . (not to enter) the school cafeteria, if he . . . (not to need) something to eat.

d) If James . . . (to be) more careful there, he . . . (not to run into) Henry.

e) If he . . . (not to crash into) Henry, Henry's tray with orange-juice, milk and cornflakes . . . (not to fall) to the ground.

f) If Henry's breakfast . . . (not to be spread) all over the floor, the waitress . . . (not to slip).

g) If the waitress . . . (not to fall down), she . . . (not to hit) a pile of plates.

What would have been different if. 76

Connect the two sentences to get one conditional sentence (type 3).

Remember: No *would* in the *if*-clause!

Example: Chris did not win the prize. He didn't fly to San Francisco.
If Chris had won the price, he would have flown to San Francisco.

a) Chris did not visit San Francisco. He didn't see the Golden Gate Bridge.

b) Chris didn't see the Golden Gate Bridge. He didn't take photos of it.

c) He did not take photos of the Golden Gate Bridge. He didn't show the photos to his friends in Germany.

d) His friends didn't see the photos. They didn't see how nice California is.

e They didn't find out how nice California is. They didn't want to visit California.

Test your grammar knowledge! 77

Use your knowledge and complete the table (Tabelle). You will get all the characteristics (Merkmale) of conditional sentences (type 1, 2 or 3).

Bedingungen: wahrscheinlich bzw. leicht erfüllbar - schwer erfüllbar bzw. unwahrscheinlich - nicht mehr erfüllbar bzw. ganz und gar ausgeschlossen

Zeiten: will future - past perfect - conditional I - simple past - conditional II - simple present

Beispielsätze: If you visit New York, you will see many skyscrapers.
If the Indians hadn't sold Manhattan to Peter Minuit, New York would not have been built.
If you stood on top of the Empire State Building, you would see the enormous size of New York.

Folgen: auf die Zukunft gerichtet - gedacht und auf die Vergangenheit gerichtet - gedacht und auf die Gegenwart oder die Zukunft gerichtet.

conditional sentence type 1	**Beispiel:** .... **Zeiten:** .... **Bedingungen:** .... **Folgen:** ....
conditional sentence type 2	**Beispiel:** .... **Zeiten:** .... **Bedingungen:** .... **Folgen:** ....
conditional sentence type 3	**Beispiel:** .... **Zeiten:** .... **Bedingungen:** .... **Folgen:** ....

78 Higgledy-piggledy - or: What a mess.

Connect *if-clauses* and main clauses to get conditional sentences. Be careful! There are *if-clauses* and main clauses from conditional sentences type 1, 2 or even 3 in this exercise. First try to find out which type of conditional sentence you get. Then write down each *conditional sentence*.

If

you arrive at New York by boat,	(1)		English people will say „city centre“ instead.	(a)
California's water system broke down,	(2)		he would have seen a wonderful carnival party there.	(b)
you asked Germans about the Fourth of July	(3)		you would get your Christmas presents on December 25th.	(c)
Americans use the word „downtown“,	(4)		you will see the Statue of Liberty.	(d)
Peter had visited New Orleans for Mardi Gras,	(5)		farming would be impossible there.	(e)
you were an American boy or girl,	(6)		only a few would know something about it.	(f)

Typ?

a) ☐ ....

b) ☐ ....

c) ☐ ....

d) ☐ ....

e) ☐ ....

f) ☐ ....

Oh, no! Translation practice ... ! 79

Die Übung sieht schwieriger aus als sie tatsächlich ist. Bedingungssätze sollen ins Englische übersetzt werden. Schwierigkeiten bereiten die deutschen Verben, deren Zeitformen nicht immer den im Englischen geforderten Zeitformen entsprechen. Wenn du Schritt für Schritt an die Übersetzung herangehst, kannst du leicht alle Fehlerquellen ausschalten.

- **Schritt 1:** Bestimme, um welchen Typ von conditional sentence es sich handelt.
- **Schritt 2:** Stelle fest, in welcher Reihenfolge if-clause und main clause erscheinen.
- **Schritt 3:** Bestimme zuerst die Zeitformen der Verben und schreibe dann die richtigen Formen der Verben auf.
- **Schritt 4:** Übersetze den ganzen Satz.

Beispiel: Wenn der Hund nicht gebellt hätte, wäre der Dieb nicht davongerannt.

Schritt 1: Typ 3

Schritt 2: if-clause - main clause

Schritt 3: past perfect - conditional II (would + have + past participle)
hadn't barked - wouldn't have run away

Schritt 4: **If the dog hadn't barked, the thief wouldn't have run away.**

a) Er würde mehr Geld verdienen, wenn er einen besseren Job hätte.

Schritt 1: . . . .

Schritt 2: . . . .

Schritt 3: . . . .

Schritt 4: . . . .

b) Wenn wir nach Washington fahren, werden wir das Weiße Hause besuchen.

Fahre fort in der angegebenen Schrittfolge.

c) Wenn du sie angerufen hättest, wäre sie sicher zu deiner Geburtstagsparty gekommen.

d) Wenn du den Fremdenführer (tour guide) fragen würdest, würde er dir sicher von der Boston Tea Party erzählen.

e) Präsident Lincoln hätte die Sklaven nicht befreit (to free), wenn er nicht den amerikanischen Bürgerkrieg (American Civil War) gewonnen hätte.

80 Make conditional sentences with *can – could – may – might – schould – must*.

In manchen Bedingungssätzen wird statt *will* oder *would* auch *ein modal auxiliary verb* (Hilfsverb) verwendet. Man kann mit *can, could, may, might, should* oder *must* unterschiedliche Bedeutungen ausdrücken:

① If we spend the weekend in New York, we can visit Chinatown in Manhattan. (Vorschlag: „können“)

② If you go to Jane's party, you could bring your CDs. („könntest eigentlich")

③ If we take a trip to the Rocky Mountains, it may be cold, („mag", d.h. gut möglich)

④ If Tracey and Shirley go out in the evening, they might buy tickets for a Broadway musical, („mögen", aber nicht so sehr wahrscheinlich)

⑤ If you want to lose weight, you should eat less, („sollen")

⑥ If you leave the house, you must lock the door, („müssen")

Die Beispiele ① bis ⑥ sind *conditional sentences* vom Typ 1. Bei Bedingungssätzen vom Typ 2 oder 3 kann *would* nur durch *might / might have* oder *could / could have* ersetzt werden.

① If we went to the White House, we might see the president.

② If we had had more time, we could have stayed longer.

Brian and Lucas in Manhattan

Brian and Lucas have spent a weekend in New York City. Now they want to go back to Boston by train. But unfortunately ...

Example:

Brian: If we **had found** the station sooner, **we might have / could have caught** the train to Boston.

a) Lucas: If we can't get to Boston today, we . . . . (to phone) our parents immediately.

b) Brian: You're right. They . . . . (to be worried) if they don't hear from us.

c) Lucas: Let's do that. But what about today? Manhattan is such an interesting place. If we . . . . (to walk) down East 42nd Street, we . . . . (to check out = to visit) the United Nations Headquarters.

d) Brian: I don't know. Peter said: „If you . . . . (to be) in Manhattan, you really . . . . (to see) Times Square and the Broadway." How about that?

e) Lucas: Why not? But first I want to go back to the youth hostel. If we stay for one more day, we . . . . (to reserve) a room for the night.

f) Brian: We really have to. If we hurry up, we . . . . (to be) at the youth hostel in thirty minutes or so.

g) Lucas: And if we are lucky, we . . . . (to get) the room we had last night and we . . . . (to enjoy) the sights of New York City for another day. Missing trains is not all that bad!

81 Oh, great! Translation practice again ... !

Translate the following *conditional sentences* (type 1, 2 and 3). Use the *modal auxiliary verbs can, could, may, might, should* or *must* instead of *will* or *would*.

a) Wenn James nächste Woche seine Eltern besuchen würde, könnte er mit seiner Tante einkaufen gehen.

. . . .

b) Wenn du morgen zu Hause bist, kannst du mich anrufen.

. . . .

c) Wenn sich Jake das Fußballspiel im Fernsehen angesehen hätte, dann hätte er nicht schwimmen gehen können.

. . . .

d) Wir gehen vielleicht ins Kino, wenn wir nicht zu müde sind (to be tired).

. . . .

e) Wenn du Onkel Tom triffst, solltest du ihm für das Geschenk danken.

. . . .

f) Ihr dürft ein Stück Kuchen essen, falls er fertig ist.

. . . .

g) Wenn die Sonne geschienen hätte, hätte Großvater im Garten arbeiten können.

. . . .

h) Du könntest meinen neuen Füller haben, wenn du mir deine Filzstifte geben würdest.

. . . .

Negated conditional sentences 82

① Ann won't lend me any money, even if I ask her.

② If Tom wasn't going away for the weekend, he would be our DJ.

③ If Columbus hadn't wanted to travel to India, America wouldn't have been discovered.

- Auch bei verneinten *conditional sentences* werden die entsprechenden Verben mit den bekannten Zeitformen verwendet.
- Je nachdem was ausgesagt werden soll, können sowohl *if-clause* als auch *main clause* oder beide Teile des *conditional sentence* verneint werden.

Immigrants, colonists, settlers ...

Connect the *if-clauses* (left) and the main clauses (right) to make negated (verneinte) *conditional sentences*. First try to find out which type of *conditional sentence* you get. Then write down each *conditional sentence* and translate it into German.

1. If people from Ireland, Sweden and Germany hadn't suffered so badly,
2. The immigrants thought if they went to America,
3. The immigrants would not have become colonists and pioneers in the West
4. If the pioneers don't want to die in the wilderness,
5. If they didn't build farms and didn't start to grow corn and vegetables,
6. The Indians would fight the settlers,
7. If the settlers hadn't moved westward,

a. if the East hadn't been so crowded.

b. if the East hadn't been so crowded.

c. if the settlers tried to take their hunting grounds.

d. they wouldn't have a place to live or food to eat.

e. America would not have stretched from the Atlantic to the Pacific.

f. they will have to work hard.

g. they would have a better life.

Example:

1 - b; Typ 3: If people from Ireland, Sweden and Germany hadn't suffered so badly, they wouldn't have come to the West.

Wenn die Menschen aus Irland, Schweden und Deutschland nicht so schwer hätten leiden müssen, wären sie nicht in den Westen gekommen

83 Conditional sentences as questions

① Would you buy a farm in Wyoming, if you were rich?

② If you had lived in the 1830s, would you have immigrated to America?

③ Will you try to find gold if you move to Alaska?

- Auch bei *condtional clauses* als Fragen werden die entsprechenden Verben mit den bekannten Zeitformen verwendet.
- Nur der Hauptsatz wird als Frage gebildet, der Nebensatz bleibt unverändert.

Who is asking all these questions?

Connect the sentence parts on the left with the sentence parts on the right to make *conditional sentences* as questions. Write the letter given on the left in the box for the sentence parts on the right. If you work correctly, the solution will name a Texan city which is very important for American space-flights (Raumfahrt).

a) If I washed Dad's car,	T	will you go skiing with your friends?	☐
b) Would Scott have come	U	would you buy a motorbike or a car?	☐
c) Will you lend me your CD player	O	if we had invited his ex-girlfriend, too?	☐
d) Would you fly to Mars,	N	if she had seen the No smoking-s\gn?	☐
e) If you had a driver's permit (BE: driving licence)	O	would you help Mom in the kitchen?	☐
f) Would she have stopped smoking,	S	if I promise to be really careful with it?	☐
g) If we have a white Christmas	H	if the NASA offered you a space shuttle?	☐

Translate. 57

Benny wants to know it all!

Benny is Simon's younger brother. He is ten and very, very curious (neugierig). In fact, he asks far too many questions, Simon thinks. Translate Benny's questions. Make sure the verb forms are correct and remember to use *auxiliary* verbs if necessary.

a) Darf ich deine CDs anhören, wenn du nicht zu Hause bist?

b) Wenn ich sechzehn wäre, könnte ich dann mit dir in die Disco gehen?

c) Wirst du deiner Freundin Ciaire einen Kuss geben, wenn du sie begrüßt? (to say hello)

d) Wenn es gestern geregnet hätte, hättest du mich dann mit dem Auto zu Francis gebracht?

e) Könntest du Eiscreme für mich kaufen, wenn du ins Einkaufszentrum (AE: mall - BE: shopping centre) gehen würdest?

f) Sollte ich es dir sagen, wenn ich dein neues Fahrrad nehmen will?

g) Wenn ich zu fragen aufhören würde, wärst du dann froh? (to be glad)

ALLES AUF EINEN BLICK

Bedingungssätze treten in verschiedenen Formen auf:

- **als Aussagesätze:**

① Many people will be out of work if that factory closes down.

② If Tom had forgotten to clean his bike, mother would have been angry with him.

③ If I found $100 in the street, I would keep it.

- **als verneinte Sätze:**

④ If you went to bed earlier, you wouldn't be so tired every morning.

⑤ Our friends will be very disappointed if we don't invite them to our party.

⑥ Tom wouldn't have eaten so much if he hadn't been very hungry.

- **als Fragesätze:**

⑦ Would you have bought the expensive shirt if you had seen the cheap one first?

⑧ If you were a millionaire, what would you do?

⑨ Will Sarah be angry with me if I take her bike without asking?

Die hier zusammengestellten *if*-Sätze haben eine ganze Reihe von Gemeinsamkeiten:

☞ Ein *if*-Satz hat zwei Teile, den *if*-Teil (*if-clause*) und den Hauptteil (*main clause*).

☞ Die Reihenfolge der beiden Teile spielt keine Rolle. Immer wenn der *if*-Satz an erster Stelle steht, dann werden *if*-Satz und Hauptteil durch ein Komma getrennt (②, ③, ④, ⑧).

☞ Im *if*-Satz wird eine *if*-Bedingung (*condition*) als Nebensatz aufgestellt. Der Hauptteil nennt dann die tatsächliche oder manchmal auch nur gedachte Folge für die Vergangenheit, die Gegenwart oder die Zukunft. Um dies zu erreichen, werden unterschiedliche Zeitformen in festen Paaren verwendet:

Typ	*if*-Satz (*if-clause*)	Hauptteil (*main clause*)	Beispiel
1	*simple present*	***will + infinitive*** **(Grundform)**	①, ⑤, ⑨
Bedingung wahrscheinlich oder leicht erfüllbar *if*-Satz auf die **Zukunft** gerichtet			
2	*simple past*	***would + infinitive*** **(Grundform)**	③, ④, ⑧
Bedingung sehr unwahrscheinlich oder nur schwer erfüllbar *if*-Satz nur gedacht und auf **Gegenwart** oder **Zukunft** gerichtet			
3	*past perfect*	***would + have + past participle*** **(3. Form)**	②, ⑥, ⑦
Bedingungen nicht mehr erfüllbar *if*-Satz nur gedacht und auf die **Vergangenheit** gerichtet			

8 Konjunktionen

85 Which conjunction fits best?

Bill's father is a lawyer, **and** his mother works in a hospital.

Jolene lost her way in the wilderness **because** she could not read a map.
The hikers walked on **as soon as** the thunderstorm was over.
The burglar was able to climb into the house **after** he had smashed a window-pane.
The burglar had to smash a window-pane **before** he could climb into the house.
The burglar was able to climb into the house **because / as** he had smashed a window-pane.

Konjunktionen (*conjunctions*) dienen dazu, Hauptsätze (main clauses) bzw. Hauptsätze und Nebensätze (*subordinate clauses*) miteinander zu verknüpfen.

The following conjunctions introduce:

main clauses
and (und)
or (oder)

clauses of time
when (als)
whenever (wann auch immer)
while (während)
after (nachdem)
before (bevor)
as soon as (sobald)
since (seit)

clauses of purpose and result
that (dass)
so that (sodass)

clauses of place
where (wo)
wherever (wo auch immer)

clauses of condition
if (wenn, falls)
even if (selbst wenn)
unless (wenn nicht)

clauses of comparison
as if (als ob)

clauses of reason
because (weil)
as (da)
since (da, da ja)

clauses of concession
though (obwohl)
although (obwohl)
whereas (während)

subordinate clauses in reported speech
that (dass)
whether (ob)
if (ob)

The right letters in ( ) describe a special type of country. Put them into the boxes below.

(c) Although
(d) When
(a) After
(f) If

Pocahontas was an Indian princess, the English King and Queen welcomed her to the court.

John Rolfe grew tobacco in Virginia

(o) after
(e) though
(x) while
(g) whether

he had seen the Indians smoke their pipes.

Pocahontas could not return to Virginia

(l) as
(u) if
(f) and
(h) as soon as

she caught smallpox and died in England.

A lot of tobacco plantations were founded in Virginia

(r) because
(o) so that
(t) before
(i) as

negro slaves were needed to do all the work.

Jamestown was not reconstructed

(n) after
(r) if
(q) while
(v) because

it had burnt down in 1693.

Some people in Virginia tried to murder Captain John Smith,

(h) before
(s) when
(b) whether
(y) because

they did not like him setting up rules for their community.

Answer: ☐ ☐ ☐ ☐ ☐ ☐

86 Combine the following clauses by means of a conjunction.

1. Many farmers cannot do without cars
2. The businessman decided to fly to New Orleans
3. Teenagers like going to concerts
4. The drunkard drove on after the accident
5. Many blacks did not know what to do
6. New hardships began for many immigrants from Europe
7. Some areas in the big cities are dangerous
8. Gerd and Claudia would never have gone to St. Louis

though • if • after • so that • whenever • because • as if • as soon as

a) he had not yet recovered from his illness.
b) their favorite pop groups play.
c) tourists should not go there.
d) their uncle had not invited them.
e) they had arrived in the New World.
f) they live too far from the nearest towns.
g) nothing at all had happened,
h) they had been set free.

Translate the following sentences. 87

After **he** had sold his house in Oregon, **Brian Hill** moved to Atlanta.
*Nachdem **Brian Hill** sein Haus in Oregon verkauft hatte, zog **er** nach Atlanta.*

> Bei der Herübersetzung von Satzgefügen wird das Nominalsubjekt zuerst genannt.
> **Nicht:** Nachdem **er**..., zog **Brian Hill**....

Since he was seventeen, **Matthew** has driven big and expensive cars.
***Seit Matthias** siebzehn war, fährt **er** (schon) große und teuere Wagen.*
***Seit seinem** siebzehnten Lebensjahr fährt **Matthias** (schon) große und teuere Wagen.*

If he had enough money, **Mr Braine** would spend the winter in California.
***Wenn Herr Braine** genügend Geld hätte, würde **er** den Winter in Kalifornien verbringen.*

Paul asked me **if** I had enough money to spend the winter in California.
*Paul fragte mich, **ob** ich genügend Geld hätte, um den Winter in Kalifornien zu verbringen.*

> *Die Konjunktionen since* und *if* haben je nach dem Zusammenhang, in dem sie auftrete unterschiedliche Bedeutung:

since	a)	**seit**	b)	**da ja**
if	a)	**wenn** (in Konditionalsätzen)	b)	**ob** (in indirekten Fragesätzen)

When Neil Armstrong first stepped onto the moon in 1969 he said, „This is one small step for a man, one giant leap (Sprung) for mankind."

Beachte: when = als
Als Neil Armstrong ...

a) The principal (Rektor) asked Jessica if she liked her new school.
b) Since he came to New York in 1963, Christopher has never thought of living anywhere else.
c) Even if all drugs were prohibited (verboten) by the Government, there would still be a lot of drug-addicts.
d) The immigration officer wanted to know if Jonathan Biggs was going to stay in America for more than two months.
e) Before he left Germany for good (für immer), Axel Schulz made sure that he would have a job and an apartment (BE: flat) in Detroit.
f) After he had checked my papers, the police officer asked me if I had not seen the traffic sign.

Lernbereich RECHTSCHREIBUNG

Mit den folgenden Übungen zu einigen wichtigen Bereichen der Rechtschreibung kannst du deine Ergebnisse bei Diktaten verbessern und verhindern, dass du bei anderen Aufgaben Punkte verlierst, weil du Wörter falsch geschrieben oder verwechselt hast.

1 Zweiteilige Wörter: Verwendung des Bindestrichs, Zusammen- und Getrenntschreibung

Bei der Verwendung des Bindestrichs oder bei der Frage, ob zweiteilige Wörter getrennt oder zusammengeschrieben werden, besteht kein Zusammenhang zwischen deutscher und englischer Schreibweise. Einige Regeln können dir aber helfen:

- Neben einer ganzen Reihe von Substantiven werden folgende Wörter immer **zusammengeschrieben:**
  anyone, anything, anyway, anywhere, cannot, downhill, downstairs, everybody, everyone, everywhere, nobody, somebody, someone, something, sometimes, somewhere, uphill, upstairs, whenever, whereas, wherever
- Immer **getrennt** werden dagegen die folgenden Wörter geschrieben:
  after all, all right, any more, each other, even so, no one, one another
- Mit **Bindestrich** geschrieben werden: Eine ganze Reihe von **Substantiven, Zehner und Einer** (*seventy-five, ninety-nine, sixty-one, thirty-four*), **zusammengesetzte Adjektive** (*a well-behaved child, a good-looking girl, a sixteen-year-old teenager, a well-known politician, a blood-curdling crime, a fast-working computer*) und die meisten Verbindungen mit folgenden Vorsilben oder Wörtern:

ex-...: *ex-politician, ex-husband, ex-football player*
half-...: *half-empty, half-finished, half-sister, half-truth*
ill-...: *ill-mannered, ill-natured, ill-timed, ill-used*
self-...: *self-catering, self-centered, self-control, self-defense, self-portrait*
well-...: *well-built, well-chosen, well-informed, well-known, well-paid*

Make one word out of two. 1

Zusammengeschriebene zweiteilige Wörter (Teil I)

Add one of the following words to the words given from a) to j).

mail • yard • bike • board • man • paper • book • friend • storm • card

a) air ....
b) motor ....
c) news ....
d) thunder ....
e) fisher ....
f) back ....
g) cup ....
h) boy ....
i) text ....
j) post ....

Zusammengeschriebene zweiteilige Wörter (Teil II)

Make one word out of two. Put two of the following words together.

play	apple	bed	mud	speaker
skate	week	writing	head	ground
end	loud	pine	guard	hand
police	master	man	board	room

a) .... f) ....

b) .... g) ....

c) .... h) ....

d) .... i) ....

e) .... j) ....

Zweiteilige Wörter mit Bindestrich

Add one of the following words to the words given from a) to l).

known	conditioning	wife	timed	respect	hand
handed	working	pool	bag	player	space

a) ill- .... g) empty- ....

b) second- .... h) air- ....

c) swimming- .... i) ex- ....

d) well- .... j) self- ....

e) hard- .... k) record- ....

f) school- .... l) parking- ....

Zahlen - mit und ohne Bindestrich

Write the following numbers in full words.

2469 **two thousand, four hundred and sixty-nine**

a) 3123 ....

g) 1121 ....

b) 755 ....

h) 101 ....

c) 35th ....

i) 101st ....

d) 274th ....

j) 248 ....

2 Die Verwendung des Apostrophs

1 John**'s** car is an old Ford Mustang, his parent**s'** car is a new Chrysler.

2 What**'s** that noise over there? Let**'s** have a look.

3 Who**'s** got a green pen? It can**'**t be mine. My pen**'**s dark blue.

- Der Apostroph steht im s-Genitiv
  (**'s** bei einem Besitzer und -**s'** bei mehreren Besitzern).
- Der Apostroph wird auch für Kurzformen verwendet: *cannot = can't*; *who has - who's*; *my pen is = my pen's.*
- Bei Gegenständen, Sachen usw. verwendest du **nicht** den s-Genitiv, sondern - wie auf Seite 152 dargestellt - die **of-phrase**

Translate. 2

Translate the following German phrases or sentences and mind the correct position of the apostrophe.

a) Harrys Freunde ....

b) die Fahrräder der Mädchen ....

c) die Bäume des Waldes ....

d) der Bart des Mannes ....

e) die Eier der Hühner ....

f) das Haus meiner Eltern ....

g) die Party der Kinder ....

h) die Geschichte Amerikas ....

3 Schreibregeln: Schreibung -s oder -es

Revision

① text – texts; roof – roofs

② to put – he / she puts; to help - he / she helps

③ speech – speeches; hero – heroes; half – halves; wolf – wolves

④ to catch – he / she catches; to miss – he / she misses

Die Beispielsätze zeigen, dass der Plural von Substantiven und die 3. Person Singular von Verben auf -s oder es enden können. Folgende Regeln musst du beachten:

-s enden der regelmäßige Plural von Substantiven wie *books* oder *shops* und die **3. Person Singular** von **Verben** im ***simple present***

-es verwendest du bei Substantiven im Plural und bei Verben in der 3. Person Singular **nach Zischlauten** (*box - boxes; bus - buses; to rush -he / she rushes*), bei einigen **Substantiven auf** -o (z. B. *potatoes, aber: pianos, discos, photos*) und bei den Verben **to do** und **to go**. Einige Substantive auf **-f** und **-fe** haben Pluralformen auf **-ves** (z. B. shelf - shelves), andere bilden die normale Pluralform auf **-s** (z. B. *cliff - cliffs*).

Fill in the correct plural form. 3

a) **wife**
b) **stereo**
c) **potato**
d) **knife**
e) **beach**
f) **bush**
g) **casino**
h) **negro**
i) **calf**
j) **thief**
k) **buffalo**
l) **search**
m) **life**
n) **studio**
o) **tomato**

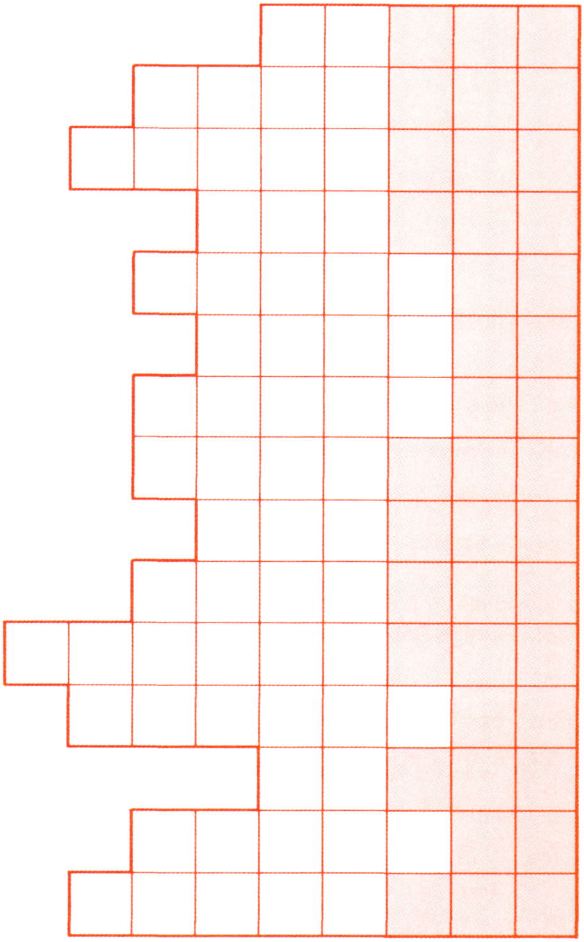

Add the third person singular form. 4

Example:	I beat	**he / she**	**beats**
a) I fetch		**he / she**	. . . .
b) I rush		**he / she**	. . . .
c) I talk		**he / she**	. . . .

d) I teach **he / she** . . . .

e) I pull **he / she** . . . .

f) I push **he / she** . . . .

g) I speak **he / she** . . . .

h) I watch **he / she** . . . .

5 Make plural forms of nouns ending with -ey or -y.

① enjoy – he / she enjoy**s** – enjoy**ed** – enjoy**ing**

② marry – he / she marr**ies** – marr**ied** – marr**ying**; lorry – lorr**ies**

③ chimney – chimney**s**

④ easy – eas**ier** – eas**iest** – eas**ily**

Wie dir die Beispiele ① bis ④ zeigen, gibt es bei Substantiven, Verben und Adjektiven bzw. Adverbien auf -y einige Regeln zu beachten:

-ys enden der Plural von Substantiven wie *chimney* oder *journey* und die **3. Person Singular** von **Verben** im ***simple present*** (①, ③).

-ies wird beim Plural von Substantiven und in der 3. Person Singular von Verben im *simple present* verwendet, wenn **vor** dem **-y** am Wortende ein **Konsonant** steht (②).

-yed enden das simple **past** und das **past participle** bei den regelmäßigen Verben, wenn vor dem **-y** am Wortende ein **Vokal** steht: *enjoy -enjoyed* (①).

-ied wird verwendet, wenn **vor** dem **-y** am Wortende ein **Konsonant** steht (②).

-y bleibt vor der Endung -ing immer erhalten: *enjoying - marrying* (①, ②).

-y wird zu -ier und -iest bei der Steigerung von zweisilbigen Adjektiven (außer wenn vor dem -y ein Vokal steht: *grey - greyer - greyest* (④).

-y wird zu -ily, wenn vom Adjektiv das Adverb abgeleitet wird: *easy - easily* (④), so auch: *happy - happily*.

Complete the singular forms of the follwing nouns with -ey or -y. Then add the correct plural form.

a) hobb........ plural: ....

b) part........ plural: ....

c) monk........ plural: ....

d) communit........ plural: ....

e) vail........ plural: ....

f) centur........ plural: ....

g) colon........ plural: ....

h) jock........ plural: ....

i) diar........ plural: ....

j) troll........ plural: ....

Add the third person singular. 6

Example: I play **he / she plays**

a) I carry **he / she** ....

b) I apply **he / she** ....

c) I buy **he / she** ....

d) I study **he / she** ....

e) I destroy **he / she** ....

f) I qualify **he / she** ....

g) I empty **he / she** ....

h) I fly **he / she** ....

i) I pay **he / she** ....

j) I try **he / she** ....

4 Unregelmäßige Plurale

Der Plural wird in der Regel durch Anfügen von -s an die Singularform des Substantivs gebildet.

Einige Pluralbildungen weichen jedoch von dieser Regel ab:

Singular		Plural				
bush	–	**bushes**				
wish	–	**wishes**				
baby	–	**babies**	aber:	boy	–	**boys**
city	–	**cities**				
potato	–	**potatoes**	aber:	piano	–	**pianos**
buffalo	–	**buffaloes**		photo	–	**photos**
wife	–	**wives**	aber:	roof	–	**roofs**
knife	–	**knives**		handkerchief	–	**handkerchiefs**
man	–	**men**	aber:	German	–	**Germans**
gentleman	–	**gentlemen**		Roman	–	**Romans**
chairman	–	**chairmen**				
woman	–	**women**				
chairwoman	–	**chairwomen**				
foot	–	**feet**				
tooth	–	**teeth**				
goose	–	**geese**				
child	–	**children**				
ox	–	**oxen**				
mouse	–	**mice**				
louse	–	**lice**				
sheep	–	**sheep**				
deer	–	**deer**				
fish	–	**fish**	aber:	**fishes** = Fischarten		
trout	–	**trout** (Forelle/n)				
salmon	–	**salmon** (Lachs)				
Japanese	–	**Japanese**				
Chinese	–	**Chinese**				
Swiss	–	**Swiss**				
the people	–	**the peoples**	(Volk / Völker)			
		people	(die Leute)			

Word-Search Game 7

There are twenty-nine plurals hidden in the word-search game. Try to find them and write them in your exercise book. It's a challenge

d	k	i	l	o	n	h	i	l	m	o	e	f	h	u	t	o	r	p	e	i	w	j	s	h	z	w	u	g	w	t	e	o	r	i	d	j	i
n	o	r	i	c	l	a	s	s	e	s	i	k	o	n	u	t	m	p	o	l	i	r	a	m	w	o	k	n	r	o	m	i	p	e	g	u	s
a	b	r	e	f	o	n	o	o	n	m	o	k	u	l	e	k	a	w	q	u	e	r	s	t	e	t	r	o	o	n	o	r	t	u	m	l	o
c	u	c	h	i	l	d	r	e	n	m	e	f	r	o	t	u	i	s	d	e	r	t	s	p	o	t	r	p	o	t	a	t	o	e	s	m	u
e	t	v	o	s	u	k	m	o	r	t	o	m	o	s	t	u	p	p	e	r	c	l	o	s	e	r	t	o	f	i	t	o	x	e	n	m	i
w	o	e	l	h	p	e	f	d	o	e	r	s	t	o	p	i	t	a	t	z	q	u	w	h	o	s	e	m	s	k	l	m	p	o	r	t	k
o	p	c	h	a	i	r	m	e	n	n	e	o	r	p	s	t	u	w	p	o	t	a	t	s	i	v	e	n	a	p	i	a	n	o	s	t	u
t	r	i	a	n	g	c	p	e	k	l	a	p	o	t	r	a	n	s	h	w	r	e	o	r	t	o	n	k	i	l	e	t	m	i	r	t	l
t	o	z	r	a	b	h	t	r	p	t	u	z	q	u	e	s	h	e	e	p	p	l	k	w	e	o	r	u	t	i	w	o	m	e	n	r	e
m	o	r	s	t	w	i	v	e	s	a	p	o	t	r	i	t	s	a	r	o	p	t	i	c	u	r	t	o	p	a	k	e	l	o	p	n	m
n	i	r	t	a	v	e	m	t	m	i	k	l	a	m	p	h	o	t	o	s	t	u	r	t	i	l	k	a	b	o	y	s	m	n	o	l	p
a	s	p	e	r	i	f	e	e	t	a	p	o	k	l	m	i	g	o	e	m	o	k	l	i	t	r	a	l	m	o	n	i	k	a	l	t	o
p	i	m	o	r	t	s	v	e	m	k	o	r	p	o	m	e	n	o	s	m	n	k	o	r	k	i	n	a	m	l	o	p	w	e	o	r	i
h	u	r	t	o	l	c	i	t	i	e	s	b	k	n	i	v	e	s	m	o	l	t	k	r	o	p	e	o	w	l	r	i	u	z	n	a	t
m	n	o	i	l	k	p	i	h	o	l	p	l	s	t	c	e	m	k	o	l	t	p	r	o	i	e	u	w	j	s	k	e	o	r	t	u	w
n	a	h	s	i	e	u	r	k	o	f	w	i	s	h	e	s	j	d	k	i	t	z	u	r	p	l	o	z	l	j	s	k	i	r	l	t	k
n	a	s	u	e	i	h	s	t	e	l	a	v	o	e	r	t	u	t	z	o	l	r	t	o	p	s	g	j	e	i	r	t	u	l	e	p	r
g	e	r	t	o	r	t	p	b	a	b	i	e	s	a	s	p	r	t	u	t	i	f	o	l	r	t	a	r	u	p	o	s	t	i	l	k	k
m	s	o	r	t	u	w	e	n	e	o	r	s	n	s	j	e	u	i	r	z	t	k	m	s	l	o	q	q	h	s	j	e	i	r	u	e	z

5 Gleiche Aussprache, verschiedene Schreibweise:

Wörter mit e – ee – ea – ie –ei

Für den Laut [i:] gibt es unterschiedliche Schreibweisen:

fever – deep – meal – believe – receive

Complete the sentences 8

a) In a car you should always use a ...
b) A soft and gentle wind ...
c) Geronimo is a famous Indian ...
d) To tell a lie is to .... other people.
e) Something you shouldn't tell other people is a …

f) Grassland for cattle is called ...

g) Mr Jones paid the money and got a ...

h) The ... of the soccer club take place every Monday afternoon.

s.....t-belt	br.....ze	ch.....f
dec.....ve	[i:]	s.....cret
f.....ld	rec.....pt	m.....tings

9 Translate the words and find them in the word-search game!

Wörter auf -or, -er, -ar, -ure und - our

Für Wörter, die auf den Laut [3] (in AE [sr]) enden, gibt es unterschiedliche Schreibweisen:

mirr**or**	fath**er**	cell**ar**	nat**ure**	col**our**
visit**or**	manag**er**	begg**ar**	pict**ure**	neighb**our**

Im amerikanischen Englisch wird die Schreibweise *our* durch *or* ersetzt: *harbor, neighbor*

Example:

Hubschrauber – helicopter

a) Universitätslehrer – ....

b) Gefallen – ....

c) Abenteuer – ....

d) regelmäßig – ....

e) Turm – ....

f) Arbeit – ....

g) Zukunft – ....

h) Anweiser, Lehrer – ....

i) beliebt – ....

j) Statue, Plastik – ....

k) Schulleiter – ....

l) Seemann – ....

m) Broschüre, Prospekt – ....

n) Hafen – ....

o) Druck, Zwang – ....

p) Besitzer – ....

q) Vorfahre – ....

P	H	E	L	I	C	O	P	T	E	R	G	I	T	G
R	M	O	P	Y	W	O	K	Y	B	W	J	I	A	B
E	Z	F	S	T	P	Y	H	K	R	O	M	N	L	T
S	H	W	V	U	K	L	E	T	O	I	Y	S	K	I
S	A	I	L	O	R	Y	A	N	C	E	S	T	O	R
U	V	A	J	N	E	R	D	K	H	L	I	R	Y	S
R	R	K	N	O	G	P	M	N	U	M	X	U	V	C
E	W	U	Z	G	U	N	A	B	R	Y	W	C	K	U
O	W	N	E	R	L	Y	S	L	E	I	F	T	G	L
I	K	N	O	A	A	W	T	Y	H	J	A	O	N	P
H	A	R	B	O	R	Y	E	O	L	I	V	R	Z	T
T	H	O	J	M	W	Y	R	I	W	H	O	M	K	U
P	R	O	F	E	S	S	O	R	B	E	R	H	K	R
L	F	U	T	U	R	E	K	S	Y	K	R	I	U	E
P	R	Y	G	A	D	V	E	N	T	U	R	E	R	Z

6 Homophone: ähnliche Wörter - schwierige Wörter

Homophone sind Wörter, die gleich ausgesprochen, aber verschieden geschrieben werden und unterschiedliche Bedeutung haben. Aus dem Satzzusammenhang lässt sich aber erkennen, welche Bedeutung gemeint ist.

[breik]	break	-	Pause
	brake	-	Bremse
[haul][houl]	hole	-	Loch
	whole	-	ganz

10 Choose the right word !

a) The Smiths traveled to San Francisco . . . . **(buy / by)** car to visit their . . . . **(sun / son)** and to do some sightseeing.

b) First they went to a jumble- . . . . **(sale / sail)** and Mrs Smith bought something nice to . . . . **(were / wear)**.

c) Afterwards they strolled . . . . **(threw / through)** many shops and then they wanted to . . . . **(see / sea)** the Museum of Modern Art.

d) Finally they were . . . . **(two / too)** tired and . . . . **(weak / week)** to go any . . . . **(farther / father)** (sind im AE keine Homophone!).

e) They took a . . . . **(brake /break)** and had a nice lunch in a snack bar.

f) Instead of walking back to . . . . **(their / there)** car they paid the money for the . . . . **(fair / fare)** and took a cable car.

g) Having arrived at the car they noticed that someone had tried to . . . . **(steal / steel)** it.

Fill in the proper word. 11

The Oscar is an American prize for really good films and actors.
Bob Miller had to pay a high price for his new house.

Choose the proper word. What is it in German?

a) .... years ago a friend of mine went .... America. She intended .... visit Canada, ..., but in the end she did not go there because time was .... short and it was .... expensive, ...

to – *nach* .... too – *auch* .... two ....

b) Mind, the buckle of the strap comes .... Don't .... your camera. That would be a great ....

to lose .... loose .... the loss ....

c) There was a .... in the garden wall. It took me a .... day to repair it.

whole .... hole ....

d) I do not yet know .... I can come to your party. It depends on the ....

whether .... weather ....

e) Martin Luther King fought for .... and equality among people of different colors (BE: colours) in America. His famous speech „I have a dream ..." has meanwhile become a of American literature.

piece .... peace ....

f) First people lived downtown (BE: in the city centre), ... they moved into the suburbs where life was less expensive .... in the center.

then .... than ....

12 Which words can you form with the letters below?

Bilde aus den vorgegebenen Buchstaben Wörter, die im Englischen ähnlich ausgesprochen werden, aber unterschiedliche Schreibung und Bedeutung aufweisen. Schreibe das deutsche Wort dahinter. Tipp: Du brauchst nicht immer alle Buchstaben, um ein Wort zu bilden.

a) e t q i u

. . . . = ...

. . . . = ...

b) i r a e a

era = Zeitalter

. . . . = ...

. . . . = ...

c) ebyu

. . . . = ...

. . . . = ...

d) g l e o c l e u g a

. . . . = ...

. . . . = ...

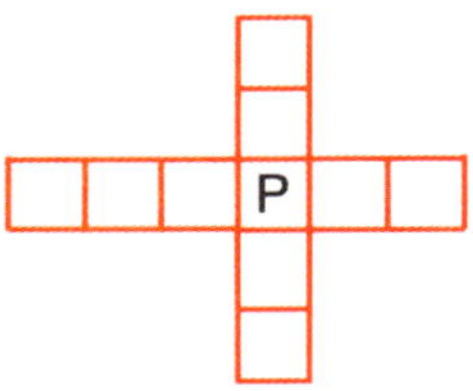

e) j o r a m y

. . . . = ...

. . . . = ...

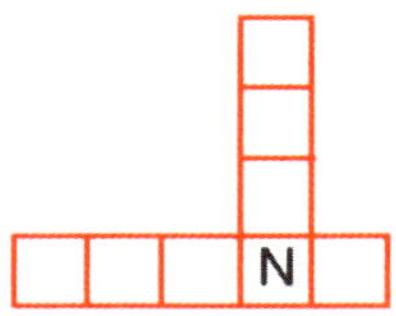

f) BE: . . . . = AE: student

g) men, women, children = ...

h) What you intend to do:. . . . .

i) What you fly with:. . . . .

j) 4 . . . .

14 . . . .

40 . . . .

Fill in the right form of the following verbs. 13

Fortunately, she **stopped** smoking.
The Washington Post **revealed** the Watergate Scandal in the 1970s.

Vor einer vokalisch anlautenden Endung (-ed, -ing, -er) wird der Endkonsonant einer Silbe nach **betontem** und **einfachem** Vokal verdoppelt.

stop — stopped; aber: reveal — revealed

Ordne die Verben zunächst in die beiden Spalten ein und bearbeite anschließend die Übung.

to refer • to suffer • to offer • to occur • to prefer • to conquer • to develop

Endsilbe betont	Endsilbe betont
/ ___________ ______	/ ___________ ______
....	....
....	....
....	....
....	....

Beachte:

BE:	to travel	–	travelled	–	traveller	–	traveller's cheque
AE:	to travel	–	traveled	–	traveler	–	traveler's check
BE:	to worship	–	worshipped	–	worshipper		
AE:	to worship	–	worshiped	–	worshiper		
BE:	to quarrel	–	quarrelled				
AE:	to quarrel	–	quarreled				
BE/AE:	to handicap	–	handicapped				

a) When Karin was in the USA she . . . . going to National Parks to visiting big cities.

b) When you come to an American house you will first be . . . . a drink.

c) The rich and highly . . . . countries should help people in . . . . countries.

d) Society should do more for mentally and physically . . . . people.

14 **Spot the mistake. Write the correct form of the word the line below.**

a) A strange incident occured near the warehouses of New York harbor.

. . . .

b) In 1066 William of Normandy conquerred Britain. That's why he is normally called William the Conqueror.

. . . .

c) As a young boy Jack Sneeze regularly sufferred from hay fever in spring and summer.

. . . .

d) In his inaugural address President Bill Clinton refered to the arguments which had been brought forward by his political opponents.

. . . .

7 Wörter mit „stummem“ Vokal oder „stummem“ Konsonanten

„Stumme“ Laute - Vokale oder Konsonanten - kommen am Wortanfang, mitten im Wort und am Wortende vor:

knight	lis**t**en	clim**b**
hour	desi**g**n	althou**gh**
write	fas**t**en	colum**n**

Find and mark twelve words with a silent letter. 15

lamb	quick	fruit	sword	enough
mustn't	uncle	guilty	surfing	often
board	foreign	felt-pen	talking	wrong
fasten	classroom	knowledge	weapon	speaker
girlfriend	island	toast	would	expensive

Translate the words and find them in the word-search game! 16

Example: Stunde – hour

a) Gitarre – . . . .

b) Zeichen, Schild – . . . .

c) Messer – . . . .

d) Herbst (im BE!) – . . . .

e) belegtes Brötchen – . . . .

f) ganz, das Ganze – . . . .

g) halb – . . . .

h) durch – . . . .

i) Mittwoch – . . . .

j) Gebäude – . . . .

k) Zweifel – . . . .

l) zuhören – . . . .

W	Y	B	U	I	L	D	I	N	G	G	K	T	U	D
E	G	M	J	K	U	B	M	L	U	L	T	Z	R	I
D	W	G	K	N	I	F	E	F	I	S	H	A	L	F
N	V	C	M	N	A	O	R	P	T	P	R	L	I	K
E	Y	W	K	E	S	G	T	H	A	G	O	R	S	M
S	A	N	D	W	I	C	H	L	R	I	U	Y	T	K
D	K	A	O	M	G	I	T	Z	H	T	G	S	E	M
A	U	T	U	M	N	K	L	O	V	Y	H	W	N	T
Y	T	O	B	J	K	H	O	U	R	H	T	F	T	E
P	K	W	T	O	U	N	M	T	W	H	O	L	E	F

14 Find sixteen spelling mistakes and correct them!

Black people in America

In the sevententh century the first Africans were . . . .

carryed from West Africa to America as slaves. . . . .

They were cheep to buy, their work was needed . . . .

and didn’t cosst the farmers anything. . . . .

Black men and woman had to do all the work on . . . .

cotton and tobacco plantations in the hot wheather . . . .

of the American South. ....

Some planters treated their workers well and ....

gave them houses to life in and enough food to eat ....

Others, however, saw them as „things“ that coud ....

be sold, punnished and even killed. ....

After the Civil War had been won buy the ....

solldiers of the North, the black people were no ....

longer slaves but that didn’t mean that they were ....

completly free. ....

White Americans in the South tried to pass laws to ....

seperate black Americans from white Americans ....

In the 1960s and 1970s politicans like Martin ....

Luther King and Malcom X fought for eqaul ....

rights - a fight wich hasn’t come to an end yet. ....

Lernbereich WORTSCHATZ

1 Schwierige Wörter

2 British English - American English

1 Schwierige Wörter

Choose the right word. 1

Beachte die unterschiedliche Bedeutung der Wörter.

a) The Americans export . . . . , which is also called Indian . . . ., to all parts of the world. You can buy it in cans or you will find it as . . . . .on the cob . . . . , especially wheat, barley and oats, is an essential element of the Americans' daily food.

gram . . . . **corn** . . . .

b) Harry Peele put the. . . . . with his meal into the. . . . . Then he listened to some. . . . . and forgot all about it. In the end everything was black and burnt and the kitchen was hot as if a. . . . . had been on.

oven . . . . **stove** . . . . **plate** . . . . **record** . . . .

c) „I . . . . where Madison Square Park is", murmured the old lady. A gentleman took a. . . . . of New York out of his. . . . . and showed her the way. She. . . . . to see that it was only two. . . . . away.

block . . . . **map** . . . . **to wonder** . . . .

to be surprised (at / that) . . . . **briefcase** . . . .

d) The participants in the conference which. . . . . at Charlotte Congress Center . . . . at the breakfast table. Apart from fried eggs ('sunny side up'), bacon and sausages, they had. . . . . (gooseberry, strawberry, raspberry, etc.) and of course . . . .

to take place . . . . **to take one´s seat** . . . .

marmalade . . . . **jam** . . . .

e) All over the country the FBI . . . . the . . . . of the old millionaire, whose . . . . had meanwhile been taken to the cemetery. After the police had found out that a physical education teacher of the local high school had . . . . him, they . . . . the school building and the . . . . They finally found a . . . . full of dollar notes hidden behind a . . . . wall.

concrete	**to look for s.o.**	**coffin** . . . .
gymnasium	**to search s.th./s.b**	**suitcase** . . . .
murderer	**to murder**	**the murder** . . . .

f) The . . . . near the airport are often broken into by burglars and shoplifters frequently steal goods in . . . . These are . . . . the . . . . themes which . . . . in the newspapers write about in their . . . . of the police organization.

criticism	**actually**	**warehouse** . . . .
critic	**department store**	**topical** . . . .

2 Translate.

a) In each match the tennis champion uses a completely new racket.
Yesterday another rocket was launched from Cape Canaveral.

. . . .

. . . .

racket . . . . **rocket** . . . .

b) Jolene is a very sensitive young lady. She will often worry about incidents of minor importance. But she can be very sensible if problems of her job are concerned.

sensitive . . . . **sensible** . . . .

c) The note says that the students will get their school reports next Friday. Raymond doesn't mind; he has made quite an effort during the last term so that he has become a good student and has got excellent grades (BE: marks) in his exams.

note . . . . **grade** . . . .

to get . . . . **to become** . . . .

d) During the horse races the visitors could buy beverages and sandwiches at the stalls near the stables.

stable .... **stall** ....

e) Sheila is very shy and self-conscious; her father was just the opposite, he was a very strong and self-confident personality.

self-conscious .... **self-confident** ....

2 British English - American English

Fill in the American or British spelling. 3

Zwischen dem britischen Englisch und dem amerikanischen Englisch bestehen einige Unterschiede in der Schreibung.

Füge in die folgende Auflistung die jeweils fehlende englische oder amerikanische Schreibweise ein.

British English	American English
-our	**-or**
....	color
favour	....
....	favorite
....	honor
honourable	....
....	neighbor
-ter	**-ter**
centre	....
....	theater
litre	....

-ence	**-ense**
licence	....
....	defense
offence	....
-logue	**-log**
dialogue	....
....	catalog
prologue	....
-mme	**-m**
programme	....
-gg-	**-g-**
....	wagon
-elling	**-eling**
travelling	....
....	quarreling
-ise / - ize	**-ize**
to realise / realize	....
....	to organize
.... / to analyze	....
-ise	**-ice**
....	to practice

Einzelwörter

British English	American English
whisky	whiskey
to plough, the plough (pflügen, der Pflug)	to plow, the plow
doughnut	donut
light	informal: lite
socks	informal: sox

Different words. Complete! 4

Wortschatzunterschiede zwischen britischem und amerikanischem Englisch

In manchen Fällen werden im britischen Englisch andere Wörter bevorzugt als im amerikanischen Englisch.
Ergänze die jeweils fehlenden Wörter aus der Liste auf Seite 135. Die zugeordneten Kennbuchstaben ergeben die Namen von neun amerikanischen Bundesstaaten.

British English		American English
I. Traffic and transport		
lorry	O_	....
....	_A	trucker
motorway	H_	....
....	_A	subway
railway	A_	....
petrol	I_	....
....	_N	gas station
dual carriageway	A_	....
....	_X	driving instruction
driving licence	A_	....

tram	C_	....
....	_I	sidewalk

II. Urban life

lift	F_	....
....	_N	apartment
city centre	I_	....
groundfloor	I_	....
....	_I	bookstore
block of flats	S_	....
dustbin	A_	....
....	F_	sales clerk
to post a letter	I_	....
cheque	R_	....
....	_A	traveler's check
postman	V_	....

III. Food

biscuit	R_	....
....	_N	can
....	_A	French fries
crisps	N_	....
....	_R	corn

IV. Miscellaneous words

autumn	A_	....
jumper	K_	....
....	_E	vacation
class	V_	....
....	_A	to guess

(O) to mail a letter • (B) maize • (K) truck • (0) elevator • (A) shop-assistant • (I) check • (O) petrol station • (A) streetcar • (D) to think, to suppose • (G) cookie • (A) grade • (E) driving lessons • (A) downtown • (O) highway • (R) flat • (N) holiday • (I) mailman • (S) driver's license, driver's permit • (M) underground • (I) apartment house • (S) fall • (O) first floor • (A) sweater • (E) chips • (T) divided highway • (N) garbage can • (R) railroad • (I) chips • (D) traveller's cheque • (I) tin • (Z) gas, gasoline • (L) lorry driver • (L) pavement • (U) bookshop

Lösungswörter:

☐☐☐☐☐☐☐☐ ☐☐☐☐☐☐ ☐☐☐☐☐
☐☐☐☐☐☐☐☐☐☐ ☐☐☐☐☐☐☐☐
☐☐☐☐☐☐☐ ☐☐☐☐☐☐☐
☐☐☐☐☐☐☐☐ ☐☐☐☐☐

Which words in the following sentences are not American English? Fill in the correct words. 5

a) The trucker stopped at the gas station to buy some biscuits and a tin of coke.

BE: biscuits AE: cookies

BE: .... AE: ....

b) In Chicago Kate and David went to the city centre by underground. They wanted to go to the theater to see „Victor, Victoria“, a famous musical. The programme said that Julie Andrews, Kate's favourite actress, was starring. They enjoyed the performance because of the many funny dialogues in the play.

BE: .... AE: ....

BE: .... AE: ....

BE: .... AE: ....

BE: .... AE: ....

BE: .... AE: ....

c) In America you will often find white or coloured neighborhoods where people of different ethnic or racial origin have their flats.

BE: .... AE: ....

BE: .... AE: ....

6 Rewrite the following sentences in British English.

For their party Sean and Beata, two sixteen-year-old students from Key West bought French fries, chips, and cookies. As they were still too young to buy any alcoholic drinks like beer or whiskey they bought some cans of lemonade and Diet Coke.

For their party Neil and Fiona, two sixteen-year-old pupils from Wantage, Oxfordshire, bought

....

....

....

Rewrite the following sentence in American English.

When travelling through Britain during their autumn holidays our neighbours realized that in suburban London motorways and railway lines run quite close to the blocks of flats in poor dwelling areas.

When .... the United States during

....

.... that in suburban Chicago

....

....

....

7 Translate the following sentences into British English and American English.

a) Der LKW-Fahrer zeigte dem Polizeibeamten seinen Führerschein.

BE: ....

....

AE: ....

....

a) Der Tourist bezahlte den Pullover mit einem Reisescheck.

BE: ....

....

AE: ....

....

Rewrite the text in American English, 8

The following text is written in British English. Underline all the words and expressions which can be replaced by American words, and rewrite the text in American English.

Last autumn Claus and Beatrice, two eighteen-year-old pupils from Gelsenkirchen, wanted to spend their holidays in Britain. Claus had only just got his driving licence and Beatrice was still taking driving lessons. Thus they decided not to go by car but to travel around the country by train. „I think railways are safer than motorways with all these lorries though British lorry drivers are said to be friendly and considerate (rücksichtsvoll) towards foreign car drivers", Claus said. „Going by train might be cheaper, anyway", Beatrice added, „petrol in Britain is supposed to be very expensive, and there are not too many petrol stations in rural (ländlich) areas."
After having travelled through different regions of Britain they finally arrived in London where they booked into the „Saxon King Hotel". Their rooms were on the ground floor, so that they could not see a lot from their windows, but they took the lift to the roof terrace from where they had a wonderful view - over the blocks of flats around the suburban (Vorstadt-) hotel. They went to the city centre by underground. There was an awful lot of traffic at Piccadilly Circus. It was almost impossible to cross the streets without using the subways (Unterführung; AE: pedestrian underpass). „What presents are we going to buy for our families?" asked Claus. „I think I will get some biscuits and sweets (Süßigkeiten; AE: candy) for my little sisters", said Beatrice, „they are still kids, so they might like them." „And I will buy a bottle of whisky for my father and a jumper for my mother, both things will keep them warm in a way, I think," answered Claus. „Let's go into the department store over there. We can pay by cheque, so we'll have enough money left for our last meal in Britain tonight."

Lernbereich Prüfungstraining

	Grammatik	Rechtschreibung	Wortschatz	
1. Test	• conditional sentences type 2 • conjunctions • indefinite article • adjective or adverb? • infinitive with to (superlatives, ordinal numbers) • mixed exercise		• synonyms and opposites	283
2. Test	• definite article • infinitive with to (verb + object) • conditional sentences: mixed types • conjunctions • reported speech and reported questions • mixed exercise	• irregular plurals		286
3. Test	• infinitive with and without to • mixed tenses • conditional sentences type 3 • of-genitive • mixed exercise		• American English and British English	290
4. Test	• conditional sentences: mixed types • infinitive with make and let • conjunctions • mixed exercise	• irregular plurals • difficult words	• definitions and paraphrases	293

Tipps:

- Die folgenden vier Tests sollen in etwa deinen schriftlichen Prüfungen (Klassenarbeiten, Schulaufgaben) entsprechen.
- Betrachte die Tests als Prüfungstraining. Versuche, sie in ungefähr 45 Minuten (vielleicht „gegen die Uhr“) zu bearbeiten. So kannst du „den Ernstfall proben“ und Routine und Sicherheit gewinnen.

1. Test

Make conditional sentences (type 2). 1

If I visited California ...

a) Wenn das Wetter in der Sierra Nevada zu kalt wäre, würde ich mich an den kalifornischen Stränden entspannen (to relax).

b) Wenn ich ein Foto der Golden Gate Bridge machen wollte (to want to ...), würde ich nach San Francisco reisen.

c) Wenn die Cable Cars funktionieren würden (to work), würde ich sie für eine Besichtigungstour durch die Stadt nutzen.

d) Wenn ich noch etwas Geld übrig hätte, würde ich meine Ferienreise in Disneyland beenden (to end up).

Find the synonym or the opposite. 2

a) Terry and Jane are very **active** children because they run around a lot. Joanne only sits around a lot – she is quite . . . .

b) Lessons at school are **interesting** most of the time. Sometimes, however, they can be very . . . .

c) Yesterday Jill saw a nice T-shirt for only $ 10 in a shop. „Rather **inexpensive**", she thought. „Ten dollars is really . . . . for such a nice T-shirt."

d) The white settlers and the Indians didn't manage to live together as **friends**. In many conflicts they fought each other as . . . .

e) Albert Einstein was a really **clever** man. People often said: „He is the most . . . . man on earth."

f) Benjamin's bike had a flat tire. He couldn't **mend** it himself, so he asked his brother to . . . . it.

g) Charlie is **short** and **weak**, but the big boys at school are afraid of him because his brother Clarence is . . . . and . . . .

h) Susan **forgot** her shopping list at home. At the supermarket she couldn't . . . . all the things she wanted to buy.

3 Choose the suitable conjunctions from the list below.

where • whether • after • so that • since • when • if • although • for • because • while • though • and • as soon as • as • whenever • as long as

a) The Pilgrims left Europe, ... they wanted to practice (BE: practise) their religion in freedom.

b) . . . . they were crossing the Atlantic Ocean, they had to endure many hardships.

c) A heavy storm drove their ship far north, ... they could not land in Virginia.

d) . . . . they came near the American coast, they signed a document in order to organize life in the new colony.

e) They landed near Cape Cod, ... thanked God for the safe crossing of the sea.

f) . . . . the Pilgrims were intruders, the Indians were not hostile towards them on their arrival.

g) . . . . the climate on the East coast was very harsh, the Pilgrim Fathers were never sure . . . . they would survive their first winter or die from hunger and cold.

h) Many tourists will visit the replica (Nachbildung) of their ship, ... they come to Plymouth, Massachusetts.

4 Fill in the indefinite article if necessary.

a) Henry Ford was . . . . American industrialist and . . . . President of the Ford Motor Company, which, already at the beginning of our century (Jahrhundert), was producing two thousand Model T cars . . . . day.

b) Before Jimmy Carter became . . . . President of the United States in 1977 he was . . . . peanut farmer and . . . . Governor of Georgia.

c) What . . . . surprise. Half . . . . year ago I still thought Stanley would never finish his studies at . . . . university, and now he is such . . . . gifted veterinarian (BE: veterinary surgeon, vet).

d) Neil O'Conner's father was . . . . Irishman who came to New Hampshire as . . . . immigrant. Though Neil is . . . . Catholic he doesn't go to . . . . church more than once month on . . . . average.

Translate. Adjective or adverb? 5

a) Harry hatte recht. Die Pizza roch und schmeckte fantastisch.
Harry was right. ...

b) Harry sagte: „Nächste Woche werde ich eine aufregende Floßfahrt (rafting trip) auf dem *Colorado River* machen. Möchtest du mitkommen?"
Harry said: „I am going to ...

c) Betty antwortete: „Nein danke. Das hört sich sehr gefährlich an. Ich bin immer viel zu aufgeregt für solche (such) Dinge." Harry lächelte Betty freundlich an.
Betty answered: „No, thanks. It...

d) Es war eine wundervolle Geburtstagsparty. Betty ging gegen Mitternacht (around midnight) langsam nach Hause. Sie war müde, aber auch sehr glücklich.
It was ...

Complete the sentences with an infinitive with *to* in the active or in the passive voice. 6

a) The fastest typist . . . . (write) with a personal computer is Gregory Arakelian from Virginia.

b) The cheapest car ever . . . . (build) was the *Red Bud Buckboard*. It cost between $ 125 and $ 150 in 1922.

c) The first man . . . . (visit) both the North Pole and the South Pole was the American Dr Albert Paddock Crary.

d) The most frequent family name . . . . (use) in the USA is *Smith*. More than 2.4 million Americans are called by that name.

e) The largest sum of money . . . . (pay) to an American actor was offered to Jack Nicholson for his part (Rolle) in *Batman*.

7 Complete the text. Use the words in brackets.

a) Jeremy and Carl moved from . . . . (the / —) delta of the Mississippi to Laramie, a town in . . . . (the / —) Rocky Mountains.

b) If the weather had been nice last weekend, they . . . . (to go fishing) to . . . . (the / —) Bluewater Lake.

c) Carl was the first . . . . (to / —) discover that beautiful lake, the only one . . . . (to find / to be found / founded) in the whole area surrounded . . . . (complete / completely) by deep forests.

d) The friends visit. (the / —) Bluewater Lake. . . . . (frequent / frequently), ... (also / whether / although) it is difficult to reach.

e) The water of the lake is. . . . . (incredible / incredibly) blue, its trout (Forellen) are . . . . (heavy / heavily) in size and they taste . . . . (fantastic / fantastically).

f) Jeremy and Carl are in love with their little lake. They would buy it immediately if they . . . . (to have) enough money.

2. Test

1 Fill in the definite article if necessary.

a) . . . . Monday is an awful day for . . . . most people.

b) . . . . Charlotte, the biggest city of . . . . North Carolina, lies in the county of Mecklenburg.

c) The summer vacations in . . . . most countries are in . . . . July and August.

d) . . . . Monticello, near Charlottesville, Virginia, one of . . . . most famous villas in . . . . USA, was planned and built by Thomas Jefferson during almost forty years.

e) . . . . Michigan Avenue in . . . . Chicago is often called ' . . . . Magnificent Mile'.

f) In . . . . United States of America . . . . education is compulsory. Thus children have to go to . . . . school between the age of 6 to the age of 14 or 16.

g) As both . . . . school and . . . . church are far away from his parents' farm in Iowa, Jack Miller goes to . . . . school by . . . . bus during . . . . week and on . . . . Sunday(s) the whole family goes to . . . . church by . . . . car.

Make sentences with verb – object + infinitive with *to* 2

Nothing but good advice?

James Jennings from Boston, Massachusetts wants to spend a few weeks with some friends in El Paso, a Texan city near the Mexican border. Before he leaves his family and friends have good advice for him.

Write down what they say to him. Use verb - object + infinitive with to and the following verbs: **advise - ask - expect - remind - tell - want - warn - wish.**

a) his mother: Mexican food tastes strange. Don't eat too many tacos and burritos!

b) his father: And don't waste all your money on drinks and cigarettes! You could buy a nice Mexican souvenir instead.

c) his friend Luke: Take your sunglasses and your *Nirvana* T-shirt with you. You look cool with them.

d) his sister Trisha: You should visit your friends in Florida. It's a lot nicer there.

e) his brother Bob: I think you should take as many pictures as possible. We could have a great time with them when you are back.

f) his friend Toby: Don't forget to buy a bottle of real tequila for my parents. And visit my pen-friend Nick - he is waiting for you.

Fill in the proper nouns. Mind the irregular plurals. 3

Japanese • man • oxen • deer • child • German • fish • mouse • Swiss • trout • people • photo • oxen • potato • wife • Chinese • buffalo • man • salmon

a) . . . . often think that their . . . . should only do their housework and look after the . . . .

b) The first settlers in America hunted . . . . in the forests and . . . . in the prairies. They also caught . . . . like . . . . and . . . . in the rivers. Later on they plowed (BE: ploughed) the fields with their . . . . and grew corn and . . . .

c) John Steinbeck's famous play-novelette is called "Of . . . . and . . . . ". (*Von Mäusen und Menschen*)

d) from all over the world, ... and . . . . , ... and a lot of . . . . visit Pennsylvania Dutch Country every year where they take . . . . of the carriages and plows (BE: ploughs) drawn by horses and . . . .

4 Complete the conditional sentences (mixed types) with the correct form of the given verb.

a) If the police . . . . (to arrive) earlier, the thief would not have escaped.

b) Mr Miller . . . . (to buy) the sports car if he has enough money.

c) If Steve listened to his teachers, he . . . . (to learn) something.

d) You . . . . (to like) this CD a lot, if you love techno music.

e) Unless Tony . . . . (to bring) the book to the library tomorrow, he will have to pay a fine (Strafe).

f) If you wished to see some of van Gogh's paintings, I . . . . (to send) you some tickets for the New York Museum of Modern Art.

g) You would not have fallen down the stairs if you . . . . (to watch) your step.

h) If the price of gas (BE: petrol) . . . . (to go up), people will have to pay more at the gas station (BE: petrol station).

i) If the Chicago Bulls hadn't played so well, I . . . . (to leave) the stadium earlier.

j) Our picnic at Lake Superior would have been a great success if it . . . . (not to rain).

5 Combine the two sentences by means of a conjunction.

Use one of the following conjunctions and think of adapting the tenses if necessary. There might be more than one possibility.

when • after • whenever • although • as soon as • as • since • because

a) Frederick Olson dared to leave his native country Sweden.
He did not know whether he would be able to make a living in America.

b) He bought a piece of land in South Dakota where he could grow wheat.
Then he built a small farmhouse.

c) He succeeded in making some profit.
Only then did he make his wife and his three children move to America.

d) His son and his two daughters had problems at school.
They did not speak English at all.

e) They all finished high school successfully.
Then they went into college.

f) They got married.
At that time they all had good jobs and fairly high incomes.

g) People will often speak about the American Dream.
Then Frederick Olson tells them how hard this dream is to be fulfilled.

The newscaster - Use reported speech. 6

London

The State Opening of Parliament took place yesterday. At 11 o'clock the Queen drove from Buckingham Palace to Westminster. Thousands of people, many of them tourists, were standing along the Mall. An elderly lady from Ystalyfera, South Wales, said to our reporter: „I already came to London yesterday. I've never seen such a colourful (AE: colorful) event in my life."

Washington, D.C.

„Mr Congressman, what measures is your party going to take in order to cope with unemployment in our country?", our reporter asked several Republicans on the steps to the Capitol.
„We will have to improve the educational standards of our schools, especially in socially underprivileged urban areas," most of them answered.

Tomorrow's weather

Heavy thunderstorms have caused serious damage in some parts of Oregon. Today it is rainy and cloudy, but, hopefully, we'll have some sunny periods as well. The temperature will be around 89 degrees. (89° Fahrenheit = 31.6° Celsius)

Frederick K. Malone from Newport, Oregon, could not listen to the news on TV. His wife Jane told him later what the newscaster had said.

The newscaster said that...

7 Fill in the blanks if necessary.

a) . . . . man has always considered a high rise building a sign of . . . . progress, but if James Otis . . . . not invented the first passenger elevator (BE: lift) in 1857, ... people in America would not have . . . . any skyscrapers at all.

b) Many . . . . skyscraper can be looked at as . . . . melting pot, ... the . . . . and grand . . . . of former immigrants (Englishmen, ... , ... , ... , ... , etc.) live together peacefully.

c) They all want the American Dream . . . . true.

d) In his famous speech of 1963 Martin . . . . King described this hope for black . . . . when he said that he . . . . a dream that his four little children . . . . one day live in a nation . . . . they . . . . not. . . . . judged by the . . . . of their skin . . . . by the content of their character.

3. Test

1 Infinitive with to or infinitive without to?

Insert *to* where necessary.

a) Robert used . . . . smoke twenty cigars a day but then the doctor advised him . . . . stop and his wife Maud made him . . . . throw the rest of his cigars away.

b) Maud expects her husband . . . . carry her bags from the supermarket and . . . . open the door for her whenever she enters or leaves a room. On the other hand she lets him . . . . go to his golf club as often as he wants . . . .

c) Robert can . . . . play the piano quite well. When he was fourteen he wanted . . . . become a musician but his father persuaded him . . . . go to university instead and . . . . study economics there.

d) Robert was the only child of his family . . . . get a university degree. He often heard his father . . . . tell his friends in the pub how proud he was of him.

Fill in the correct tenses. 2

a) In 1927 Carles Lindbergh . . . . (to fly) non-stop from New York to Paris in his plane the *Spirit of St Louis*.

b) Abraham Lincoln . . . . (to be) a lawyer before he . . . . (to become) President in 1861. In 1863 he . . . . (to declare) that the slaves . . . . (to be freed) soon.

c) Look at this painting. The artist . . . . just . . . . (to finish) it. Its colors (BE: colours) . . . . (to be) still wet.

d) The Indians . . . . (to live) on the American continent for centuries (Jahrhunderte) before Columbus . . . . (to discover) the New World in 1492.

Translate.

e) Ich werde dir heute Abend einen Brief schreiben. Dann wirst du ihn übermorgen bekommen.

f) Mein Vater liest seit Stunden Zeitung.

Make some conditional sentences (type 3). 3

When it is too late, people often think „If only I had ...“ or „If only I hadn’t...“.
Make *conditional sentences* (type 3) to say what you think in these situations.

Example:

You are on a long bicycle tour. It is hot and your bottle of lemonade is at home ...
If only I’d (I had) remembered to bring some lemonade.
If only I hadn’t picked a sweater (BE: jumper) to wear.
If only I had decided to stay at home.

a) Your friend invites you to the cinema. You have to pay for the tickets and the film is really boring ...

b) You take your friend’s bike, fall off, break your arm and damage the bike ...

c) The English teacher surprises you with a little test. You do really badly in it...

d) Your favorite football team loses another match. You have paid a lot of money to be in the stadium ...

4 Complete the following sentences.

a) If I had been ill, I . . . . (to go) to the . . . .

b) If the . . . . (to give) me a prescription, I would have taken it to the . . . .

c) If Jolene is hungry, she . . . . (to buy) some bread at the . . . . and some sausages at the . . . .

d) If Dennis and Jackie were in America in November, they . . . . (to enjoy) the Thanksgiving dinner with turkey, sweet potatoes and pumpkin (Kürbis) pie at their . . . . (grandparents) in Great Falls, Montana.

Translate.

e) Die Pullover meiner Kinder sind immer schmutzig.

f) Boise, die Hauptstadt von Idaho, wurde von französischen Siedlern gegründet.

g) Bevor der Pilot startet, ruft er einen seiner Freunde in Carson City, Nevada, an, um den heutigen Wetterbericht zu bekommen.

5 Headlines from American or English Newspapers

Is it BE or AE? Put a cross in the right column.

	AE	BE
a) Fire during theater performance - Building severely damaged.	☐	☐
b) Lorry driver caused accident - Police took driving licence.	☐	☐
c) Rent increase for flats in multi-storey buildings - Tenants worried.	☐	☐
d) Fifteen people caught in elevator - Rescued by fire-department after four hours.	☐	☐
e) Bomb alert in railway and underground station - Traffic jam in city centre.	☐	☐
f) Theft in hotel room - Traveler's checks and jeweler's sample case (Musterkoffer) stolen.	☐	☐
g) Serious offence - Europe's favourite pop star wrongly accused of stealing song.	☐	☐

4 Complete the text. Use the words in brackets.

) Tom Trevor is his . . . . (father's / fathers') youngest son. His parents expect him . . . . (to / —) become a computer specialist or famous scientist, so they make him . . . . (to / —) study hard for his high school exams.

b) If Tom had worked harder for his subjects, his . . . . (parent's / parents') friend Georgios Papandreo . . . . (to invite) him to Greece.

c) Bad luck for Tom. Instead of relaxing in the Mediterranean, he . . . . (had / will have to) study geometry and algebra with Teresa, a friend of his . . . . (sister's / sister).

d) So far Tom . . . . (finished / has finished) more than ten pages in his exercise book. This afternoon he . . . . (has worked / worked / has been working) for more than three hours now.

e) . . . . Tom solved the math problems . . . . but then he . . . . had to concentrate . . . . to find the correct answers, (fill in: often / in the beginning / hard / easily).

f) He would have continued with his work, if the telephone . . . . (not to ring). Leo Smith, a friend of . . . . (him / his) wanted Tom . . . . (to / —) show him how . . . . (to /—) load a new computer program.

g) So Tom went over to the . . . . (Smith's / Smiths') house after he . . . . (has been saying / said / had said) good-bye to Teresa and his parents.

4. Test

Find definitions and paraphrases. 1

Match the words from list 1 with the definitions in list 2.

1. to describe	a) to start something
2. to reach	b) to find the correct result
3. to appear	c) to get
4. to become	d) to be afraid of
5. to explore	e) to come out and be seen
6. to found	f) to look at someone long and hard
7. to receive	g) to look around and discover new things
8. to calculate	h) to say what something is like
9. to fear	i) to get to a place
10. to stare	j) to turn into something

Explain the words in bold print.

a) Every morning at 9 o'clock Mr Jones **enters** his office.
b) The Indians helped the Pilgrims **to survive** the winter with corn and meat.
c) The Smiths own a big house and three cars. They are quite **wealthy**.
d) The math **instructor** made Tony do all the exercises again.
e) Jeremy is a **smart** kid. He always gets good grades at school.
f) Usually the **climate** in the Mojave Desert is very dry and very hot.

2 Test your knowledge: conditional sentences (mixed types).

What kind of sentence is it: A - statement; B - negated; C - question; and what type of conditional sentence (1, 2, 3)?

a) If Tony . . . . (to go) on vacation (BE: holiday), he will need some money.

b) What would you do if your bike . . . . (to steal)?

c) If you . . . . (to set) the alarm clock, you wouldn't have been late.

d) John will buy a computer if he . . . . (to save) enough money.

e) Will you buy the new CD if it . . . . (to be) still in the shop?

f) If Jane . . . . (to hurry), she would have caught the train.

g) If Jack . . . . (to come) to the party earlier, he would have met his girlfriend.

h) Tim . . . . (to write) to Helen if he knew her address.

i) The bees . . . . (not to attack) the bear if it hadn't tried to take the honey.

3 Defining words

1) Young . . . . go to kindergartens.

2) French fries are made from . . . .

3) Male human beings (3 letters).

4) Spoons, forks, and . . . . are called cutlery (Besteck).

5) Hens, ducks, and . . . . live on the farm.

6) Impolite, even offensive word for 'black people'.

7) When the cat's away, the . . . . will play.

Make sentences. Use infinitives without *to*. 4

Complete the following sentences with **make** or **let** and one of the following verbs:

eat • go to a disco • go to bed • look after • play • read • ride • say good night • say yes • stay out • stay up • take • wash • watch

a) Last Wednesday Michelle's parents . . . . her . . . . her little sister Louise.

b) Michelle's mother said: „Don't . . . . her . . . . too long. You should Louise . . . . around 8.30."

c) After Michelle's parents had left the house. Michelle . . . . Louise with her Barbie doll.

d) Louise . . . . Barbie . . . . on a pony and then she . . . . her . . . . a bath.

e) After playing for more than an hour, Michelle . . . . Louise . . . . some pizza for dinner. Then she . . . . her . . . . TV.

f) Little Louise got tired and so Michelle didn't . . . . her . . . . any comic books.

g) Before Michelle took Louise to bed, she . . . . her . . . . her face and brush her teeth. Then she . . . . her . . . . to all her teddies.

h) Afterwards Michelle thought: „Usually Mom and Dad don't . . . . me . . . . on Sunday. This weekend it could be different. They won't . . . . me . . . . all night, but Mom could . . . . Dad . . . . to an evening at the *Techno Dreams*. That would be great."

Spot the mistakes and write a correct version of the sentences. 5

a) The *Wall Street Journal* daily publishes the most actual news about the economical situation in America and the world.

b) Being very self-conscious the candidate was quiet sure that he would win the elections.

c) The chairman took place and opened the debate on the critics of the financial policy which had been published in some newspapers.

d) The white-collar criminals were being searched by the policy all over the country.

e) As she is a very sensible girl, she will always cry whenever she reads the moving story of *The Legend of Sleepy Hollow* by Washington Irving.

6 The following text is stylistically bad and boring. Try to improve its style. Use conjunctions and put two or more sentences together.

Abe Rosenberg is a Jewish scientist.

Abe Rosenberg is a college professor at Chicago University.

He has been living in Illinois for many years.

His parents came to America as immigrants in 1973.

He owns a large, but old house in Oak Park.

He could buy a new and more modern and comfortable house.

He loves his neighborhood.

Many of his colleagues from the university live there, too.

3 Translate.

a) Millionen von Einwanderern, Engländer, Franzosen, Italiener, Deutsche, Schweizer, Chinesen und viele andere kamen im 19. und 20. Jahrhundert nach Amerika.

b) Die amerikanische Regierung ließ (zulassen) Männer, Frauen und Kinder einwandern, solange das Land Menschen und vor allem Arbeitskräfte (manpower) brauchte.

c) Heute lässt (veranlassen) die Polizei illegale Einwanderer in ihr Heimatland zurückreisen.

d) Wenn der Süden den Amerikanischen Bürgerkrieg gewonnen hätte, wären die Sklaven wahrscheinlich nicht so früh befreit worden.

e) Obwohl Afro-Amerikaner und Indianer gleichberechtigte Bürger sind, ist ihre wirtschaftliche Lage tatsächlich seit jeher ein aktuelles Problem.

Lernbereich
GRAMMATIK (S. 152-251)

1 Wem / Wozu gehört was?

a) President Clinton's wife is called Hillary Rodham, **b)** America's biggest city is New York, **c)** The children's toys are spread all over the floor in the kindergarten, **d)** John F. Kennedy's most famous saying was, "Ich bin ein Berliner." **e)** The elevator of the skyscraper is out of order, **f)** Baron von Steuben's name is still remembered by most Americans, **g)** The park of the White House cannot be visited by the public, **h)** The women's right to vote did not yet exist in the 19th century, **i)** People do not like the dog's biscuits. **j)** The British army was defeated by George Washington's soldiers.

2 Gebrauche den s-Genitiv.

a) I have (got) a toothache and must go to the dentist's (auch: dentist), **b)** I want to buy a pound of sausages at the butcher's, **c)** My friend is one of the Mayor's sons, **d)** I'm spending my vacation at my aunt's and my uncle's, **e)** I'm going to buy some bread at the baker's, **f)** Dr Braine is a brother of my French teacher's, **g)** Susan is a granddaughter of the Smiths' and (is) one of their neighbors (a neighbor of theirs).

3 Verwende ein Possessivpronomen an Stelle des s-Genitivs.

a) This mobile home belongs to a friend of theirs, **b)** You have just met a daughter of theirs, **c)** You have just met a daughter of his. **d)** You have just met a daughter of hers.

4 Welches Wort passt nicht in die Reihe?

Lösungswort: a b s t r a c t

5 Wähle den richtigen Lösungsbuchstaben.

Lösung: p e o p l e + m a n

6 Füge den bestimmten Artikel ein, wenn nötig.

a) — — **b)** — **c)** The **d)** — **e)** — **f)** the **g)** — **h)** — **i)** the **j)** — —

7 Entscheide, ob der bestimmte Artikel nötig ist oder nicht.

a) — — — — the **b)** — **c)** — the **d)** The the — — — **e)** — **f)** — — — — — — the — **g)** the **h)** — — the

8 Setze, wenn nötig, den bestimmten Artikel ein.

on — education; **College Lecturer:** — The —; **Father:** — The, the; **Schoolteacher:** — — the, the; **College Lecturer:** the — The, — the; **Mother:** — the —; **Schoolteacher:** — —

9 Übersetze die folgenden Sätze. Achte auf den Gebrauch des bestimmten Artikels.

a) Die meisten Leute vertragen es nicht, von anderen kritisiert zu werden, **b)** Die Menschen werden über die Auswirkungen der Weg werf mental ität nachdenken müssen, **c)** Mr Blake wird der Mann sein, der die wirtschaftliche Lage unserer Firma verbessern kann. **d)** Viele Leute in diesem Industriegebiet sind arbeitslos; die Hälfte von ihnen wird nie wieder einen Arbeitsplatz bekommen, weil sie ohne Ausbildung oder einfach zu alt sind, **e)** Nach dem Unglück in dem Atomkraftwerk wurden die meisten Wissenschaftler zur Untersuchung ins Krankenhaus gebracht. Das am nächsten gelegene Krankenhaus konnte bald keine Patienten mehr aufnehmen. **f)** Der Unterricht beginnt früher als der Gottesdienst, aber die Kirche ist weiter entfernt als die Schule. Deshalb müssen wir selbst am Sonntag früh aufstehen.

10 Der unbestimmte Artikel - ordne die Wörter in die richtige Spalte ein.
a / ǝ /: tepee, rear light, university degree, T-shirt, Yankee, vacation, unicorn, unit, warehouse; an / an /: OPEC agreement, unhappy girl, unforgettable performance, emergency, uncomfortable seat, earthquake, unsinkable ship, interstate highway, oven, unpleasant event, essential element

11 Füge den unbestimmten Artikel, wenn nötig, in die Lücken ein.
a) an, an, a — **b)** — an, a, a — a **c)** a, a — a **d)** a, a — a, a, a, a, a, a, a **e)** a, a, a, an, a **f)** I'm sorry, I don't speak English. My name is Günther Bannwarth. I'm a psychologist and president of the German Umweltschutzverein (Association for the Protection of the Environment). I'm a Catholic and as a liberal I am a member of the F.D.P.. My wife is English. As a doctor she is the environmental health officer of Duisburg.

12 Sonderangebote — der unbestimmte Artikel bei Maß- und Zeitangaben.
a, $ 2.45 a pound, $ 2.10 a piece, $ 11.30 a basket, $ 18.45 a box, $ 25.40 a bottle, $ 0.65 a can, $ 12.85 a bunch, $ 935.00 a person a week

13 Durcheinandergewürfelte Wörter - bilde Sätze mit der richtigen Wortstellung.
a) Jack O'Brien built his new farmhouse within half a year, **b)** Americans own two cars and three TV sets on an average, **c)** Moving to the West was quite an adventure for many a settler, **d)** As he was in a hurry Terry had to sell his car at a loss, **e)** However expensive a dress is / may be my wife will buy it. **f)** First Barbara and Howard went for a ride, after that they went for a swim, and finally they had a drink near the pool.

14 Übersetze die folgenden Sätze.
a) That was too awful an accident. I can't forget it. (That was too awful an accident for me as to forget it.) **b)** Marilyn Monroe was quite a talented actress, **c)** "I have (got) a stomachache" said Lewis in a low voice, **d)** This is such an exciting story. Newspaper and TV are already interested in it / have already taken an interest in it.

15 Wer ist das? Füge, wenn nötig, den bestimmten oder unbestimmten Artikel in die Lücken ein.
the – a, an, a – – a, a, a – the – the, the, the, an, an, an; Lösung: Mark Twain

16 Setze das passende Pronomen ein.
a) Its ... my **b)** his, His, his, she, he, our, yours **c)** her d) Her, their, their, my **e)** yours, mine **f)** you, your **g)** mine, his, its **h)** Their **i)** They, my, mine **j)** Your, you, my, their **k)** his, me, my, our **l)** their, mine **m)** yours, theirs **n)** mine, hers, mine, his

17 Achte auf das Reflexivpronomen. Übersetze.
1. Ich kann mich (selbst) im Spiegel sehen. **2.** Clare kennt Chicago so gut, weil sie schon selbst dort war. **3.** Der Hund kratzte sich (gerade) hinter dem Ohr. **4.** Seid ihr immer noch hungrig, Jungs? Auf dem Tisch sind belegte Brötchen. Bedient euch (selbst)!

5. Die Kinder bastelten die Modellflugzeuge selbst. **6.** Können wir uns in der Küche nützlich machen? **7.** Paul, du solltest keinen Brief an Mary schreiben. Du solltest selbst mit ihr reden. **8.** Erinnern Sie sich / Erinnerst du dich an mich? Wir trafen uns letzten Sommer in Dallas. **9.** Wayne blieb gestern im Bett, weil er sich nicht wohlfühlte. **10.** Sally fragte sich, wie viel Geld sie letzte Woche ausgegeben hatte.

18 Mache noch eine Übersetzungsübung!

a) Last week Dave and Luke joined the American Football club at their high school. **b)** They like American Football itself very much, but it is also important to them to play for their high school team, **c)** First they introduce themselves to the coach and the team. **d)** Luke shows an old football helmet which his father used many years ago. **e)** Dave dresses himself very carefully in his padded clothes, **f)** Both want to protect themselves against injuries – American Football can be very dangerous, **g)** Often Luke trains alone and he wonders when he will be on the team, **h)** Dave and Luke feel very happy in the club. They can't imagine living / life without American Football.

19 Lerne einige englische Sprichwörter kennen.

1 – c); 2 – d); 3 – a); 4 – e); 5 – b) Lösungswort: New Orleans

20 Ein Berg von Adverbien

adverbials/adverbs of definite time: **last month**, in the afternoon, next Friday, tomorrow
adverbials/adverbs of place: at school, **outside**, above, there
adverbs of degree: completely, partly, almost, **quite**
adverbs of indefinite time: late, **early**, soon, long ago
adverbs of manner: politely, **badly**, well, wonderfully
adverbs of frequency: **often**, weekly, frequently, scarcely

21 Adjektiv oder Adverb?

a) short **b)** busy, quickly, delicious **c)** slowly, carefully **d)** different, easily, different **e)** helplessly (auch *helpless* möglich), enormous, angrily, busily, quickly **f)** soft, helpless **g)** quietly, shortly **h)** endless, incredibly slowly, patiently, terribly loudly, unhappily

22 Lerne mehr über Adverbien.

a) politely **b)** fanatically **c)** monthly **d)** extremely **e)** horribly **f)** comfortably **g)** economically **h)** truly **i)** early **j)** fully **k)** fast **l)** heavily **m)** completely **n)** daily **o)** sensibly **p)** exclusively **q)** in a friendly way **r)** wholly

23 Übersetze.

a) When Betty arrived at the birthday party she felt nervous at first, **b)** She opened the door carefully and looked around quickly, **c)** All her friends were there and looked happy, **d)** Betty said hello to Chris and Helen. The girls answered politely, **e)** The party soon became very lively. Betty danced with Peter, then with Harry, **f)** Harry said: "You dance perfectly. I'll bring / get a glass of lemonade and a piece of pizza for you quickly, the pizza is / tastes fantastic."

24 Komparativ und Superlativ von Adverbien

a) **rapidly** – more rapidly – most rapidly **b)** easily – more easily – **most easily** **c)** badly – **worse** – worst **d)** heavily – **more heavily** – most heavily **e)** early – **earlier** – earliest **f)** well – better – **best**

25 Finde und verbessere die Fehler!
a) quickly **b)** less **c)** as badly as **d)** worst **e)** more aggressively

26 Setze die Adverbien an der richtigen Stelle ein.
a) She sat down carefully and started the engine quickly, **b)** The engine ran smoothly and Diana was extremely pleased with herself, **c)** How wonderfully quickly the car drove down the street! **d)** "Don't drive too fast, Miss Wilson", the driving instructor's soft voice warned politely. **e)** (Immediately) Diana (immediately) reduced the speed of the car (immediately).

27 Adverbien der Zeit und des Ortes - finde die richtige Wortstellung.
a) 2 – 1 – 4 – 3 **b)** 4 – 1 - 2- 3 **c)** 1 – 4 – 2 – 3 **d)** 1 – 4 – 3 – 2 – 5 **e)** 3 – 2 – 4 –1 – 5 **f)** 2 – 1 – 3 – 4 **g)** 1 – 4 – 2 – 3 **h)** 5 – 1 – 2 – 3 – 4 – 6

28 Adverbien der Häufigkeit und des Grades.
a) The team didn't play badly last summer, **b)** The team practiced extremely hard on the playing field during the summer, **c)** Luke ran incredibly fast in his first match for the team, **d)** In the first quarter he often could get through the defense quickly, **e)** Luke easily scored two touchdowns in the beginning. **f)** Surprisingly Dave didn't play successfully, **g)** After the match he left the field rather slowly because he was disappointed.

29 Und zum Schluss - mach' dich bereit für eine Übersetzungsübung.
a) Jacqueline completely forgot to buy bread, cheese and wine, **b)** After his appointment at the dentist's Raymond could hardly talk. **c)** I always go to church on Sundays. **d)** Thomas sometimes smokes a cigar at parties, **e)** I clean my apartment once a week or at least three times a / every month, **f)** The doctor advised Mr Jennings to take the medicine four times a / every day. **g)** The exercise is nearly finished, **h)** You are quite an expert in using adverbs now.

30 Wähle die richtige Zeitform.
haven't seen, went, did, did you go, had, has been, has been working, Did ... fly, didn't, went, see, did ... take, was, wasn't, wasn't, were flying, were serving (served), were showing (showed), passed, Did ... stay, is coming

31 Übersetze die folgenden Sätze.
a) Chicago is one of the biggest cities in the USA. **b)** Paul Bradley has been working as a policeman in New York for five years, **c)** In 1492 Columbus discovered America, **d)** Mrs Elliot has missed her train. The next train will leave tonight at 8.13. That's why she is going to take a taxi, **e)** Mrs Batson wohnt schon seit zwanzig Jahren in Seattle. Jetzt will (wird) sie nach Kalifornien (um-)ziehen, wo es wärmer sein wird, **f)** Herr Hillerman will (beabsichtigt), ein neues Auto (zu) kaufen. Er hat sein altes Auto seit 1992. Damals kaufte er es gebraucht von seinem Nachbarn.

32 Füge die Verben in der richtigen Zeitform in die Lücken des Dialogs ein.
didn't, has been living, went, was, married, came, stayed, have not been, hope, 'll come, was doing, were showing, Did ... see, are, went, had, are visited, had not been, Did ... go, did, spent, was, Is, has not had, have ... been, haven't, think, will

33 Verwende das *past perfect* und verbinde die Sätze.

After he had bought a map of New York, Harry Biggs walked up Broadway. After he had walked up Broadway, he visited the Rockefeller Center. When he had visited the Rockefeller Center, he looked around Central Park. After he had looked around Central Park, he had lunch at a fast food restaurant. As soon as he had had lunch at a fast food restaurant, he went up the Empire State Building by elevator. After he had gone up the Empire State Building by elevator, he took a lot of photos. After he had taken a lot of photos, he went on a boat trip on the East River. After he had gone on a boat trip on the East River, he visited the Statue of Liberty. When he had visited the Statue of Liberty, he walked around Chinatown. After he had walked around Chinatown, he had dinner in Little Italy.

34 Bilde Sätze und verwende dabei das *present perfect progressive* und *for / since.*

A secretary had been typing letters for two hours, ... A doctor had been examining patients since 10.00, ... A detective had been questioning a suspicious person since 9.30,... A window cleaner had been cleaning windows for an hour and a half,... A lawyer had been dictating letters since 9.00, ... A businessman had been sitting in front of the computer for an hour, ... A musician had been rehearsing songs since 9.30, ... A journalist had been writing reports for three hours, ... A housewife had been doing the laundry for two and a half hours, ... A waitress had been serving meals since 6.00, ...

35 Vergleiche den Gebrauch des Infinitivs im Englischen und im Deutschen.

Bill: Was für ein Morgen! Die meisten meiner Mathematikaufgaben waren falsch und der Lehrer sagte mir, dass ich sie noch einmal machen muss/müsse.

Craig: Musst du nach der Schule an den Aufgaben arbeiten?

Bill: Ja, und es gibt niemanden, der mir dabei hilft.

Craig: Das bedeutet, dass du nicht mit mir Tennis spielen kannst, richtig?

Bill: Leider nicht. Die Hausaufgaben kommen zuerst dran - und Vater hat mir aufgetragen, das Auto zu waschen und das Gras im Garten zu mähen. Pech gehabt. Wo ist eigentlich John? Ich möchte meine Comic-Hefte zurückhaben. Hast du ihn gestern getroffen?

Craig: Nein, hab' ich nicht. Aber ich habe ihn heute gesehen. Er hatte den Bus verpasst und bat seine Mutter, ihn zur Schule zu fahren. Ich sah ihn im Auto seiner Mutter ankommen. Er hatte es eilig und vergaß deshalb, mir deine Comic-Hefte zu geben.

Bill: John scheint ziemlich viele Dinge zu vergessen. Vor zwei Tagen wollte er Baseball mit uns spielen. Aber er vergaß seinen Baseballschläger mitzubringen und konnte deshalb nicht mitspielen. Sein Fehler.

Craig: Richtig. Hast du die Schulglocke gehört? Es ist Zeit, in unser Klassenzimmer zu gehen. Chemie - es ist ja interessant, die ganzen Experimente zu sehen, aber bitte mich ja nicht, sie zu erklären. Manchmal verstehe ich wirklich kein einziges Wort

36 Betrachte die Verben, denen ein Infinitiv mit to folgt.

a) decided to – hoped to **b)** offered to– consented to **c)** decied to – promised to **d)** managed to – seemed to **e)** refused to – wanted to **f)** hesitated to – tried to **g)** agreed to **h)** prepared to

37 Übersetze.

① Sie bat ihn, die Tür zu schließen.
② Kate wollte, dass ihre Schwester etwas Brot kaufte.
③ Der Polizeibeamte warnte die Kinder, nicht die Straße zu überqueren.
④ Mr Smith erwartet, dass sein Sohn Arzt wird.
⑤ Helens Eltern erlaubten ihr, auf die Party zu gehen.

38 Bilde Sätze.

a) Tom reminded me to buy some lemonade, **b)** Christine (had) wanted it to be a surprise, **c)** He will ask / asked Louise to marry him. **d)** Did you allow your son to go there? **e)** They invited the Parkers to stay with them, **f)** The radio warned the drivers to drive slowly, **g)** Did you expect the Chicago Bulls to win?

39 Übersetze die folgenden Sätze.

Die Puritaner in Massachusetts

a) Als die Puritaner beschlossen England zu verlassen, wählten sie Virginia als ihre neue Heimat aus. **b)** Sie erwarteten, dass die Reise auf der Mayflower lang und rauh sein werde. **c)** Ein Sturm trieb die Mayflower weit nach Norden, weg von Virginia. Der Kapitän bot den Puritanern an, sie wieder in den Süden hinunterzubringen, **d)** Die Puritaner befahlen dem Kapitän, an die Küste zu segeln und baten ihn, das Schiff verlassen zu dürfen, **e)** Die Puritaner trafen bald Indianer, die ihnen erlaubten, sich auf ihrem Land niederzulassen, **f)** Die Indianer halfen den Puritanern, den ersten harten Winter in Amerika zu überleben, **g)** Im Frühling rieten die Indianer den Puritanern, Mais anzubauen und sie erlaubten ihnen, mit ihnen zu jagen, **h)** Im Herbst hatten die Puritaner eine gute Ernte. Sie dankten Gott und luden die Indianer ein, Erntedankfest mit ihnen zu feiern.
40 Verbinde die Satzteile und übersetze.

40 Verbinde die Satzteile und übersetze.

a) We missed the plane to Washington and there was no other flight for us to arrive on time.
Wir verpassten das Flugzeug nach Washington und es gab für uns keinen anderen Flug, mit dem wir rechtzeitig angekommen wären.

b) It is important for young people to get a good education.
Es ist für junge Menschen wichtig, eine gute Erziehung/Ausbildung zu erhalten.

c) 5.30 in the morning is too early for me to get up.
Halb sechs Uhr morgens ist für mich zu früh, um aufzustehen.

d) They wanted to help the old man, but he talked too quickly for them to understand.
Sie wollten dem alten Mann helfen, aber er redete zu schnell, sodass sie ihn nicht verstehen konnten.

e) In many towns in America there is no place for teenagers to meet.
In vielen Städten Amerikas gibt es keine Einrichtung, in der sich Jugendliche treffen können.

f) Leave the door of the sitting-room open for us to hear the doorbell.
Lass' / Lasst die Wohnzimmertür offen, damit wir die Türglocke hören können.

g) In Disneyland there are so many things for the visitors to see.
In Disneyland gibt es für die Besucher so viele Dinge zu sehen.

Lösungswort: Rocky Mountains

41 Bilde Sätze. Benutze den Infinitiv mit to und Fragewörter.

a) She does not to know where to find a taxi at the airport, **b)** In her new apartment she does not understand how to switch on the dishwasher, **c)** Later a friendly neighbor shows her how to use the ticket machine for bus tickets, **d)** At the bank Justina asks when to pick up the new credit card, **e)** A man in the street tells her where to find a good supermarket, **f)** In the supermarket Justina decides what to buy for the next few days. **g)** In the evening she cannot decide whether to cook some spaghetti or some soup, **h)** For the next day she plans to find out when best to call her relatives in Karlsruhe.

42 Vervollständige die Sätze.

a) where to find **b)** how to order **c)** where to rent **d)** when to pay **e)** how to switch off **f)** which bus to take **g)** what to wear

43 Vervollständige die Sätze. Benutze den Infinitiv mit to nach Superlativen und Ordnungszahlen.

a) to become **b)** to be found **c)** to be launched **d)** to live **e)** to be eaten

44 Der Infinitiv mit to in Nebensätzen. Bilde Sätze.

a) The shop in 159 Willbury Road is the place to go/you must go to. **b)** The film to see/you should see this week is the latest with Arnold Schwarzenegger, **c)** Cape Cod is a nice place to spend/where you can spend a few days, **d)** *O'Henry's Cocktail Bar* is the place to be/where you must be. **e)** Mr Porter next door is the man to help/who can help. **f)** My number is the number to call/you should call.

45 Der Infinitiv mit *feel, hear, see, notice, watch.* Verbinde die Sätze.

Lösungswort: Colorado

46 Der Infinitiv ohne *to* nach *can, must, may.*

a) Darf ich bitte deinen Füller benutzen? **b)** Sicher. Du kannst ihn eine Weile haben, aber du darfst ihn nicht verlieren. Übrigens – hast du nicht gestern Kevins Füller genommen? **c)** Ja, das hab' ich. Und ich muss dir sagen, dass ich ihn nirgends finden kann. Aber – das brauchst du Kevin nicht zu erzählen, O.K.? **d)** Ich werde ihn das nicht erfahren lassen, aber du solltest besser den Füller suchen, **e)** Ich habe genug davon, nach diesem dummen Ding zu suchen. Ich würde ihm lieber einen neuen Füller kaufen. **f)** Ich würde eher noch einige Tage warten. Der Füller kann ja irgendwo wieder auftauchen.

47 Übersetze das Gespräch.

a) Doing homework! I had rather play football outside. May I have another glass of lemonade? **b)** Sure. But you shouldn't drink too much. You could get sick. **c)** You needn't worry. Can you give me your exercise book? **d)** If I were / was you I'd sooner do the exercises on my own. **e)** Math is always very difficult. I can't understand a lot of things. **f)** You mustn't give up so quickly, **g)** I hate algebra exercises. I'd sooner work in the garden for the whole afternoon. Are we allowed to use / May we use pocket calculators for the class test? **h)** No, of course not! That's why you had better concentrate on your exercises now.

48 Der Infinitiv ohne to nach make und let.

Commercials, commercials!

a) *Sharkies* make you jump higher than Michael Jordan, **b)** *Barko-Barko* makes your dog run faster than the cats in the neighborhood, **c)** *Supergas* makes your car go better. **d)** *Hairy Harry* makes your hair grow like weeds.

Daniel's dreary day!

e) The bus lets Daniel wait for half an hour in the rain, **f)** Geoffrey doesn't let Daniel copy the math (BE: maths) homework, **g)** Daniel's mother doesn't let him practice the drums in the afternoon, **h)** Later Shirley makes Daniel carry all the heavy shopping bags, **i)** The man at the entrance to the club doesn't let Daniel and Shirley enter the *Techno Factory.*

49 Markiere die Passivformen und schreibe sie heraus.

was broken – were taken away – were seen – was stained – has been found – have not been arrested

50 Benutze das Passiv. Achte auf die richtige Zeitform.

The first day at work

a) are paid **b)** may be bought **c)** are sold **d)** is being designed

What people don't like

a) being asked **b)** being invited **c)** being polluted **d)** being hurt **e)** being left **f)** being bitten

At the garage

a) The brakes and the lights were checked thoroughly and the air and oil filters were replaced, **b)** All the windows were cleaned and the air pressure of the tires was increased. **c)** The spark plugs were changed and the hubcaps and bumpers were polished. **d)** Some rust was removed and some parts were painted.

Cowboys

a) The cows were being branded, **b)** Whiskey is being drunk at the saloon, **c)** Folk songs are being sung at the camp fire, **d)** Ham and beans are being eaten for breakfast.

An old ghost town

a) The door of the saloon has been stolen, **b)** The windows of several houses have been broken by storms, **c)** The wheels of the stage-coach have been damaged, **d)** The stable near the sheriff's office has been burned down and many houses have been pulled down.

New at UCLA

a) The debate about feminism will be held in about two weeks. **b)** New methods in education will be discussed at the Roosevelt Study Center, **c)** The discussion on agricultural problems will be started tomorrow, **d)** Political economy will be taught by Professor Rutherford-Keynes.

A new house

a) A new carpet will be put down in the bedroom, **b)** A new garage is going to be built. **c)** The telephone will be connected, **d)** The lights are going to be checked.

Mixed tenses
a) are ... kept **b)** was given **c)** may be called **d)** were taken **e)** would have been injured

51 Übersetze und benutze das Passiv.
a) My car was stolen yesterday, **b)** An Italian restaurant will be opened next week, **c)** My football club should be given a second chance, **d)** The new town hall can't be built.

52 by-agent: benutzen oder nicht benutzen ...?
a) My tennis racket had been stolen before I went / got back to the tennis court, **b)** The *Theory of Relativity* was discovered by Albert Einstein, **c)** Cake can be bought at the supermarket, **d)** The *Empire State Building* was built in 1931. **e)** The door of the gym was left open yesterday, **f)** The power of nuclear energy was dicovered by American scientists, **g)** A class test will be written on Wednesday, **h)** Tomorrow the books will be returned to the library by Bart and Lucy.

53 Bilde Passivsätze. Achte auf die Verben mit Präpositionen.
a) Pedro "Hammer" Alvarez had been knocked out by Jimmy "Fist" Murray in round three, **b)** The cinema was closed down yesterday, **c)** The fire is going to be put out quickly by the fire brigade, **d)** I was rung up in the middle of the night, **e)** The harvest is being brought in by the farmers now.

54 Welche Fragen und Antworten passen zusammen?
G-E, O-R, G-E, W-A, S-H, I-N, G-T, O-N (GEORGE WASHINGTON)

55 Frage nach den unterstrichenen Satzteilen.
a) What do Helen Broady and her friends read at school every morning? Where do Helen Broady and her friends read the notes every morning? When do Helen Broady and her friends read the notes at school? **b)** Who does the taxi driver take to the airport at five o'clock? Where does the taxi driver take the passengers at five o'clock? When does the taxi driver take the passengers to the airport? **c)** When did the Mayflower carry 102 colonists to Cape Cod? Who did the Mayflower carry to Cape Cod? How many colonists did the Mayflower carry to Cape Cod? Where did the Mayflower carry 102 colonists? Why did the Mayflower carry 102 colonists to Cape Cod? What did the colonists want to start in America? Where did the colonists want to start a new life?

56 Kennzeichne den Fragetyp.
A, A, A, B, B, A, B, C, C

57 Bilde die zugehörigen Fragen.
Do you use **CLEANFIX** regularly? Where do you use it? Does your husband use it? What about your children? Do they use **CLEANFIX**? Do you really allow your children to play with **CLEANFIX**? How often do you use **CLEANFIX** in the bathroom? Where do you normally buy it? Do you think it is too expensive?

58 Gebrauche die indirekte Rede.
Mr King says (that) he was born in 1918, it will be his eightieth birthday next week, his parents lived in Ohio, they had a small farm there and they were rather poor people, he had an elder brother and two younger sisters, his brother died some years ago, he had

(S. 220-225)

worked on his father's farm, his sisters are still alive, when they were young they moved to New Orleans and got married there, they have come here with their families for his birthday, when he was young life was hard, but quiet, there were not so many cars, ..., they had to get up early and help their parents ..., they walked to school, it was a very small school and the teacher was very strict, but they learnt (auch: learned) a lot, he became a carpenter, after he'd got married he moved to St. Louis, he opened his own business ... his family and he have been living here ever since, he wouldn't work as much as he did, he'd travel a lot, and he'd retire earlier to enjoy life more.

59 Wandle die folgenden Sätze in die indirekte Rede um. Beachte die Adverbien der Zeit.

a) Father said (that) the children had been working hard that day. **b)** The police officer said (that) the police had arrested the suspect two days before, **c)** The coach said (that) the team would certainly win the baseball match the following day. **d)** The engineer on the oil rig thought (that) the supply ship had come on Wednesday the week before and (that) it would be there again on Thursday the following week, **e)** The director announced (that) the performance would start at a quarter past eight that night.

60 Schritt für Schritt

a) they, had opened, before, that **b)** he, would sell, that day, those **c)** they, were going, that night, those **d)** they, their, would start, the following week, those **e)** they, they, their, had packed, had followed, the year before, those **f)** they, they, had arrested, would search, the night before, the following morning, those

a) The ranger in the national park explained (that) they had opened that exhibition only two years before. **b)** The sales representative said (that) he would sell those items at a lower price that day. **c)** The ambulance men said (that) they were going to take those injured persons to different hospitals that night. **d)** Last year the President said (that) they would start their campaign against hunger in those underdeveloped countries the following week. **e)** On his arrival in California the gold prospector said (that) they had followed the Santa Fe trail to the West after they had packed all those things on their wagons the year before.

61 Finde die Fehler in den folgenden Sätzen und trage die falsche sowie die richtige Form in die Lücken ein.

a) has bought (–), had bought (/) **b)** has lived (-), had lived (/), next month (–), the following month (/) **c)** will not pay (–), would not pay (/), would not be represented (–), were not represented (/), now on (-), then on (/) **d)** improved (–), had improved (/), I (–), he (/), will publish (-), would publish (/), tomorrow (-), the next day (/) **e)** will inform (–), would inform (/), our (–), its (/), next week (-), the following week (/), has found (–), had found (/), this (–), that (/)

Mr Anderson said (that) he had bought his new house in 1986 as soon as he had saved enough money, **b)** Last April my uncle in Philadelphia wrote that he had lived in America for fifteen years and that he would come to visit us in Europe the following month, **c)** In 1773 the Bostonians declared (that) they would not pay taxes any longer if they were not represented in the English Parliament from then on. **d)** Last month the President declared (that) the economic situation of the USA had improved since 1992 and (that) he would publish the newest statistics the next day. **e)** The *Washington Post* wrote in 1976 that it would inform its readers the following week whether it had found out further details about that scandal (the Watergate Affair).

62 Verwende in den folgenden Sätzen die indirekte Rede. Beachte die Veränderung der Pronomen.

a) The foreign politician said in the interview (that) the financial situation of his country was getting worse from day to day. **b)** The Indian woman said (that) she had been living on the reservation since she had been (was) born. She then said (that) she didn't really like the life which they lived, **c)** She added that her grandfather had been the chief of their tribe and that he had been hunting buffalo in the prairies until the railroad had come. **d)** The teacher promised (that) they would certainly go on an excursion to (the) Yosemite National Park, **e)** The homeless woman said (that) she had been working in that firm for fifteen years and (that) she had lost her job in 1993. She added that she had been living in the streets ever since and that she hoped (that) times would soon be better, **f)** The mayor announced (that) they would do everything to solve the problems of homeless and unemployed people, **g)** The winner of the Nobel Prize said (that) she had written her book in order to show the social injustices in her home country.

63 Verwende in den folgenden Sätzen die indirekte Rede. Beachte auch die Veränderung der Adverbien.

a) Jill said (that) she would go downtown and do some shopping for the party the following week **b)** The weatherman reported (that) there had been heavy storms on the Atlantic coast the night before and he announced (that) there wouldn't be any sunshine in that part of the country before the following day. **c)** Mr and Mrs Howard said (that) the year before they had spent their holidays at Durango, Colorado, but (that) the following year they would go to Florida, **d)** Alan thought (that) the day before he had had a terrible headache. He hoped (that) he would feel better again that day. **e)** The captain said (that) the week before they had flown to Hong Kong, (that) the next day they would fly to Tokyo, and (that) the following week they would fly to Singapore, **f)** The young man said (that) he had been waiting there for two hours then and (that) he had been reading that newspaper article over and over again. He said (that) he was not going to wait any longer and (that) he would certainly not come back the following day. **g)** The journalist wrote that social conditions in the slum areas of that city had been extremely bad the year before. He was sure (that) they had not improved that year and (that) they would be even worse the following year.

64 Über sich selbst sprechen.

Maren said (that) she lived at Evanston, (that) her father had been a lecturer at the University of Illinois for three years and her mother had been working as a psychologist in a hospital for two years, (that) her elder sister had got married the month before, (that) she would move to Florida the following week together with her husband, (that) two years ago she had flown to Cologne on the Rhine on a students' exchange, (that) her German had not been too good up to then, but (that) it had improved a lot while she had been staying with a German family.

Enrico said (that) he had been living with his mother since his parents had got divorced in 1993, (that) his mother had been working in a cafeteria since then, (that) he had not met his father in the last few years, (that) his father was a truck driver and that he therefore was often away, (that) some months ago he had started to do a paper route (BE: round)

(S. 225-226)

(S. 226-228)

every morning. He said (that) that gave him some pocket money which he spent on books about computers. He further said (that) they lived in a mobile home and (that) he didn't think they would stay there in New Mexico. He hoped (that) they would certainly move to Baltimore where his grandparents had bought a house last year.

Stan told us that he was from Charleston, (that) his native town was the place where the Civil War had begun more than a hundred years ago, (that) tourists who came there would see many traces of our / their Old South .... He then said (that) his father was a lawyer and (that) his mother had died in a car accident when he was still very young. He added that after graduation from high school he wanted to go to college in order to become a doctor. He told us (that) he had been quite good at playing basketball in his school team until he had broken his leg last year. He said (that) he didn't think he would ever be able to play again.

José said (that) he didn't really know who his parents were. He told us (that) he had got lost or that they had left him behind after they had crossed the Mexican border illegally. gJ He told us (that) a trucker had found him near the highway and (that) he had taken him home and (that) he had been living with him, his wife and their two children ever since. He said (that) he worked as a car mechanic in a big garage for the time being, but (that) he was going to be a trucker as well later on. He thought (that) that would be more exciting.

Kathleen said (that) her mom and her dad had met at (the) Mesa Verde National Park eighteen years ago. She explained to us (that) her mother had been working there as a guide for tourists. She said (that) her mother was Indian and (that) her mother's family still lived near the park. She said (that) they didn't want to move away from there. Kathleen then told us (that) her parents had a big house in Dallas and (that) her father had been in the oil business since they had moved there in 1987. She said (that) she didn't think she would stay there for good.

65 Schreibe einen Bericht.

a) Policeman: "Yesterday there was a serious street accident. Two persons were injured. One of the car drivers was obviously drunk. As he fled after the accident we are looking for a green car whose front part was damaged in the accident, **b)** A fire broke out in the knitwear factory at 7.35 last night. The fire brigade had extinguished the fire by midnight. No one was hurt in the incident. We are not yet sure why and how the fire broke out – perhaps it happened through a short circuit, perhaps through arson, **c)** A burglar or several burglars broke into a house in Lincoln Street. They broke a window while the owners of the house were on vacation. They opened the safe and stole jewelry as well as cash. Neighbors who had heard some noise called the police, **d)** We were able to arrest a bank robber after we had got an anonymous hint at a certain house. We searched the house and found some money from last week's bank robbery. We arrested the owners of the house – a man and a woman, but the woman may not be guilty, **e)** A fourteen-year-old girl had been missing for ten days when we found her in a lonely hut near Willows' Lake yesterday morning. She said that she had worried about her school report. Her parents were glad to have her back after all.

The spokesman of the police said that yesterday there had been a serious street accident. He went on to say that two persons had been injured, (that) one of the car drivers had obviously been drunk. He said (that) as the driver had fled after the accident the police were looking for a green car whose front part had been damaged in the accident.

b) The police officer said that a fire had broken out in the knitwear factory at 7.35 last night. He was glad to say that the fire brigade had extinguished the fire by midnight. He said (that) no one had been hurt in the incident. He admitted (that) the police were not yet sure why and how the fire had broken out – perhaps it had happened through a short circuit, perhaps through arson.
c) The spokesman reported that one or several burglars had broken into a house in Lincoln street, (that) they had broken a window while the owners of the house had been on vacation, (that) the thieves had opened a safe and had stolen jewelry as well as cash. He added (that) neighbors, who had heard some noise, had called the police, **d)** The officer said (that) the police had been able to arrest a bank robber after they had got an anonymous hint at a certain house. He said (that) they had searched the house and had found some money from last week's bank robbery. He reported (that) they had arrested the owners of the house – a man and a woman, but he admitted that the woman might not be guilty, **e)** Finally he told us about a fourteen-year-old girl who had been missing for ten days when they (had) found her in a lonely hut near Willows' Lake yesterday morning. According to the policeman the girl had said (that) she had worried about her school report. He added (that) her parents had been glad to have her back after all.

66 Schreibe den Text in direkter Rede.

The mayor: It is not possible to build a new cultural center for concerts and theater performances. The town does not have enough money to realize such an expensive project. **Mr Whitman:** The council decided to build the center many years ago. There has been enough time to get the financial means ready. **Mrs Bentry:** I agree with the mayor's argument. I think that a new school building for the junior high school will be more essential than a cultural center where especially young people will not go. **Mrs Niemec:** Society is obliged to do something for young people in order to keep them off the streets. It is a necessity to offer young people something to do during their spare time, above all in rural areas. **Mr Warren:** Sixteen-year-old boys and girls cannot be bothered with cultural values. These people will rather go to discos or enjoy sports events than boring theater performances. **The mayor:** I have been listening to different arguments for two and a half hours and I discovered an hour ago that the majority is against building the center. I, too, think that a new school building will be of the utmost urgency.

67 Übersetze.

Er sagte, die Südstaatler hätten Negersklaven besessen, die auf ihren Plantagen gearbeitet hätten. Die Sklaverei sei jedoch in den Nordstaaten verboten gewesen. Er sagte, im Jahre 1860 sei Abraham Lincoln, der schon immer gegen die Sklaverei gewesen sei, Präsident geworden. Die Südstaaten hätten dann ihre eigene Regierung gebildet, weil sie befürchteten, die Sklaverei würde abgeschafft werden. Er sagte, deshalb habe der Bürgerkrieg angefangen und viele Soldaten auf beiden Seiten hätten ihr Leben verloren. Schließlich habe der Norden den Krieg gewonnen und die Sklaven im Süden seien freigelassen worden. Nur einige Tage nach dem Ende des Krieges sei Präsident Lincoln von einem fanatischen Südstaatler getötet worden.

68 Indirekte Fragen

Lösungswort: GRAMMAR

69 Gebrauche die indirekte Rede in der Übersetzung.

He says that the Romans built good and broad roads from one town to the next. He says that thus the Roman soldiers could march quickly from one place to the other. He says that the Romans did not only live in towns and military camps, but also in small villages and farmhouses. He says that the Roman baths had a kind of central heating, which you can see here. He says that the Romans came to these baths to have a bath, but also to play games, to have a drink and to talk to each other. He says that that is enough for today and that tomorrow he is going to show us some other buldings of the Roman settlement.

The archaeologist said that the Romans had built good and broad roads from one town to the next. He went on to say that thus the Roman soldiers had been able to march quickly from one place to the other. He then told us that the Romans had not only lived in towns and military camps, but also in small villages and farmhouses as well. He said that normally a bath had belonged to such a farmhouse and that the Roman baths had had a kind of central heating, which we could see there. He said that the Romans had come to those baths to have a bath, but also to play games, to have a drink and to talk.

70 Vervollständige die Bedingungssätze.

a) eat **b)** will steal **c)** catch **d)** will find **e)** will go skiing

71 Bilde Bedingungssätze (Typ 1).

a) If the children hurry up with their homework, they will have time to play, **b)** If the sun shines, they will not / won't stay inside the house, **c)** If the boys and girls have enough money, they will go downtown by bus. **d)** If the bus is not crowded, everyone will have a seat, **e)** If the children are hungry in town, they will eat a hamburger at a fast food restaurant, **f)** If the children have more time, they will visit the zoo.

72 Vervollständige das Gespräch. Benutze if-Sätze (Typ 2).

a) made – would get **b)** owned – would drive **c)** had – would buy **d)** allowed – would invite

73 Übersetzungsübung: Wenn ich Kalifonien besuchen würde ...

a) If I had enough money, I would fly to the USA next summer, **b)** If I had a lot of time, I would travel around in California, **c)** If I was interested in computers, I would visit Silicon Valley, **d)** I would spend a day in an old town of the times of the gold rush if I found such a town, **e)** I would go camping in Yosemite National Park if I met some friends, **f)** If I saw a bear there, I would surely be very much afraid.

74 Bilde Bedingungssätze (Typ 3).

a) 2 – f: Wenn John die rote Verkehrsampel gesehen hätte, dann hätte er den Wagen rechtzeitig angehalten, **b) 3 – i:** Wenn wir früher nach Hause gekommen wären, hätten wir die Fernsehnachrichten sehen können, **c) 4 – h:** Wenn Susi die Tür des Kühlschranks zugemacht hätte, wäre die Eiskrem nicht geschmolzen, **d) 5 – g:** Wenn sie das Kino gefunden hätten, dann hätten sie sich eine Eintrittskarte für *Terminator I* kaufen können. **e) 6 – d:** Wenn ich Tanja getroffen hätte, dann hätte ich sie zur Party eingeladen, **f) 7 – a:**

Wenn sich Mutter an meinen Geburtstag erinnert hätte, dann hätte sie mir ein Geschenk gegeben, **g) 8 – c:** Wenn die Katze den Hund gesehen hätte, wäre sie schnell den Baum hochgeklettert, **h) 9 – b:** Wenn Herr Brown seinen Wagen abgeschlossen hätte, dann wäre er nicht gestohlen worden.

75 Vervollständige die Sätze.

a) had got up – would have had **b)** had eaten – would not have been **c)** would not have entered – had not needed **d)** had been – would not have run into **e)** had not crashed into – would not have fallen **f)** had not been spread - would not have slipped **g)** had not fallen down – would not have hit

76 Was wäre anders gewesen, wenn ...?

a) If Chris had visited San Francisco, he would have seen the Golden Gate Bridge, **b)** If Chris had seen the Golden Gate Bridge, he would have taken photos of it. **c)** If he had taken photos of the Golden Gate Bridge, he would have shown the photos to his friends in Germany, **d)** If his friends had seen the photos, they would have seen how nice California is / was. **e)** If they had found out how nice California is / was, they would have wanted to visit California.

77 Prüfe dein Grammatikwissen!

conditional sentence (type 1):
Bedingungen: wahrscheinlich bzw. leicht erfüllbar; Zeiten: simple present - will-future; **Beispielsatz:** If you visit New York, you will see many skyscrapers.; **Folgen:** auf die Zukunft gerichtet.

conditional sentence (type 2):
Bedingungen: schwer erfüllbar bzw. unwahrscheinlich; Zeiten: simple past - conditional I; **Beispielsatz:** If you stood on top of the Empire State Building, you would see the enormous size of New York.; **Folgen:** gedacht und auf die Gegenwart oder die Zukunft gerichtet.

conditional sentence (type 3):
Bedingungen: nicht mehr erfüllbar bzw. ganz und gar ausgeschlossen; Zeiten: past perfect – conditional II; **Beispielsatz:** If the Indians hadn't sold Manhattan to Peter Minuit, New York would not have been built.; **Folgen:** gedacht und auf die Vergangenheit gerichtet.

78 Drunter und Drüber - oder: Was für ein Durcheinander.

a) 1 – d; TypI **b)** 2 – e; Typ II **c)** 3 – f; Typ II **d)** 4 – a; Typ I **e)** 5 – b; Typ III **f)** 6 – c; Typ II

79 Oh, nein! Eine Übersetzungsübung ...!

a) Typ II; main clause – if-clause; conditional I – simple past; would earn – had; He would earn more money if he had a better job. **b)** Typ I; if-clause – main clause; simple present – will-future; travel / drive – will visit; If we travel / drive to Washington, we will visit the White House, **c)** Typ III; if-clause - main clause; past perfect – conditional II; had called / phoned – would have come; If you had called / phoned her, she surely would have come to your birthday party, **d)** Typ II; if-clause - main clause; simple past – conditional I;

asked – would; If you asked the tour guide, he would surely tell you about the Boston Tea Party, **e)** Typ III; main clause – if-clause; conditional II – past perfect; would not have freed – hadn't won; President Lincoln would not have freed the slaves if he hadn't won the American Civil War.

80 Bilde Bedingungssätze mit *can – could – may – might – should – must.*

a) should / must phone **b)** may be worried **c)** walked – could check out d) are – must / should **e)** should / must reserve **f)** can / could be **g)** may / can get – can / could enjoy

81 Oh, toll! Noch eine Übersetzungsübung ...!

a) If James visited his parents next week, he could go shopping with his aunt, **b)** If you are at home tomorrow, you can call / phone me. **c)** If Jake had watched the football match on television, he could not have gone swimming, **d)** We may go to the cinema if we are not too tired, **e)** If you meet Uncle Tom, you should thank him for the present. **f)** You may / can eat a piece of cake if it is done / finished, **g)** If the sun had been shining, grandfather could have worked in the garden, **h)** You could / might have my new pen if you gave me your felt-pens.

82 Verneinte Bedingungssätze

2 – g; Typ II: Die Einwanderer dachten, dass sie ein besseres Leben hätten, wenn sie nach Amerika gehen würden.
3 – a; Typ III: Wenn der Osten nicht so dicht bevölkert gewesen wäre, dann wären die Einwanderer keine Kolonisten / Siedler und Pioniere im Westen geworden.
4 – f; Typ I: Wenn die Pioniere in der Wildnis nicht sterben wollen, werden sie hart arbeiten müssen.
5 – d; Typ II: Wenn sie keine Farmen gebaut und nicht begonnen hätten, Getreide und Gemüse anzubauen, dann hätten sie keine Wohnung und nichts zu essen gehabt.
6 – c; Typ II: Die Indianer würden mit den Siedlern kämpfen, wenn die Siedler versuchen würden, den Indianern die Jagdgründe wegzunehmen.
7 – e; Typ III: Wenn die Siedler nicht in westlicher Richtung gezogen wären, dann hätte sich Amerika nicht vom Atlantik bis zum Pazifik ausgedehnt.

83 Bedingungssätze als Fragen

Lösungswort: HOUSTON

84 Übersetze.

a) May I listen to your CDs if you are not at home? **b)** If I was sixteen, could I go to the disco with you then? **c)** Will you kiss your girlfriend Claire / give your girlfriend Claire a kiss when you say hello to her? **d)** If it had been raining yesterday, would you have taken me to Francis by car? **e)** Could you buy some ice-cream for me if you went to the mall? **f)** Should I tell you if I want to take your new bike? **g)** If I stopped asking questions, would you be glad?

85 Welche Konjunktion passt am besten?

Antwort: COLONY

86 Verbinde die folgenden Teilsätze durch Konjunktionen.

1 because f), 2 though a), 3 whenever b), 4 as if g), 5 after h), 6 as soon as e), 7 so that c), 8 if d)

87 Übersetze die folgenden Sätze.

a) Der Rektor fragte Jessica, ob ihr ihre neue Schule gefalle, b) Seit Christoph im Jahre 1963 nach New York kam, hat er nie daran gedacht, irgendwo anders zu leben (leben zu wollen), c) Selbst wenn alle Drogen durch die Regierung verboten würden, gäbe es immer noch viele Drogenabhängige, d) Der Einwanderungsbeamte wollte wissen, ob Jonathan Biggs länger als zwei Monate in Amerika bleiben wolle (würde), e) Bevor Axel Schulz Deutschland für immer verließ, stellte er sicher, dass er einen Arbeitsplatz und eine Wohnung in Detroit haben würde, f) Nachdem der Polizist meine Papiere überprüft hatte, fragte er mich, ob ich das Verkehrsschild nicht gesehen hätte.

Lernbereich
RECHTSCHREIBUNG (S. 253-271)

1 Bilde aus zwei Wörtern eines.

Zusammengeschriebene zweiteilige Wörter (Teil I)

a) airmail b) motorbike c) newspaper d) thunderstorm e) fisherman f) backyard g) cupboard h) boyfriend i) textbook j) postcard

Zusammengeschriebene zweiteilige Wörter (Teil II)

a) playground b) pineapple c) skateboard d) loudspeaker e) weekend f) headmaster g) bedroom h) handwriting i) policeman j) mudguard

Zweiteilige Wörter mit Bindestrich

a) ill-timed b) second-hand c) swimming-pool d) well-known e) hard-working f) school-bag g) empty-handed h) air-conditioning i) ex-wife j) self-respect k) record-player l) parking-space

Zahlen - mit und ohne Bindestrich

a) three thousand, one hundred and twenty-three b) seven hundred and fifty-five c) the thirty-fifth d) the two hundred and seventy-fourth e) one thousand, one hundred and twenty-one f) one hundred and one g) the (one) hundred and first h) two hundred and forty-eight

2 Übersetze.

a) Harry's friends b) the girls' bikes c) the trees of the forest d) the man's beard e) the hens' eggs f) my parents' house g) the childrens' parties h) the history of America

3 Setze die richtige Pluralform ein.

a) wives b) stereos c) potatoes d) knives e) beaches f) bushes g) casinos h) negroes i) calves j) thieves k) buffaloes l) searches m) lives n) studios o) tomatoes

4 Füge die Form der 3. Person Singular hinzu.

a) fetches b) rushes c) talks d) teaches e) pulls f) pushes g) speaks h) watches

5 Bilde die Pluralformen von Nomen auf -ey oder -y.
a) hobby – hobbies b) party – parties c) monkey – monkeys d) community – communities e) valley – valleys f) century – centuries g) colony – colonies h) jockey – jockeys i) diary – diaries j) trolley – trolleys

6 Füge die 3. Person Singular hinzu.
a) carries b) applies c) buys d) studies e) destroys f) qualifies g) empties h) flies i) pays j) tries

7 Wörtersuchspiel
wives, babies, knives, photos, classes, roofs, children, sheep, lives, pianos, deer, cities, men, tomatoes, fish, thieves, heroes, mice, potatoes, wishes, teeth, chairmen, feet, oxen, babies, lives, handkerchiefs, boys, women

8 Vervollständige die Sätze.
a) seat-belt b) breeze c) chief d) deceive e) secret f) field g) receipt h) meetings

9 Übersetze die Wörter und finde sie im Wörtersuchspiel!
a) professor b) favor c) adventure d) regular e) tower f) labor g) future h) instructor i) popular j) sculpture k) headmaster l) sailor m) brochure n) harbor o) pressure p) owner q) ancestor

10 Suche das richtige Wort aus!
a) by – son b) sale – wear c) through – see d) too – weak – farther e) break f) their - fare g) steal

11 Füge das richtige Wort ein.
a) Two (zwei), to (nach), to (zu), too (auch), too (zu), too, too (auch) b) loose (lose), lose (verlieren), loss (Verlust) c) hole (Loch), whole (ganz) d) whether (ob), weather (Wetter) e) peace (Frieden), piece (Stück) f) then (danach, dann), than (als)

12 Wortbildungen
a) quite (ganz), quiet (ruhig) b) era (Zeitalter), area (Gebiet), air (Melodie) c) buy (kaufen), bye (Auf Wiedersehen) d) college (Universität), colleague (Kollege / Kollegin) e) major (Major), mayor (Bürgermeister) f) pupil g) people h) plan i) plane j) four, fourteen, forty

13 Füge die richtige Form der folgenden Verben ein.
Endsilbe betont: referred, occurred, preferred; Endsilbe unbetont: suffered, offered, conquered, developed
a) preferrred b) offered c) developed, underdeveloped d) handicapped

14 Finde den Fehler.
occurred, conquered, suffered, referred

15 Finde und markiere zwölf Wörter mit einem „stummen" Buchstaben.
lamb – sword – mustn't – guilty – often – foreign – talking – wrong – fasten – knowledge – island – would

16 Übersetze die Wörter und finde sie im Wörtersuchspiel!

a) guitar b) sign c) knife d) autumn e) sandwich f) whole g) half h) through i) Wednesday j) building k) doubt l) listen

17 Finde sechzehn Fehler und verbessere sie!

seventeenth – carried – cheap – cost – women – weather – to live in – could – punished – by – soldiers – completely – separate – politicians – equal – which

Lernbereich WORTSCHATZ (S. 273-281)

1 Wähle das richtige Wort.

a) corn (Mais), corn, corn, grain (Korn, Getreide) b) plate (Teller), oven (Backofen), records (Schallplatten), stove (Ofen) c) wonder (sich fragen), map (Landkarte), briefcase (Aktentasche), was surprised (sich wundern), blocks (Straßenblocks) d) took place (stattfinden), took their seats (Platz nehmen), jam (Marmelade), marmalade (Orangenmarmelade) e) was looking for (suchen nach), murderer (Mörder), coffin (Sarg), murdered (ermorden), searched (durchsuchen), gymnasium (Sporthalle), suitcase (Koffer), concrete (Beton) f) warehouses (Lagerhaus), department stores (Kaufhaus), actually (tatsächlich), topical (aktuell), critics (Kritiker), criticism (Kritik)

2 Übersetze.

a) In jedem Spiel benutzt der Tennischampion einen vollkommen neuen Schläger. Gestern wurde von Cape Canaveral eine weitere Rakete abgeschossen, b) Jolene ist eine sehr empfindsame junge Dame. Sie macht sich oft Gedanken über Ereignisse von geringerer Bedeutung. Aber sie kann sehr vernünftig sein, wenn es um Probleme ihrer Arbeit geht. c) Die Notiz (Mitteilung) besagt, dass die Schüler ihre Zeugnisse am nächsten Freitag bekommen werden. Raymond macht das nichts aus; er hat sich im letzten Tertial (Schuljahresabschnitt) sehr stark bemüht, sodass er ein guter Schüler geworden ist und in seinen Prüfungen ausgezeichnete Noten bekommen hat. d) Während der Pferderennen konnten die Besucher an den Verkaufsständen in der Nähe der Ställe Getränke und belegte Brote kaufen, e) Sheila ist sehr schüchtern und befangen; ihr Vater war genau das Gegenteil; er war eine sehr starke und selbstbewusste Persönlichkeit.

3 Ergänze die englische oder amerikanische Schreibweise.

colour, favor, favourite, honour, honorable, neighbour, center, theatre, liter, license, defence, offense, dialog, catalogue, prolog, program, waggon, traveling, quarrelling, to realize, to organise / to organize, to analyse, to analyze, to practise

4 Ergänze die fehlenden Wörter.

Lösungswörter: Oklahoma, Arizona, Texas, California, Louisiana, Florida, Virginia, Nebraska, Nevada

5 Welche Wörter sind nicht amerikanisches Englisch?

a) tin – can b) city centre – downtown, underground – subway, programme – program, favourite – favorite, dialogues – dialogs c) coloured – colored, flats – apartments

6 Schreibe die folgenden Sätze in britischem Englisch bzw. in amerikanischem Englisch.

... bought chips, crisps, and biscuits. As they were still too young to buy any alcoholic drinks like beer or whisky they bought some tins of lemonade and Diet Coke.

When traveling through the United States during their fall vacation our neighbors realized that in suburban Chicago highways and railroad lines run quite close to the apartment houses in poor dwelling areas.

7 Übersetze.

BE: The lorry driver showed his driving licence to the policeman.
AE: The truck driver (trucker) showed his driver's license to the policeman.
BE: The tourist paid for the jumper with a traveller's cheque.
AE: The tourist paid for the sweater with a traveler's check.

8 Schreibe den Text in amerikanischem Englisch.

Last fall Claus and Beatrice, two eighteen-year-old students from Gelsenkirchen, wanted to spend their vacation in Britain. Claus had only just got his driver's license and Beatrice was still having driving instruction. So they decided not to go by car but to travel around the country by train. "I guess, railroads are safer than freeways with all these trucks, though British truck drivers are said to be friendly and considerate towards foreign car drivers", Claus said. "Going by train might be cheaper, anyway", Beatrice added, "gasoline in Britain is supposed to be very expensive, and there are not too many gas stations in rural areas."
After having traveled through different regions of Britain they finally arrived in London, where they booked into the 'Saxon King Hotel'. Their rooms were on the first floor, so that they could not see a lot from their windows, but they took the elevator to the roof terrace, from where they had a wonderful view – over the apartment houses around the suburban hotel. They went downtown by subway. There was an awful lot of traffic at Piccadilly Circus. It was almost impossible to cross the streets without using the pedestrian underpasses. "What gifts are we going to buy for our families?" asked Claus. "I guess I will get some cookies and candy for my little sisters", said Beatrice, "they are still kids, so they might like them." "And I will buy a bottle of whiskey for my father and a sweater for my mother, both things will keep them warm in a way, I guess", answered Claus. "Let's go into the department store over there. We can pay by check, so we'll have enough money left for our last meal in Britain tonight."

Lernbereich
PRÜFUNGSTRAINING (S. 283-297)

1. Test

1 . Bilde Bedingungssätze (Typ 2 und 3).

a) If the weather in the Sierra Nevada was too cold, I would relax on the Californian beaches, **b)** If I wanted to take a photo of the Golden Gate Bridge, I would travel to San Francisco, **c)** If the cable cars worked, I would use them for a sightseeing tour through the town, **d)** If I (still) had some / a little bit of money left, I would end up my holiday trip in Disneyland.

2. Finde das Synonym oder das Gegenteil.
a) passive **b)** boring **c)** cheap **d)** enemies **e)** intelligent **f)** repair **g)** tall – strong **h)** remember

3. Setze die passenden Konjunktionen ein.
because – while – so that – when – and – although – as – whether – whenever

4. Setze, wenn nötig, den unbestimmten Artikel ein.
a) an, –, a **b)** –, a, – **c)** a, a, –, a **d)** an, an, a, –, a, an

5. Übersetze. Adjektiv oder Adverb?
a) Harry was right. The pizza smelled (auch smelt) and tasted fantastic, **b)** Harry said: "I am going to go on an exciting rafting trip on the Colorado River. Would you like to accompany me?" **c)** Betty answered: "No, thanks. It sounds very dangerous. I am always too excited for such things." Harry smiled at Betty in a friendly way. **d)** It was a wonderful birthday party. Betty went home slowly around midnight. She was tired, but also very happy.

6. Vervollständige die Sätze mit einem Infinitiv mit to im Aktiv oder im Passiv.
a) to write **b)** to be built **c)** to visit **d)** to be used **e)** to be paid

7. Vervollständige den Text.
a) the the **b)** would have gone fishing — **c)** to to be found completely **d)** — frequently although **e)** incredibly heavy fantastic **f)** had

2. Test

1. Setze, wenn nötig, den bestimmten Artikel ein.
a) – – **b)** – – – **c)** – – – **d)** – the the **e)** – – The **f)** the – – **g)** the the – – the – – –

2. Bilde Sätze mit Verb - Objekt + Infinitiv mit to.
Nothing but good advice?
a) Mrs Jennings advised / warned him not to eat too many tacos and burritos. **b)** Mr Jennings warned / wished him not to waste all his money on drinks and cigarettes. He told him to buy a nice Mexican souvenir instead, **c)** Luke advised / reminded him to take his sunglasses and his Nirvana T-shirt with him (because he looks cool with them). **d)** Trisha expected / wished him to visit his friends in Florida (because it's a lot nicer there), **e)** Bob advised / asked him to take as many pictures as possible (because they could have a great time with them when they are back), **f)** Toby wanted / reminded him to buy a bottle of real tequila for Toby's parents. Toby asked / expected / wished him to visit his pen-friend Nick because he is waiting for James.

3. Füge die richtigen Substantive ein. Achte auf unregelmäßige Plurale.
a) Men, wives, children **b)** deer, buffalo, fish, trout, salmon, oxen, potatoes **c)** Mice, Men **d)** People, Chinese, Japanese, Swiss, Germans, photos, oxen

4. Vervollständige die Bedingungssätze (verschiedene Typen) mit der richtigen Verbform.

a) had arrived **b)** will buy **c)** would learn **d)** will like **e)** brings **f)** would send **g)** had watched **h)** goes up **i)** would have left **j)** hadn't rained

5. Verbinde die beiden Sätze durch eine Konjunktion.

a) Frederick Olson dared to leave his native country Sweden although he did not know whether he would be able to make a living in America, **b)** After he had bought a piece of land in South Dakota where he could grow wheat he built a small farmhouse, **c)** After / As soon as he had succeeded in making some profit he made his wife and his three children move to America, **d)** His son and his two daughters had problems at school since they did not speak English at all. **e)** When they all had finished high school successfully they went into college, **f)** When they got married they all had good jobs and fairly high incomes, **g)** Whenever people speak about the American Dream Frederick Olson will tell them how hard this dream is to be fulfilled.

6. Der Nachrichtensprecher. Gebrauche die indirekte Rede.

The newscaster said (that) the State Opening of Parliament had taken place yesterday, (that) at 11 o'clock the Queen had driven from Buckingham Palace to Westminster, (that) thousands of people, many of them tourists, had been standing along the Mall. He then added (that) an elderly lady from Ystalyfera, South Wales, had said to their reporter (that) she had already come to London the day before and that she had never seen such a colourful event in her life.

The newscaster said (that) their reporter had asked several Republicans on the steps to the Capitol what measures their party was going to take in order to cope with unemployment in our country. He said (that) most of them had answered that we (they) would have to improve the educational standards of our schools, especially in underprivileged urban areas.

The weatherman said (that) heavy thunderstorms had caused serious damage in some parts of Oregon. He said (that) today it was rainy and cloudy, but that, hopefully, we would have some sunny periods as well and that the temperature would be around 89 degrees.

7. Füge, wenn nötig, passende Wörter in die Lücken ein.

a) – – had – built **b)** a a because children (grand)children Irishmen Germans Chinese Swiss **c)** to come **d)** Luther people had would where would be color but

3. TEST

1. Infinitive mit to oder Infinitive ohne *to*?

a) to, to – **b)** to, to, –, to **c)** –, to, to, to, **d)** to, –

2. Füge die richtige Zeit ein.

a) flew **b)** had been, became, declared, would be freed **c)** has ... finished, are **d)** had been living, discovered **e)** Tonight I'm going to write a letter to you. Then you'll get it the day after tomorrow, **f)** My father has been reading the newspaper for hours.

3. Bilde einige Bedingungssätze (Typ 3).

a) If only I had stayed at home. If only I hadn't had to pay for the tickets. If only my friend hadn't invited me to the cinema, **b)** If only I hadn't taken that stupid bike and damaged it! If only I hadn't fallen off that bike and broken my arm. If only I had learned to ride a bicycle properly, **c)** If only our teacher had been ill today. If only I had known about that test before. If only I hadn't forgotten all the answers for the questions of that test. **d)** If only I hadn't bought those expensive tickets. If only my wonderful team hadn't lost another match. If only I had decided to watch the match on TV.

4. Vervollständige die folgenden Sätze.

a) would have gone, doctor's **b)** doctor had given, chemist's **c)** will buy, baker's, butcher's **d)** would / could enjoy, grandparents' **e)** My children's sweaters are always dirty, **f)** Boise, the capital of Idaho, was founded by French settlers, **g)** Before the pilot takes off, he rings up a friend of his in Carson City, Nevada, to get today's weather report.

5. Überschriften aus amerikanischen oder englischen Zeitungen?

a) AE **b)** BE **c)** BE **d)** AE **e)** BE **f)** AE **g)** BE

6. Vervollständige den Text.

a) father's, to, — **b)** parents', would have invited **c)** will have to, sister's **d)** has finished, has been working **e)** in the beginning, easily, often, hard **f)** had not rung, his, to, to **g)** Smiths', had said

4. TEST

1. Finde Erklärungen und Umschreibungen.

Füge die Wörter der Liste 1 und die Erklärungen der Liste 2 zusammen.

1 – h; 2 – i; 3 – e; 4 – j; 5 – g; 6 – a; 7 – c; 8 – b; 9 – d; 10 – f

Erkläre die fett gedruckten Wörter.

a) to go into **b)** to stay alive, not to die **c)** rich, well-off **d)** teacher **e)** clever, intelligent **f)** typical weather

2. Prüfe dein Wissen: Bedingungssätze (verschiedene Typen).

a) goes – A – 1 **b)** was stolen – C – 2 **c)** had set – B – 3 **d)** saves – A – 1 **e)** is – C – 1 **f)** had hurried – A – 3 **g)** had come – A – 3 **h)** would write – A – 2 **i)** would not have attacked – B – 3

3. Wörter definieren.

1. children 2. potatoes 3. men 4. knives 5. geese 6. negroes 7. mice

4. Bilde Sätze mit Infinitiven ohne to.

a) made her look after **b)** let her stay up, make Louise go to bed **c)** let Louise play **d)** let Barbie ride; made her take **e)** made Louise eat, let her watch **f)** let her read **g)** made her wash, let her say good night **h)** let me go to a disco, let me stay out, make Dad say yes

(S. 291-295)

5. Finde die Fehler und verbessere die Sätze.

a) The Wall Street Journal daily publishes the latest news about the economic situation in America and the world, **b)** Being very self-confident the candidate was quite sure that he would win the elections, **c)** The chairman sat down and opened the debate on the criticism (critiques) of the financial policy which had been published in some newspapers. The white-collar criminals were being looked for by the police all over the country. As she is a very sensitive girl, she will always cry whenever she reads the moving story of "The Legend of Sleepy Hollow" by Washington Irving.

6. Verbinde zwei oder mehr Sätze durch Konjunktionen.

Abe Rosenberg is a Jewish scientist and a college professor at Chicago University. He has been living in Illinois since his parents came to America as immigrants in 1973. He owns a large, but old house in Oak Park though he could buy a new, more modern and comfortable house. But he loves his neighborhood because many of his colleagues from the university live there, too.

7. Übersetze.

a) Millions of immigrants, Englishmen, Frenchmen, Italians, Germans, Swiss, Chinese and many others came to America in the 19th and 20th centuries, **b)** The American government let men, women and children immigrate (into the country), as long as the country needed people (men) and above all manpower, **c)** Today the police make illegal immigrants go back to their native countries, **d)** If the South had won the American Civil War the slaves would probably not have been freed so early, **e)** Though Afro-Americans and Indians (native Americans) are equal citizens their economic situation has actually always been an issue of current interest.

(S. 295-296)